The European Periphery and the Eurozone Crisis

This book provides a new understanding of the eurozone crisis across three of the worst hit cases: Greece, Portugal, and Ireland.

In contrast to accounts that stress the 'immaturity' of the European 'periphery', as well as more critical narratives that understand these countries as victims of German and core 'economic domination', this book recognises that individual peripheral countries have followed dramatically different paths to crisis, making it difficult to speak of the eurozone crisis as a single phenomenon. Bringing literature from Comparative Political Economy into dialogue with scholarship on Europeanisation, this book contributes the concept of 'divergence via Europeanisation'. It explores the much-overlooked ways in which the negotiation of a 'one size fits all' project of European financial integration has been generative of precarious patterns of economic growth across Greece, Portugal, and Ireland. The book shows that far from their failure or inability to do so, it has been the European periphery's attempt to 'follow the rules' of European integration that explains their current difficulties.

This novel understanding of the eurozone crisis should appeal to students and scholars in International Political Economy, European and European Union Studies, Comparative Political Economy, Irish Politics, Greek Politics, and Portuguese Politics.

Neil Dooley is a Lecturer in Politics at the University of Sussex. His articles appear in *New Political Economy, Millennium: Journal of International Studies* and *Third World Thematics: A TWQ Journal*. Neil has written for *The Washington Post*, *The Conversation*, and *Le Monde Diplomatique*.

RIPE SERIES IN GLOBAL POLITICAL ECONOMY

Series Editors: James Brassett (*University of Warwick, UK*), Eleni Tsingou *(Copenhagen Business School, Denmark)* and Susanne Soederberg *(Queen's University, Canada)*

The RIPE Series published by Routledge is an essential forum for cutting-edge scholarship in International Political Economy. The series brings together new and established scholars working in critical, cultural and constructivist political economy. Books in the RIPE Series typically combine an innovative contribution to theoretical debates with rigorous empirical analysis.

The RIPE Series seeks to cultivate:

- Field-defining theoretical advances in International Political Economy
- Novel treatments of key issue areas, both historical and contemporary, such as global finance, trade, and production
- Analyses that explore the political economic dimensions of relatively neglected topics, such as the environment, gender relations, and migration
- Accessible work that will inspire advanced undergraduates and graduate students in International Political Economy.

The *RIPE Series in Global Political Economy* aims to address the needs of students and teachers.

For more information about this series, please visit: www.routledge.com/RIPE-Series-in-Global-Political-Economy/book-series/RIPE

The Language of World Trade Politics
Unpacking the Terms of Trade
Edited by Klaus Dingwerth and Clara Weinhardt

Power in North-South Trade Negotiations
Making the European Union's Economic Partnership Agreements
Peg Murray-Evans

The European Periphery and the Eurozone Crisis
Capitalist Diversity and Europeanisation
Neil Dooley

Informal Economies and Power
Anna Danielsson

"This is an important book not just because it provides an original and convincing account for the way the Eurozone crisis played out across three different countries, but also because it combines insights from across comparative political economy and EU studies to produce a sophisticated conceptualization of how states and societies are shaped by European integration."

Rebecca Adler-Nissen, University of Copenhagen, Denmark

"Dooley's book brilliantly addresses flaws in major arguments on the origins of the Euro-crisis. Rather than sorting countries into groups, Dooley recognizes the unique features of countries within the Euro-zone periphery that made them susceptible to the crisis in different ways; this susceptibility was driven, ironically, by their success in adopting EU banking reforms before and after the launch of the Euro. While the European project has promoted convergence, Dooley aptly identifies that Europeanization has led to a divergence in stable and sustainable financial development between the E(M)U's member-states, an outcome that has yielded dangerous consequences."

Alison Johnston, Oregon State University, USA

"Neil Dooley's book demonstrates impressively the strengths of a nuanced approach to the study of the European political economy, interweaving themes of diversity and commonality via a discussion of the asymmetric impact of the Eurozone crisis. This is of particular importance for current debates about 'core' and 'periphery' but also European capitalism more generally. Therefore, the book is of strong relevance for literatures on 'peripheral' Europe, the multiple developmental trajectories that constitute European capitalism, and EU crisis management failures."

Ian Bruff, University of Manchester, UK

"This is an excellent book, which adds much needed nuance to the intricacies of what became known as the European sovereign debt crisis. Dooley persuasively argues that Europe's periphery suffered disproportionately from the crisis, not due to their own immaturity or German economic domination, but because their political economies were ill adapted to follow the EU rules in the first place. Anyone wanting a deeper understanding of the Eurozone's predicament will greatly benefit from reading this book."

Matthias Matthijs, Johns Hopkins University, USA

The European Periphery and the Eurozone Crisis

Capitalist Diversity and Europeanisation

Neil Dooley

Routledge
Taylor & Francis Group
LONDON AND NEW YORK

First published 2019
by Routledge
2 Park Square, Milton Park, Abingdon, Oxon OX14 4RN

and by Routledge
52 Vanderbilt Avenue, New York, NY 10017

First issued in paperback 2020

Routledge is an imprint of the Taylor & Francis Group, an informa business

British Library Cataloguing-in-Publication Data
A catalogue record for this book is available from the British Library

Library of Congress Cataloging-in-Publication Data
Names: Dooley, Neil, author.
Title: The European periphery and the Eurozone crisis : capitalist diversity and Europeanisation / Neil Dooley.
Description: Abingdon, Oxon ; New York, NY : Routledge, 2019. | Series: RIPE series in global political economy | Includes bibliographical references and index.
Identifiers: LCCN 2018032822| ISBN 9781138048010 (hardback) | ISBN 9781315170466 (e-book)
Subjects: LCSH: Financial crises—European Union countries. | Eurozone. | European Union countries—Economic policy—21st century. | European Union countries—Politics and government—21st century.
Classification: LCC HB3782 .D66 2019 | DDC 337.1/42—dc23
LC record available at https://lccn.loc.gov/2018032822

ISBN 13: 978-0-367-58355-2 (pbk)
ISBN 13: 978-1-138-04801-0 (hbk)

Typeset in Times New Roman
by Swales & Willis Ltd, Exeter, Devon, UK

For my parents

Contents

Figures

Tables

Abbreviations

CEE	Central and Eastern Europe
CMEs	Coordinated Market Economies
CPCS	Standing Committee for Social Concertation
CPE	Comparative Political Economy
EC	European Community
ECB	European Central Bank
EDP	Excessive Deficit Procedure
EEC	European Economic Community
EMU	Economic and Monetary Union
EU	European Union
FDI	Foreign Direct Investment
FSAP	Financial Services Action Plan
GDP	Gross Domestic Product
GNP	Gross National Product
ICTU	Irish Congress of Trade Unions
IDA	Industrial Development Agency
IFSC	International Financial Services Centre
IFSRA	Irish Financial Services Regulatory Authority
IMF	International Monetary Fund
LMEs	Liberal Market Economies
MMEs	Mixed Market Economies
MNC	Multinational Corporation
ND	New Democracy
NFC	Non-Financial Company
OAE	Organismos Anasygkrotiseos Epicheiriseon (Business Reconstruction Organization)
OECD	Organisation for Economic Co-operation and Development
PASOK	The Panhellenic Socialist Movement
PIIGS	Portugal, Ireland, Italy, Greece, Spain
PD	Progressive Democrats
PSD	Partido Social Democrata (Social Democratic party)

RBS	Royal Bank of Scotland
REER	Real Effective Exchange Rate
SEA	Single European Act
SMEs	small and medium-sized enterprises
VoC	Varieties of Capitalism

Acknowledgements

I graduated from University College Dublin in 2009, the year that revelations about Greece's public finances kick-started the eurozone crisis, and a year before the troika came to Ireland. At the time, I could not have known to what extent the next decade or so of my life would be consumed by bond yields, current account imbalances, and sovereign debt. This book is the result, and – appropriately – I have numerous debts of my own to acknowledge to all of those who contributed to its completion.

First, to all my colleagues in the departments of Politics and International Relations at the University of Sussex. I could not have asked for more supportive, convivial, and stimulating environments in which to write this book. I would especially like to thank Fabio Petito and Kevin Gray, it is to them that I most owe my intellectual development. Their support and guidance over the past number of years have made it possible for me to produce something that I hope they can be proud of. My sincerest gratitude also goes to (in no particular order) Paul Taggart, Claire Annesley, Justin Rosenberg, Sam Knafo, Andreas Antoniades, Beate Jahn, Louiza Odysseus, Cynthia Weber, Rorden Wilkinson, and Anna Stavrianakis for their generous engagement, directly and indirectly, with this project over the years.

I am especially grateful to series editors Susanne Soederberg, Eleni Tsingou and James Brassett, and to Claire Maloney and Robert Sorsby at Routledge for their incredible support as editors and in bringing this book to fruition. I wish to acknowledge Taylor & Francis Group for kindly permitting me to include versions of two articles as part of this book. First, 'Who's Afraid of the Big Bad Wolf? Rethinking the Core and Periphery in the Eurozone Crisis' by Neil Dooley, *New Political Economy* (2017) Taylor & Francis Ltd, is reprinted by permission of the publisher. Second, 'Divergence via Europeanisation: Rethinking the Origins of the Portuguese Debt Crisis' by Neil Dooley *Third World Thematics: A TWQ Journal* (2017), copyright © South Series, is reprinted by permission of Taylor & Francis Ltd, on behalf of South Series.

Outside of Sussex, I am indebted to the kindness of many colleagues who took the time to read and comment on chapters and earlier versions of this book. These are too numerous to mention, but I am especially grateful to Kevin Featherstone,

Rebecca Adler-Nissen, Niamh Hardiman, Alison Johnston, Matthias Matthijs, and Ian Bruff. I am also grateful to two anonymous peer reviewers for their generous and valuable feedback on this manuscript.

I am fortunate to have amazing friends who provided much-needed temporary 'exits from the eurozone' during the writing process. To the 'C349 crew', Sam Appleton, Tom Bentley, Synne Dyvik, Darius A'Zami, and Felipe Antunes de Oliveira, I could not have asked for better office-mates and friends. I will always look back with great fondness to those times when we were all together, sometimes making coffee with our hazardous cafetiere, sometimes streaming the West Wing, sometimes writing. To the extended 'cheers brothers', thanks to the wonderful Sam Appleton, Jade McShane, Tristan Kirby, Kirley Soares, Paul Eastman, George Moody, Helen Johnston, and my alt-country band-mate Roger Johnson. Bonus thanks to George and to Jonathan Moss for providing particularly insightful feedback in the final stretch.

To the love of my life Jenny Mc Guill, I have even less idea how to ever thank you. I will never forget your never-ending kindness, patience, love, and friendship throughout the writing of this book. More than anyone, you have lived this book with me. You have always been there for me, supported me, and are an inspiration to me.

To my brother Colin Dooley, thank you for always doing 'whatever it takes', in so many ways. This book would not have been possible without you, and thanks also for moving to England briefly, having you here was easily the most enjoyable part of the writing process. Special thanks to my step-mother, Kay Webster-Dooley, and to my wee brother, Enda Dooley, and sister, Rachael Dooley. I feel like I have been writing this book for most of your lives, and hanging out with you back home has helped more than you probably realise.

My greatest debt is to my parents. I thank my Dad, Tom Dooley, for giving me a fascination for political economy from an early age. There was always a 'book in the garage' on every imaginable topic from uneven and combined development to theoretical and experimental studies of slender oscillating water columns, and plenty of conversations on dialectics in the Joes' bar in Dromiskin. Heartfelt thanks to my Mom, Ann Campbell. I feel very lucky to have had your endless support and unwavering belief in me – and I could never have done this without you. You have gone above and beyond the call of duty, and this has meant more to me than I have probably ever told you outside of formal acknowledgements. I can never thank my parents for all they have done for me, materially and non-materially. I dedicate this book to them.

1 Introduction

The asymmetry of the eurozone crisis

One of the most striking aspects of the eurozone crisis is its asymmetric impact. Detrimental economic and political consequences have resonated across Europe, but 'peripheral' member states have been affected more severely than others (Hardiman and Dellepiane 2010, 473). The embattled Greek economy makes up just about 2 percent of the overall eurozone economy. And yet, the shock-waves from its crisis have appeared to threaten the disintegration of the entire European project. Not only this, but individual peripheral countries have followed dramatically different paths to crisis. While the Greek state may have perilously over-borrowed and widened its budget deficit, the Republic of Ireland[1] appeared to be among the most fiscally responsible economies in Europe. As banks fuelled overheating in Ireland, the Portuguese economy stagnated. As an International Monetary Fund (IMF) economist playfully put it, all happy countries are alike; but each unhappy peripheral country is 'unhappy in its own way' (Selassie 2012).

As such, regardless of whether the eurozone crisis is understood as a story of fiscal, financial, or competitiveness imbalances, it is vital that existing literature reflects on the assumptions it makes about the crucial role of the European periphery. Moreover, for this explanation to be persuasive, the dramatically different paths to crisis the European periphery has followed must be accounted for. The crisis has been and is playing out in very different ways across Europe (Bruff and Ebenau 2014, 4), but much existing analysis emphasises core-periphery divergence at the expense of divergence between the countries of the European periphery themselves. This book zooms in on this intellectual puzzle: why has the eurozone crisis appeared to manifest as a fiscal crisis in Greece, economic stagnation in Portugal, and a banking crisis in Ireland? What explains the asymmetry of the eurozone crisis?

Europeanisation, capitalist diversity, and the asymmetry of the eurozone crisis

This book seeks to make a novel contribution. Within a single study, it investigates the asymmetric origins of the eurozone crisis across three of the worst hit cases: Greece, Portugal, and the Republic of Ireland. The book offers a novel interpretation of the eurozone crisis by showing how 'following the rules' of European integration, rather than failing to, contributed to the crises of the European periphery. I outline a framework based on a combination of scholarship on Europeanisation and the Comparative Political Economy (CPE) literature on 'capitalist diversity'. This framework makes it possible to reveal the much-overlooked ways in which domestic adaptation to European integration has been generative of precarious patterns of economic growth across the European periphery. I develop the concept of 'divergence via Europeanisation' to show that, over the past number of decades, Greece, Portugal, and Ireland have attempted to adapt, with various levels of success, to a 'one size fits all' project of European integration. As such, national and supranational efforts at promoting the convergence of member states have – paradoxically – propelled these countries towards crisis.

The issue of asymmetry is becoming increasingly acknowledged as absolutely central to research into the origins of the eurozone crisis (Bruff and Ebenau 2014, 4; Jäger and Springler 2015, 1; Johnston and Regan 2016). However, I argue that much existing literature has yet to adequately take up the challenge of explaining it. Emphasis has been placed on explaining core-periphery asymmetry rather than the asymmetry between peripheral countries themselves. Moreover, there has been a tendency, even in otherwise sophisticated analysis, to fall back upon, and reproduce, one of two problematic narratives of why the periphery was 'hit hardest' by the eurozone crisis.

The first is a story about the 'lazy Greeks' and their fellow European 'PIIGS'.[2] As the story goes, Portugal, Ireland, and particularly Greece were unwilling to introduce 'painful but necessary' reforms in the decades before the crisis hit; content to irresponsibly reproduce patterns of fiscal profligacy, low productivity, and political immaturity (Bastasin 2012, 8; Lavdas, Litsas, and Skiadas 2013, 175). The second story offers a more critical take by casting Germany as the 'big bad wolf' of the tale (Dooley 2017a).[3] These approaches typically understand the eurozone as a region characterised by a core-periphery hierarchy between the 'beggar-thy-neighbour' style economic growth of the core, especially Germany, which lead to precarious, 'financialised' growth in the periphery. 'Core–periphery' analysis has been rapidly gaining momentum in academic debates on the eurozone crisis (see Dooley 2017a, 3–4) allowing many to argue that it doesn't matter what material the PIIGS built their houses from, the real problem is that a big bad wolf resides in the eurozone and is blowing them down.

These two narratives of the origins of the crisis in the periphery – labelled here as the 'immaturity thesis' and the 'beggar-thy-neighbour narrative' – have remained strongly influential.[4] The prevalence of such assumptions within a range of disparate approaches (see Chapter 2) has contributed to two major limits in the existing literature. First, existing accounts which rely on narratives of blame downplay the very different kinds of crisis the European periphery has experienced. Pointing out, as scholarship relying on assumptions of immaturity does, that every peripheral country 'failed to converge' tells us little about how and why these three specific kinds of 'divergence' emerged. Exposing the periphery's collective domination by Germany or Western Europe explains less still about these multiple paths.

Second, these narratives tend to produce scholarly and political debates that are preoccupied with assigning blame (as Hänska 2015; Papadimitriou and Zartaloudis 2014; and Ntampoudi 2014 all note). On the one hand, narratives of blame are clear in the conditionality of the European Union–European Central Bank–International Monetary Fund (EU–ECB–IMF) arrangements, as well as in the emerging European institutional response to the crisis; all of which are marked by measures designed to correct the immaturities of the peripheral states. This response has been widely admonished with even the IMF issuing more than one extraordinary apology for not recognising the damage austerity would do to Greece (see Elliott, Inman, and Smith 2013). Related to this, some have noted how public, media, and political perceptions of the periphery, particularly Greece, as being immature contributed to the notorious procrastination on the part of European elites in responding to the crisis, a serious error that raised the stakes of the crisis (Bastasin 2012, 7–11). Brazys and Hardiman (2013) have even noted how the very use of 'heuristic labels' such as the 'PIIGS' acronym have actually contributed to negative market responses towards those states.

On the other hand, transposed from academic to political discourses, narratives of victimisation have contributed to the problematic rise of anti-German sentiment within Europe. Labels such as 'Nazi oppressor and colonizer' and 'strict teacher' vie for prominence against 'immature pupil' and 'moral sinner' (see Adler-Nissen 2017; Dooley 2015b). Roberto Orsi notes that the taboo of large scale weaponisation of war memories against Germany has been broken (Orsi 2015), and populist rhetoric from all corners has emerged that others claim forms an emerging 'intra-European neo-racism' (Kouvélakis 2012, xix; see also Andreou 2012) – potentially feeding into disintegrative momentums for the European project. Although its salience was relegated well below that of factors such as immigration, anti-German sentiment likely played a role in Britain's referendum to leave the EU, especially among left-wing Brexit ('Lexit') supporters (see Lapavitsas 2018).

This book seeks to leave such problematic narratives of blame behind. Based on in-depth case study analysis of Greece, Portugal, and Ireland, I develop a different interpretation of the origins of their respective crises. These countries were 'hit hardest' not because of their 'immature' patterns of political and economic governance, nor due to their economic domination by their more powerful European neighbours. Instead, I show that the crisis in the European periphery is the product of their adaptation to a 'one size fits all' project of European integration. In each case I show how domestic adaptation to EU-led reforms of banking and finance resulted in wholesale transformations of peripheral political economies. Greece, Portugal, and Ireland have been at the centre of the crisis because their aspirations to converge with Western Europe catalysed brand new and unexpected patterns of divergence. In other words, the countries of the European periphery got into trouble by 'following the rules' of European integration, not solely by failing to.

In developing this argument, this book makes important contributions to debates on the eurozone crisis. Theoretically, I develop the concept of 'divergence via

Europeanisation' to demonstrate how insights from the CPE literature on 'capitalist diversity' can be fruitfully brought into dialogue with studies of 'Europeanisation'. While the former emphasises the persistence of national variation in the face of pressures to transform (Hancké 2009, 9), Europeanisation directs attention to the transformative effects of 'domestic adaptation to European regional integration' (Vink and Graziano 2007, 7). Their combination leads to a new understanding of how domestic adaptation to European regional integration can be generative of brand new, unpredictable patterns of transformation. In contrast to CPE, I propose that the evolving economic trajectories of the European periphery cannot solely be explained with reference to the resilience of national Varieties of Capitalism (VoC) in the face of EU-driven pressures to converge. Rather, the Europeanisation of the European periphery led to the generation of new, unanticipated, patterns of transformation. As such, this book makes a critical contribution to the literature on capitalist diversity, VoC, and CPE.

This argument implies an important distinction between convergence as a *process* and convergence as a *project*. National and EU elites alike have tended to subscribe to a common-sense belief that European integration would lead to *processes* of convergence among member states. The implication of joining the Single Market and the euro is that all member states could and should use a 'one size fits all' formula to secure economic growth, and it was believed that competitive pressures together with the stringent conditions imposed by the EU on member states would force structural reform and lead to institutional convergence (Hall 2012, 347). As Hall (2014) notes, an 'element of prophecy was built into this mythology', which remained, of course, unfulfilled (Dooley 2017b). Greece, Ireland, and Portugal all participated in *projects* of convergence during their membership of the EU. I argue that these projects aimed at promoting convergence were significant contributors to processes of divergence in these countries. Convergence as a process is a myth, but the emergence of projects to restructure economies in the name of convergence has had real and significant effects.[5]

Empirically, I contribute new interpretations of the origins of the eurozone crisis in Greece, Portugal, and Ireland. Existing domestic accounts have been dominated by historical narratives that are preoccupied with identifying the various obstacles to the development of mature trajectories of development in these countries. Systemic accounts have tended to eschew a domestic focus. When they do trace national crises, they privilege the structural role of 'external' over domestic pressures for change. As such, parallel national histories of the origins of specific patterns of divergence –something altogether different – have tended to be neglected. In contributing to the filling of these gaps, the case studies presented here invite new thinking on the histories of economic development and crisis in these three countries.

Taken together, these contributions suggest a way for debates on the crisis in the European periphery to move beyond problematic narratives of immaturity and German/core economic domination and to better understand the asymmetric impact of the crisis. Although it is vital that the domestic sources of the eurozone crisis be accounted for, a deeper understanding of these sources can be arrived at by recognising both their immature and non-immature components. Similarly, debates surrounding the potentially 'hegemonic' role of Germany, hierarchy and inequality within Europe, and the architectural flaws of the European project matter. I suggest that we can enrich our understandings of these issues by leaving beggar-thy-neighbour assumptions behind.

Chapter overview

The argument of this book is developed across the following six chapters. Chapter 2 recasts the political and scholarly debate on the eurozone crisis by identifying the limits of approaches that emphasise narratives of 'blame' – both those directed at the perceived 'immaturity' of the so-called 'PIIGS' and critical accounts focused on their supposed 'economic domination' by Germany. I show how these approaches draw necessary attention to the domestic and systemic character of the eurozone crisis respectively. Yet, they are each unable to adequately account for the asymmetry of the crisis. Through an analysis of trade and capital lending data, I demonstrate the inadequacy of these narratives as explanations, and highlight the political problems generated by their underpinning narratives of blame. Blaming the 'lazy PIIGS' or the German 'big bad wolf' has contributed to rising Euroscepticism, disastrous policy prescriptions, and serious problems for the future of European integration.

Chapter 3 develops the analytical framework, which is applied to the case studies of Greece, Portugal, and Ireland. The chapter begins with a critique of VoC approaches to the eurozone crisis. Such approaches convincingly show how the attempt to integrate incompatible national VoC within a flawed-in-design monetary union led to contradictions, imbalances, and ultimately crisis. While taking their insights on 'institutional stickiness' on board, I show how VoC is incomplete because it downplays processes of institutional transformation. By bringing a broadly CPE approach into dialogue with Europeanisation, I develop an analytical framework that can identify 'divergence via Europeanisation'. This framework makes it possible to trace the role of institutional path dependency in placing limits on export-led growth in Greece, Portugal, and Ireland, while also being sensitive to the possibility that Europeanisation has acted as a catalyst for the emergence of radically new structures and patterns of growth.

Chapter 4 analyses the case of Greece, beginning the first of three case studies. Scholarship on the Greek crisis has emphasised its 'exceptional' origins, typically tracing how the emergence of 'debt-fuelled clientelism' in the 1980s has resisted the attempts of modernisers and reformers to supplant it in the decades before crisis struck. In contrast, I make an analytical distinction between the fiscal and competitiveness components of Greece's crisis. I show how, although the former can be partially (but not exhaustively) explained with reference to the 'poor reform capacity' of the Greek state, the latter emerged because of implementing

EU reforms relating to liberalisation, privatisation, and deregulation of banking and finance. The Europeanisation of Greek banking facilitated the emergence of a 'debt-led' trajectory of economic growth, suggesting that Greece's problems were caused just as much by the EU-driven reforms it succeeded in introducing as by those it failed to.

Chapter 5 turns to Portugal and investigates the origins of a crisis that was characterised by the experience of 'all of the signs of overheating . . . without any acceleration of GDP' (Deutsche Bank 2010). I trace how the introduction of EC/EU-facilitated 'structural reforms' throughout the 1980s and 1990s contributed to the development of debt-led growth. In the 1990s, a rejuvenated private banking sector drove the expansion of economic growth in Portugal's non-tradable sector, damaging the country's competitiveness and creating some of the highest levels of private debt in the EU. This trajectory of economic growth contributed to a decade of stagnation in the 2000s, ensuring that Portugal was particularly vulnerable to contagion from the Greek and Irish crises from 2010 onwards. At the same time, patterns of institutional stickiness left Portugal's export sector vulnerable to intense competition from developing economies during the 2000s, exacerbating its decelerating economic growth. Portugal's crisis is a combination of rapid institutional change, as well as stubborn institutional path dependency.

Chapter 6 focuses on the origins of the Irish banking crisis. I make an analytical distinction between the decline of the 'Celtic Tiger' export boom and the emergence of a detrimental housing bubble in the early 2000s. While I argue that negligence on behalf of Irish governments from the late 1990s onwards played an undeniable role, I show that Ireland's implementation of reforms driven by its preparations for joining the Single Market and Economic and Monetary Union (EMU) facilitated the emergence of a highly liberalised and aggressive banking sector from as early as the late 1980s. While European integration may have been vital to Ireland's development of export-oriented growth in the 1990s, it also created the conditions for a severe banking crisis a decade later.

Chapter 7 brings the three case studies together and concludes with an account of the book's contribution to new theories of the origins and asymmetry of the eurozone crisis. More specifically, it develops the concept of *divergence via Europeanisation*. While existing CPE approaches emphasise the role of institutional stickiness under an unfit-for-purpose euro, I expand such analysis to show how the Europeanisation of banking and finance developed a variety of equally damaging patterns of debt-led growth across Greece, Portugal, and Ireland. I demonstrate how the combination of CPE and Europeanisation answers the central research question of this book: what explains the asymmetry of the eurozone crisis?

CPE sheds light on the different institutional legacies of different peripheral VoC. To greater or lesser extents, these distinct institutional configurations placed limits on the periphery's convergence with the core, in terms of developing patterns of export-led economic growth. Europeanisation shows how domestic adaptation to European financial integration led to profound transformations to peripheral political economies. However, Europeanisation studies also recognises that these processes of domestic adaptation to European integration (Europeanisation) are by no means uniform. Greece, Portugal, and Ireland each developed distinctive forms of debt-led growth, leading to distinctive forms of crisis. Finally, the concluding chapter summarises the development of the overall argument, and reflects on its broader significance for academic and political debates on the eurozone crisis. I propose that the concept of 'divergence via Europeanisation' can deepen understandings of the crises in the European periphery, of hierarchies and inequalities within the EU, and of the eurozone crisis more generally.

This book makes three significant contributions. First, it challenges two influential notions regarding the origins of the eurozone crisis. It makes the argument that the crisis cannot be explained solely by the irresponsibility of the countries of the European periphery, and neither can it be explained exhaustively by the 'economic domination' of Germany. This book calls for scholars of the eurozone crisis to rethink settled common-sense assumptions about the politics of blame and the origins of the crisis. Second, it breaks new ground in the positioning of its analysis of the European periphery and the eurozone crisis in the intersection of CPE and Europeanisation studies. In an important sense, this book bridges a persistent divide between Political Science and Political Economy, in order to gain a deeper understanding of the crisis facing Greece, Ireland, Portugal, and indeed the EU. Finally, it contributes the concept of 'divergence via Europeanisation'. The book shows that the European periphery have been 'hit hardest' by the eurozone crisis because their attempts to 'catch up' with Western Europe by aspiring to converge their levels and forms of development with them were – paradoxically – generative of brand new patterns of unstable divergence. I show how the crises in Greece, Portugal, and Ireland were not caused solely by exceptional or immature national traits. Rather, they were, in large part, an unintended outcome of putatively 'mature' patterns of Europeanisation. This concept of 'divergence via Europeanisation' implies that the eurozone crisis is in part a crisis of the project of convergence itself, and the integration process has not been sensitive or flexible enough to the unpredictable and divergent outcomes of the attempt to promote the economic convergence of its member states.

Notes

1 The island of Ireland technically comprises of two states: The Republic of Ireland and Northern Ireland. For the sake of convenience, throughout this book, I refer to the Republic of Ireland as 'Ireland'.

2 A commonly used and regrettable acronym for the so-called 'deficit' countries of Southern Europe and Ireland: Portugal, Ireland, Italy, Greece, and Spain.

3 While Germany remains central to most research in this vein, some approaches emphasise the role of 'core Europe' and/or of transnational capital classes.

4 These two narratives of blame are clearly not exhaustive of the different 'approaches' to the study of the eurozone crisis. Rather, they operate as influential assumptions that crop up in a range of disparate theories (see Chapter 2). In Chapter 3 I show how CPE

approaches such as VoC represent a highly prominent example of an approach that does not easily succumb to such narratives of blame. What is interesting, however, is how VoC nevertheless tends to smuggle in some of the assumptions of both narratives.

5 For the sake of clarity, please note that throughout the book the term 'convergence' will refer to *projects* of convergence, and does not indicate any subscription to theories that assume the likelihood of 'convergence' as a *process* (e.g., see Hancké 2009, 5–6 for an account of liberal convergence theorists). For this reason, it is possible to speak about a 'project of convergence' (e.g., adherence to EU budget rules or transposition of EU directives on banking and finance) and to note how these projects are actually generative of *divergence*.

2 Beyond the 'lazy PIIGS' and the German 'big bad wolf'[1]

Why did the eurozone crisis impact some countries more severely than others? The shocks of the 2008 global financial crisis reverberated around the world, but why were the faults so pronounced in the countries of the European periphery? EMU has any number of well-known design flaws, but why did these create disproportionate problems for Greece, Ireland, and Portugal? And why did these worst-affected cases experience such markedly different kinds of crisis? A highly prominent strategy to explain this asymmetric impact of the eurozone crisis has been to focus how and why the crisis-hit countries of the periphery have lost *competitiveness* vis-à-vis the relatively unscathed countries of the European core (see Jones 2016; Johnston, Hancké, and Pant 2014 for summaries). I focus on two competing versions of the 'competitiveness hypothesis' in this first chapter: the 'official narrative' and 'core–periphery analysis'. I show how both accounts fall short of explaining asymmetry, in large part due to a shared preoccupation with 'narratives of blame'.

Section one focuses on the 'official narrative'. Much like their namesakes in the fairy tale, the so-called 'PIIGS' built their houses out of straw, risking the survival of the eurozone in the process.[2] The countries of the European periphery were hit hardest because of their supposed hubris, profligacy, corruption, and general lack of the kind of mature political culture found in core Europe. Section two focuses on the competing approach of core–periphery analysis, casting Germany as the 'big bad wolf' of the tale (see especially Lapavitsas et al. 2012). In this version of the story, Germany is accused of uniquely and perhaps deliberately benefitting from a foundational inequality of EMU, at the inevitable expense of the periphery (Lapavitsas et al. 2012; Moravcsik 2012). By replacing one scapegoat with another, this 'beggar-thy-neighbour' narrative challenges existing assumptions by blaming the German big bad wolf instead of the PIIGS.

In this chapter I show how 'competitiveness hypothesis' scholarship, which relies on notions of either peripheral immaturity or German beggar-thy-neighbour assumptions, cannot adequately explain the asymmetry of the eurozone crisis. While the official narrative stages a problematic 'morality play' between Northern 'saints' and Southern 'sinners' (Matthijs and McNamara 2015; Adler-Nissen 2017; Fourcade et al. 2013), narratives of German dominance will be shown to lack empirical support for their positing of a beggar-thy-neighbour relationship between core and periphery. Drawing out these limitations makes it possible to argue in the subsequent chapter that a revised competitiveness hypothesis, drawing on CPE and Europeanisation, can indeed explain the asymmetry of the eurozone crisis.

Official narratives of 'immaturity' in the European periphery

To explain the asymmetry of the eurozone crisis, or why the epicentre was in the European periphery and not elsewhere, a range of influential approaches have argued that focus should be on the different national sources of weak competitiveness and fiscal profligacy in the worst-hit countries. As distinct from systemic accounts that focus on the design flaws of EMU (such as Papadimitriou and Wray 2012) or on global capital flows 'gone wild' (such as Jones 2016), these approaches advise that to explain variation in experience of the global credit crunch or the eurozone crisis, the appropriate unit of analysis is the different institutions, practices, and policies within states. The most prominent version of this approach is labelled here as the 'official narrative', which underpins a policy response of austerity and structural reform. It has been developed by the European Commission, the ECB, and the IMF, as well as by academics (Sinn 2014; Lane 2012), think tanks, and, as Matthijs and McNamara note (2015), several German economists and political figures.[3]

In this section, I show that while this narrative can explain why the periphery may have had public finance issues and lacked institutions similar to those underpinning export-led growth regimes in the core of Europe, it cannot tell the whole story. In short, it can only explain why the European periphery's growth regimes did *not converge* into export-led models. Due to an excessive focus on pre-identified 'obstacles to export-led growth', or what is dysfunctional or *immature*, the official narrative cannot fully explain the parallel emergence of 'debt-led growth', which I show in subsequent chapters is, to a major extent, a product of 'getting the policies right'.

Official narratives of the crisis in Greece, Ireland, and Portugal

Former head of the Eurogroup Joeren Dijsselbloem faced calls to resign in March 2017 for refusing to apologise for his remarks that crisis-hit countries such as Greece, Portugal, and Ireland had wasted their money on "drinks and women" (Khan and McClean 2017). Such comments have been standard fare since the outbreak of this crisis. Peripheral states have been presented in segments of the international press as "the (corrupted) *other* of the (rational) western society" (Antoniades 2013). Social and cultural 'national traits' have been reified and pathologised, and used as a convenient explanation for the problems encountered by the peripheral states (Patomäki 2013, 13; Dooley 2014). It has proven remarkably resilient too. As political events in Italy threatened to 'reawaken' the eurozone crisis in the summer of 2018, *Der Spiegel* published a column referring to Italians as ungrateful 'beggars' – failing to recognise that Italy is a net contributor to the EU budget and, at the time of writing, has not been subject to the kind of bailouts seen in Greece, Portugal, and Ireland (Fleischhauer 2018). As Wolfgang Münchau writes in the *Financial Times*, narratives matter, and can contribute to a toxic combination of mistrust and untruths (2018). These kinds of sentiments are informed (or perhaps more fairly, misinformed) by an explanation of the eurozone crisis identified here as 'the official narrative', sometimes labelled the 'fiscal recklessness' hypothesis (Johnston et al. 2014) or the 'immaturity thesis' (Dooley 2014); an explanation that has gained considerable traction among European political leaders and policy makers (Johnston et al. 2014; Matthijs and McNamara 2015) since the crisis broke out.

Stepping back from the more sensationalist echoing of this explanation in political and media discourse, this 'official narrative' is most clearly apparent in the analysis and prescriptions of the EU–ECB–IMF arrangements, as well as in the EU institutional response to the crisis; all of which are marked by measures designed to correct key 'immaturities' of the peripheral states (Dooley 2014). Although tailored to fit the specific cases (as noted by Hardiman et al. 2017), the official narrative tends to comprise of three key steps. First, fiscal policy in the European periphery was mismanaged. Second, labour markets have been mired by rising wage costs, rigidity, and falling productivity. Third, there has been political unwillingness to make painful but necessary reforms.[4]

Greece

The official narrative first emerged within analysis of the Greek crisis. Jason Manolopoulos writes that:

> modern Greek society and economy . . . is a monster . . . This is a systemic, cultural dimension of the Greek saga; it is not just a case of a few unconnected scandals. It is institutionalised.
>
> (2011)

More than a few agree (see, e.g., European Commission 2010; Katsimi and Moutos 2010; Mētsopoulos and Pelagidēs 2012).[5] Notions of Greek exceptionalism underpin the argument that a country such as Greece should never have been allowed to join the euro in the first place. Greece is not only accused of being responsible for its own mess; its immaturity has risked the very survival of the European project.

There are three main steps to the tale of Greek immaturity. The first is to recognise, at the most basic level, that the Greek sovereign debt crisis of 2009 was mostly fiscal: it was a crisis of Greek public finances, and of its consistently exorbitant levels of public debt and budget deficits. Greek public debt has been close to 100 percent of Gross Domestic Product (GDP) or more since the late 1980s, and its budget deficit has never been balanced while a member of the euro (European Commission 2010, 3–4; Alogoskoufis 2012,

2; Featherstone 2011; Pisani-Ferry, Sapir, and Marzinotto 2010, 4). Greece is accused of endemic tax evasion, systematic overspending, and persistently overoptimistic tax projections (European Commission 2010, 3–4).

Worse still, fiscal misbehaviour was not only a problem for the solvency of the Greek state. The European Commission (2010, 3–4; see also Oltheten et al. 2013, 330–1; Featherstone 2008, 19) argues that Greece's fiscal problems are a cause of its competitiveness problems, as a ballooning yet inefficient public sector distorts and crowds out private sector activity. Greece has relatively high unit labour costs, meaning real wage growth consistently outstrips productivity (European Commission 2010). Competitiveness problems are primarily the result of Greek workers being paid too much, especially in sheltered sectors, while being relatively unproductive, and of the state spending unwisely which disincentives mature, modern economic activity (ibid). Fiscal profligacy has thus been a central cause of Greek public deficits, indebtedness, but also has contributed to current account deficits through falling competitiveness.

Secondly, Greece's fiscal problems have their origins in the highly-charged populist agendas of its major political parties since the late 1970s/1980s, who tend to consolidate their support once in power through expansionary fiscal policies and the construction of systems of clientelism. PASOK and later New Democracy (ND) transformed the Greek state into a complex system of clientelism/patronage. Electoral support was traded for favours, employment, and particular lifestyles. Major sections of society accordingly became bound up in a system of clientelism, and bribery and corruption in the everyday provision of public services became a 'national pastime' (Manolopoulos 2011, 103–4). Put very simply, there exists a broad 'culture of entitlement' across Greek society.

The final analytical step posits the 'end of Greek history'; the next thirty years of Greek history are, in any meaningful sense, static; the clientelistic state that had become consolidated during the 1980s proved impossible to supplant throughout the 1990s and 2000s (see Diamandouros 2011). Although exceptions are well noted, it is widely considered that no meaningful reforms succeeded during the 1990s and 2000s (see Diamandouros 2011) because the debt-fuelled clientelism had become endemic and impossible to supplant. The state's growth, and the interests of society at large, not to mention powerful interest groups, were all too dependent on the 'Greek' model (see, e.g., the discussion in Triandafyllidou, Gropas, and Kouki 2013, 1–21; Diamandouros 2011, 1994; Tsoukalas 1995).

Portugal

The Portuguese crisis is understood as a story of three main factors: "chronic fiscal misbehaviour" (Royo 2012a), weak competitiveness, and, crucially, the political unwillingness to deal with either (Pereira and Wemans 2012; Magone 2004; Baer and Leite 2003). Just prior to its bailout, the European Commission described Portugal's public finances as being on an "unsustainable trend" (2011, 9). Like Greece, Portugal's government deficit has never been below the 3 percent of GDP rule since euro membership. Its debt-to-GDP ratio has steadily increased over the 2000s, from below 60 percent in 2004, rising above 100 percent in 2011 (European Commission 2011, 9). The 2011 troika rescue package is in fact the third time Portugal has been bailed out since its democratic revolution in 1974. Successive Portuguese governments are accused of failing to get a handle on their public finances, even temporarily introducing a government fiscal stimulus package in 2009 at the height of the eurozone crisis (Pedroso 2014). The European Commission also focuses in on Portugal's state-owned enterprises and use of Public Private Partnerships, which entail large fiscal risks. State-owned enterprises, many of which are loss makers, are a drain on public spending, but also distort the market by, inter alia, attracting bank lending and talent away from potential private sector competitors (European Commission 2011).

The Portuguese crisis is more widely recognised as not just a fiscal crisis, but also a crisis of competitiveness and productivity. Portugal's economy stagnated at an annual average GDP growth rate of 1 percent between 2001 and 2008, the second lowest of the EU27 (European Commission 2011; Pereira and Wemans 2012, 10). Portuguese policy makers are accused of not doing enough to improve their international competitiveness and productivity by taking advantage of the opportunities of European integration (Abreu 2006, 3). Reis (2013) notes that most literature on Portugal's crisis tends to mention various obstacles to Portugal's productivity during the 2000s; a list that typically includes low average educational attainment, low total factor productivity, an oversized government, labour market rigidities, inefficient legal system, and low export competitiveness (see also European Commission 2011, 5 for a similar list; as well as Pereira and Wemans 2012, 4–5; see also Baer and Leite 2003, 745). Portugal's tradeable sector is predominated by small to medium sized enterprises (SMEs), and low- to medium-technology goods, which are particularly sensitive to changes in price. Portugal lost market share against East Asian and Central and Eastern European competitors during the 2000s. In spite of some success with diversification, to restore competitiveness in the late 2000s, the argument is that Portugal urgently needs to reform its labour markets to attract investment and increase productivity (European Commission 2011).

Like Greece, analysis of Portugal's crisis recognises the very real attempts at reform made by the country over the years. Yet, these reforms are almost always understood as insufficient or illusory (Royo 2012, 190). As Abreu notes, in the second half of the 1990s fiscal policy was expansionary. Deficit reductions necessary to join the euro owed much to high economic growth and the substantial fall in interest rates and consequently in debt servicing costs, and were not achieved through necessary structural reforms as they should have been (Abreu 2006, 2). Much like Greece, Portugal allegedly managed to participate in the euro under false pretences, and as Magone puts it, it failed at reforming and upgrading the "cultural patterns of behaviour in Portuguese society" and politics (Magone 2004, 236).

Ireland

Ireland was forced to apply for an €85 billion bailout after two decades of being viewed as the 'poster child of the EU' (Kirby 2010, 3). During the 1990s,

Ireland's high-technology export sector contributed to economic growth rates of over three times that of most other European countries; with some of the lowest levels of government spending and borrowing in Europe (Kirby 2010; Ó Riain 2004, 2014). Yet it is typically argued that over time, different decisions by Irish governments contributed to the emergence of a banking crisis. The Celtic Tiger model was 'hijacked' by governments in the late 1990s and 2000s, who facilitated freedoms to the banking sector, spurring a housing boom, and put in place a timid and ineffective (Honohan 2010) "light-touch regulatory system seeking to encourage the market rather than restrain it" (Kirby 2010, 9; Honohan 2010). Irish pro-cyclical budgetary policy did not "lean sufficiently against the wind" (European Commission 2012a) and although budgets were generally in surplus between 2001 and 2007, public spending was mostly directed to areas that contributed to overheating and damaged competitiveness. The EU, as well as the OECD consistently warned Ireland of fiscal and macroeconomic risks related to overheating and recommended spending restraint (Regling and Watson 2010). The Irish tax base was narrow, overly reliant on construction related taxes, and incredibly vulnerable after the bubble burst (European Commission 2012b). There existed close personal as well as financial links between bankers, property developers, builders, and politicians, especially in the Fianna Fáil party (Dellepiane, Hardiman, and Las Heras 2013, 92). Elaine Byrne argues that Fianna Fáil, who were in government for most of the 2000s, developed a financial reliance on the construction sector – "[a] list of rich political donors once read like a Who's Who of Irish property developers" (2012, 205; see also McMenamin 2013, 2).

Ireland's problematic fiscal policy clearly contributed to competitiveness problems. Policy decisions that assisted in overheating the property sector helped undermine Ireland's competitiveness as investment began to be directed away from the high-technology export sector (Hardiman forthcoming, 22). Ireland is also argued to have lost competitiveness due to rising wages during the boom period. Although Ireland was recognised to have a better track record than Greece and Portugal in providing an attractive and flexible workforce, the Real Effective Exchange Rate appreciated as wage growth remained high and productivity declined (European Commission 2012b) during the boom years. This analysis of high wages driving the Irish crisis led to a short-lived troika-recommended lowering of the minimum wage in Ireland.

Nowhere was poor governance more evident than in the banking sector, where Ireland's infamous system of 'light touch regulation' did nothing to help a sector characterised by intense competition for profits in an overheating economy (European Commission 2012b). Hogan, Donnelly, and O'Rourke (2010) view the failure to heed the warnings as representing a tragically missed opportunity to exploit external fiscal commitments as political cover to help overcome the political pressures to act this way (38). Such immature governance left Ireland dangerously exposed to external shocks (Hardiman 2010, 72). As such, it doesn't matter that Ireland temporarily 'got it right'. When it came down to it, Ireland's governance became just as problematic as that of its fellow PIIGS. Ireland is understood to have squandered its 'mature' economic development during the 2000s when, as the late Minister for Finance Brian Lenihan infamously put it, "we all partied" (RTÉ Prime Time 2010).

The problem of the 'immaturity thesis'

Critics have pointed out that the official narrative's sometimes myopic focus on the fiscal nature of the crisis barely explains Greece's problems, and certainly can't explain those of Ireland and Portugal. Spain and Ireland's fiscal position was stronger than Germany's, yet this did little to halt major shifts to their bond yields, while Belgium's consistently high levels of high public debt experienced little pressure from speculation (Johnston et al. 2014, 1772). The official narrative also fails to account for the international dimensions of the crisis and is unable to recognise some deeper contradictions of the eurozone itself (Dooley 2014; Becker and Jäger 2012; Fouskas and Dimoulas 2012, 147). By downplaying these kinds of clearly important aspects of the crisis, the official narrative creates a very partial account of what went wrong in the European periphery (see Fouskas and Dimoulas 2013, 147).

These empirical limitations of the official narrative stem from an underlying assumption of 'peripheral immaturity' (Dooley 2014). This is the assumption that identifying obstacles to sound public finances and convergence in terms of competitiveness, typically a host of dysfunctional national institutions, policies, and practices, explains the asymmetry of the eurozone crisis between the creditors in the core and the debtors in the periphery. There has been an implicit assumption in much of the official narrative on Southern Europe and Ireland that if the correct sets of policies are followed, and the right institutions are built and effectively governed; each country could have converged their patterns of economic growth along the lines of their Western European neighbours. As a result, any variation across societies is assumed to be a 'perversion' of the 'mature' or 'normal' developmental trajectory. In this way, the economic trajectories of particular societies are 'othered', and this is at the heart of the official narrative's moralisations in political, public, media, and policy discourse.

The problem is not that dysfunctional peripheral institutions, policies, and practices have nothing to do with the crisis in the periphery. Very few analyses of Greece would feel comfortable denying the reality of clientelism and its role in the crisis. The problem is that identifying obstacles to fiscal solvency and competitiveness can't, by definition, tell us the whole story. Approaches utilising the immaturity thesis can theorise the asymmetry between the core and periphery as being about immaturity/maturity. But what about the asymmetry of the crisis countries themselves? The three very distinctive forms of crisis encountered by Greece, Portugal, and Ireland suggest that something is missing from this formulation. Identifying various obstacles to the emergence of export-led growth models in the periphery can only tell us the reasons why export-led growth models failed to materialise. They tell us rather less about why a banking crisis materialised in Ireland but not Greece or Portugal. These obstacles can't tell us much about why convergence along fiscal lines still left Ireland vulnerable, or why falling competitiveness lead to GDP growth in Greece during the 2000s, but stagnation in Portugal during the same time.

There is clearly more to the story than 'obstacles' to maturity. Yet the immaturity thesis discounts the possibility that something other than an obstacle, like the transposition of EU directives on banking, could also be a potential source of divergence. It also discounts the possibility that 'non-liberal' practices of governance could conceivably contribute to 'convergence' even if they are identified as obstacles (Ó Riain 2014, 39) and vice versa. Additionally, it overlooks the fact that while there may only be one single way, in theory, to achieve growth regime 'convergence', there is any number of different ways for growth regimes to diverge, and, moreover, not all of these trajectories would have necessarily led to precarious, vulnerable patterns of growth.

Due to assumptions of peripheral immaturity, the official narrative accounts for the history and the crises in the European periphery in only a partial way, emphasising the supposed mistakes, errors, and failures that have led each country to squander its opportunity to converge with its Western European neighbours. Recognising this as the key limiting characteristic of the immaturity thesis, I argue that we can only account for the asymmetry of the eurozone crisis by going beyond 'obstacles to convergence', and studying the origins of 'paths to divergence' instead.

Germany, the core, and 'beggar-thy-neighbour' narratives

In part as a response to the aforementioned limitations, important alternatives to the official narrative have emerged in recent years. Among the most prominent is VoC, which I discuss in Chapter 3. But an especially demanding challenge is made by approaches that view core euro area countries,[6] but especially Germany, as the 'big bad wolf' of the story; focusing on how Northern economic dominance of the eurozone contributed directly or indirectly to the vulnerabilities of the so-called 'PIIGS'. In this section I outline the different strands of this challenge to the immaturity thesis, before zooming in on the key analytical steps of 'core–periphery analysis', which represents the most exacting critique of Germany's role in the crisis.[7]

Germany, the core, and the eurozone crisis

Three major strands of argument can be identified regarding Germany's role in the eurozone crisis. The first strand focuses on the ways in which Germany's problematic *response* to the eurozone crisis is a big part of the reasons why the crisis took on the magnitude that it did.[8] Matthijs (2016a), for instance, outlines a number of episodes where German politicians' stubborn preference for the 'southern sinners' myth measurably contributed to acute instances of negative market reaction (Matthijs cites five episodes, see Matthijs 2016a). It is also well known that German politicians, economists, and powerful institutions such as the

Bundesbank and Constitutional Court worked to prevent the ECB from playing the 'lender of last resort' role that the Federal Reserve had in the USA in 2008 and 2009 (Matthijs and Blyth 2011). The ECB did eventually fulfil this role, but many insist that German delays and obstruction allowed the crisis to develop on a scale and scope that it likely wouldn't have otherwise (see Wren-Lewis 2015). Thompson (2013, 2015) draws attention to how highly vulnerable core banks viewed the crisis in the periphery as an opportunity to shift "the risk of default in the periphery from German and French banks to collective European and other taxpayers" (Thompson 2013, 7). Others such as Bulmer (2014) have contributed to vibrant debates on whether post-eurozone-crisis Germany is emerging as a hegemon, reluctantly or otherwise.[9]

The second strand outlines a more systematic approach, showing how various actions and institutions of Germany, the European periphery, and EMU culminated in a perfect storm. This approach has its origins in CPE and does not typically directly refer to Germany 'beggaring its neighbour' (in contrast to the third), but rather directs attention to an unfit for purpose project of monetary integration, which suited the core 'coordinated market economies' yet was intrinsically damaging for peripheral 'mixed market economies' (Johnston 2016; Hancké 2013; Hall 2018). I outline this approach in detail in Chapter 3, as it forms part of this book's analytical framework.

The third strand argues that not only did Germany benefit from EMU and make a bad situation worse, but that it directly caused the crisis in the periphery in the first place. As distinct from the other strands, which tend to identify root causes at the level of the euro and typically emphasise the negative symbiosis of both core and peripheral institutions (Hall 2014), this critical approach places the blame squarely at the feet of the core; although, more often than not, it is the role of Germany that steals the headlines. While core–periphery analysis is not just about Germany, nevertheless, it is Germany that tends to get singled out by this analysis as the main offender. It is this latter and most demanding strand that is the main focus of this section. Originating from critical political economy (Lapavitsas et al. 2012; Stockhammer 2011), perspectives as diverse as Keynesian (Patomäki 2013; Wolf 2014) post-Keynesian (Cesaratto 2013; Dejuán, Paños, and Gonzalez 2013), and neo-Gramscian (van Apeldoorn 2012) have taken up core–periphery assumptions in their work. The approach has since 'gone mainstream'. José Magone, Brigid Laffan, and Christian Schweiger (2016), in an edited volume, explore core–periphery relations in the EU from a variety of perspectives (but see especially Sepos 2016). Andrew Moravcsik's widely cited 2012 work is one of the most prominent mainstream appropriations of Lapavitsas et al.'s original argument, and Dani Rodrik (2013), Jörg Bibow (2012), Simon Wren-Lewis (2015), Paul Krugman (2013a, 2013b), Martin Wolf (2010), Joseph Stiglitz (2016, 254–6), Yanis Varoufakis (2017, 23), and Robert Skidelsky (2014) have all popularised the argument.

As evidenced by its wide take-up from a disparate range of perspectives, German beggar-thy-neighbour notions have emerged as a much-needed alternative and touchstone for critical perspectives wishing to challenge the still influential peripheral immaturity thesis. Yet, there has been a clear reluctance from within critical literature on the eurozone crisis to interrogate narratives of Germany 'beggaring its neighbour', as argued elsewhere (Dooley 2014). Flassbeck and Lapavitsas have gone so far as to accuse a recent criticism of their approach by Storm (2016) of 'sowing confusion':

> Heterodox voices in Europe certainly need conviction . . . but they need clarity even more. . . . Simply put, there could be no coherent explanation of Eurozone failure that left diverging nominal unit labour costs [between Germany and the periphery] out of account.
>
> (Flassbeck and Lapavitsas 2016)

In contrast, I show that critical or heterodox perspectives on the origins of the eurozone crisis have much to gain from interrogating, and ultimately, from jettisoning beggar-thy-neighbour narratives. To show this, I first present core–periphery analysis as involving three key analytical steps.

Three steps of core–periphery analysis

The first step focuses on how the 'uploading' of German values to the EU level contributed to the emergence of the eurozone crisis in the first place.[10] As Matthijs (2016a, 389) notes, Germany was only willing to abandon its highly symbolic Deutschemark and Bundesbank and participate in EMU if the rest of Europe agreed to create the euro in a German ordoliberal image. As a result, a 'one size fits all' model of European integration was designed with German interests firmly in mind (Thompson 2013). The periphery was unable to emulate the German model of excessive wage moderation and low inflation and thus lost competitiveness and generated current account deficits (Lapavitsas et al. 2012, 4).[11] Confronted with falling competitiveness, as members of the euro the periphery lost the power to devalue their currencies, and were similarly damaged by the ECB imposing a single, blanket interest rate, which was always too low for countries that are booming and too high for those in recession.

The second step focuses on diverging unit labour costs between the core and periphery (Moravcsik 2012, 4–6; and see also Lapavitsas at al. 2012; Bellofiore 2013). During the period of their euro membership Greece, Italy, Portugal, and Spain saw their unit labour costs rise by 1 percent per year over target, slowly rendering their economies uncompetitive. During the very same period German unit labour costs rose by an average of less than 1 percent a year, well below the ECB inflation target of 2 percent (Moravcsik 2012, 4–6; Flassbeck and Lapavitsas 2016). Germany was excessively squeezing its wages in a way that the European periphery simply couldn't match. The result was stronger competitiveness and trade surpluses in the core, declining competitiveness, and trade deficits in the periphery.

Current account deficits in the periphery are understood to be the 'mirror' of Germany's current account surpluses (Lapavitsas et al. 2012, 4). As Moravcsik puts it, "[f]orty percent of [Germany's trade surplus] comes from German trade with the eurozone – a total roughly equal to the combined deficits of the crisis countries" (2012, 4; Lapavitsas et al. 2012, 30; see also Stiglitz 2016, 253). Moreover, because the competitiveness of Germany's export model rests on low wages, low inflation, and low domestic consumption, Germany has effectively exported high unit labour costs, high inflation, and domestic demand/import dependent patterns of economic growth into the periphery. Within such an arrangement, the eurozone periphery fulfils a crucial role for Germany's model of growth, as Bellofiore notes that Germany has a "historical need to export to Southern Europe, where it realised the largest part of its profits" (2013: 505). This is the crux of core–periphery analysis, "[t]he worsening of the current account balance of the peripheral countries emerges pari passu with the improving surplus of the central countries" (Cesaratto and Stirati 2011, 59). For Lapavitsas et al. (2012, "[t]he euro is nothing less than a beggar-thy-neighbour policy for Germany" (30; see also Stiglitz 2016, 253).

The third analytical step theorises the way in which EMU has led to enormous financial imbalances stemming from capital flows from the core to the periphery. Germany is argued to have 'recycled' its current account surpluses into capital exports, "primarily bank lending and foreign direct investment . . . the main recipient of which has been the eurozone, including the periphery" (Lapavitsas et al. 2012, 4). This has had two important effects. Firstly, large capital inflows have resulted in capital account surpluses in the periphery, directly contributing to public and private indebtedness, precipitating the sovereign debt crisis (Lapavitsas et al. 2012, 5). Secondly, capital outflows from the core into the periphery have led to the promotion of financialised growth via investment bubbles and consumer booms. As such, the 'export-led model' of growth in the core has directly led to the 'debt-led' model of growth in the periphery (Stockhammer 2012; Cesaratto 2013, 113). Accordingly, peripheral import dependency and persistent external imbalances become financed, and thereby constantly reproduced by capital inflows from the core (Bellofiore et al. 2010, 136–7; Becker and Jäger 2012, 183). In other words, the current account surpluses that are necessary for the success of German neomercantilism, become financed by German lending to the periphery. This not only creates new vulnerabilities and fault lines for the periphery via the worsening of their balance of payments, but it also leads to the "destruction of their productive base[s]" (Milios and Sotiropoulos 2010, 227).

Empirical limits I: current account imbalances

Core–periphery analysis is a highly influential critique of the immaturity thesis (Fouskas and Dimoulas 2013, 144), which makes it possible to argue that the current account deficits of the periphery have their origins in Berlin, not Athens. In other words, core and German dominance of the eurozone didn't leave the so-called PIIGS with any option but to build their economies out of straw. In a way that the official narrative tends not to, core–periphery analysis brings issues of German hegemony, current account imbalances, capital flows, and the unequal/hierarchical nature of EMU to the fore. Nevertheless, as important as these issues are, core–periphery analysis suffers from some serious empirical limitations, as I now outline.

Claims that current account surpluses in the core are the 'mirror' of those in the periphery rest on three major assumptions:

1 Relative unit labour costs are the primary determinant of divergences in competitiveness between the core and periphery.
2 Most German trade takes place within the eurozone and that the core 'needs' the periphery (Young and Semmler 2011, 9) to generate its current account surpluses.
3 The periphery 'lost out' on export market share to Germany/the core.

This all seems intuitive, as Figure 2.1 shows, because the eurozone is indeed clearly characterised by current account surpluses in the core, and deficits in the periphery.

However, it is one thing to be able to recognise that the eurozone is characterised by deficit countries and surplus countries, and quite another to argue that one is responsible for the other (Milios and Sotiropoulos 2010, 227; Young and Semmler 2011; Dooley 2014). In this section I show that the assumed connection between core/German current account surpluses and the deficits in the periphery is tenuous, for three reasons.

First, unit labour costs aren't everything. A growing literature shows that relative unit labour costs are a misleading explanation for the current account imbalances displayed in Figure 2.1 (Storm 2016; Storm and Naastepad 2015; Jones 2016) for two reasons. On the one hand, Storm (2016) shows that export prices are far less responsive to changes in unit labour costs than core–periphery analysis assumes, making up less than 25 percent of the gross output price. Germany's competitive advantage and current account surplus have much more to do with non-price (technology-based) competitiveness and its superior links to trading partners in the core and outside of Europe (such as with the USA and China) (Storm 2016, 7–8). On the other hand, current account deficits in the periphery are more likely a sign of a growth in imports, fuelled by capital inflows, than a fall in exports. This is evidenced, by Storm, through the fact that current account deficits in the crisis countries precede rising unit labour costs (see Storm 2016, 7–8).[12]

Second, German exports to most countries in the eurozone periphery are in fact marginal, and are unlikely to account for the imbalances posited by Lapavitsas et al. (2012) (Milios and Sotiropoulos 2010, 234–5; Dooley 2014, 945; Bastasin 2012, 156, 157). Core–periphery literature tends to overlook *country-specific* balances of trade. For example, if the periphery were structurally necessary to Germany or other core economies as a market for its exports, we would expect that trade to peripheral economies, such as Portugal, Ireland, Greece, Spain, and Italy, would be significant. However, as shown in Figure 2.2, the reality is much more complicated.

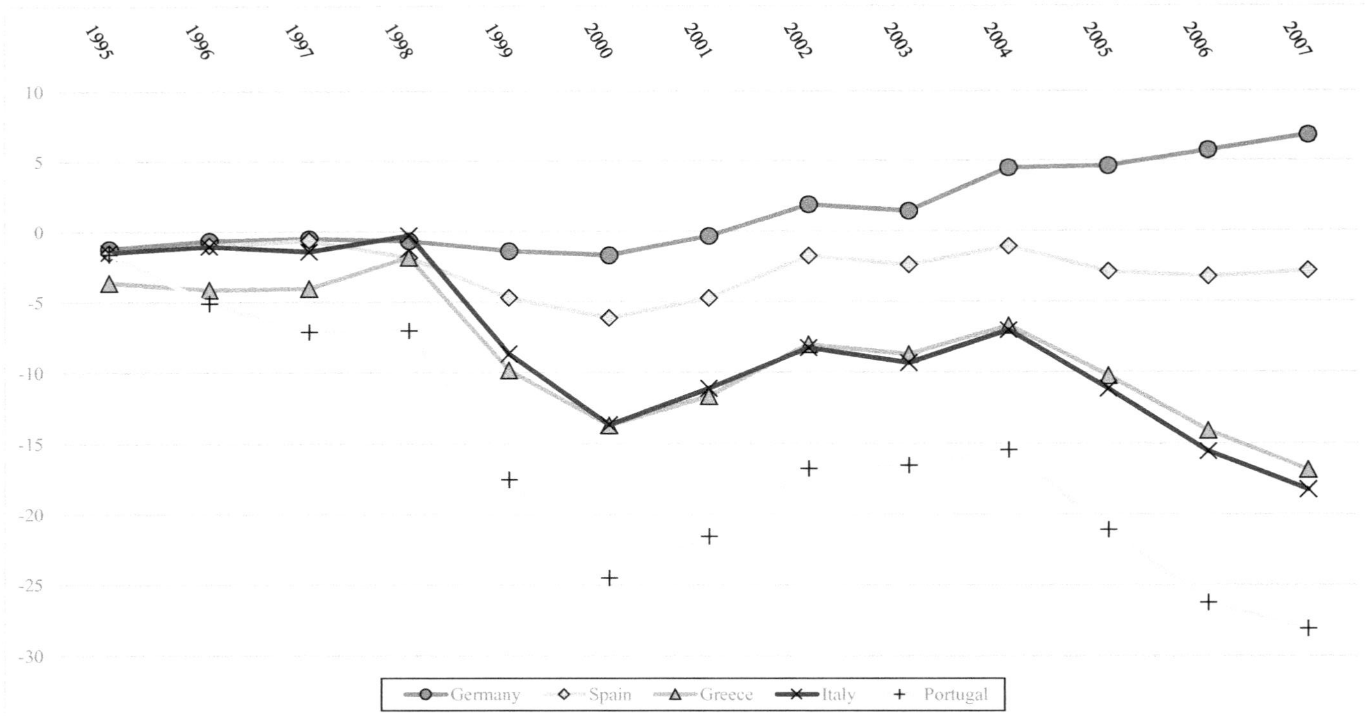

Figure 2.1 Current account balances for Germany, Spain, Greece, Italy, and Portugal (as a percentage of GDP)

Source: World Bank: Data Source indicated as International Monetary Fund, Balance of Payments Statistics Yearbook and data files, and World Bank and OECD GDP estimates.

Figure 2.2 shows Germany's trade balances with its top three partners, the four bailout countries, plus 'guilty by association' Italy for the boom period 2003–7. It shows that most of the peripheral eurozone countries account for a marginal percentage of Germany's trade surplus since the introduction of the euro. In fact, whereas the top three destinations of German exports (France, the USA, and the UK) account for 52.16 percent of the German trade surplus, Portugal, Ireland, and Greece account for only 3.03 percent of Germany's overall trade surplus, and, in fact, this includes a small trade *deficit* with Ireland. However, it must be noted that Germany has a considerably higher trade surplus with both Spain (13.49 percent) and Italy (10.77 percent) than the other three peripheral countries considered here; and when accounting for this, the five peripheral economies make up 27.29 percent of Germany's trade surplus altogether, or just about half of the contribution from core and extra-EMU trading partners. This is clearly substantial, but nevertheless reflects the relative importance of core-EMU and extra-EU partners. Spain and Italy are the next most important, but deficits in Portugal, Ireland, and Greece can in no way be said to be the 'mirror' of Germany's surplus.

The picture is complicated further by exploring the rest of the core, as Figures 2.3 and 2.4 and Table 2.1 show.[13]

Belgium (Figure 2.3) and the Netherlands (Figure 2.4) are both surplus countries. Belgium's top three trade surpluses come from France ($20.24 billion, or 110.19 percent of its world surplus), Germany ($9.41 billion; 51.21 percent), and

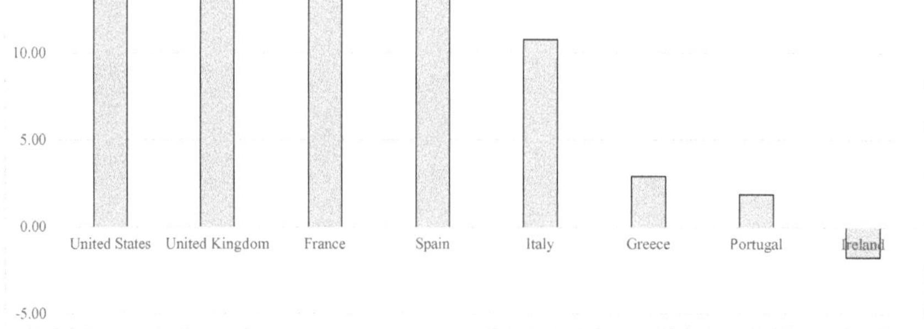

Figure 2.2 Germany trade balances with top three partners and the periphery: percentage of world surplus, average figures 2003–7

Source: IMF Direction of Trade Statistics

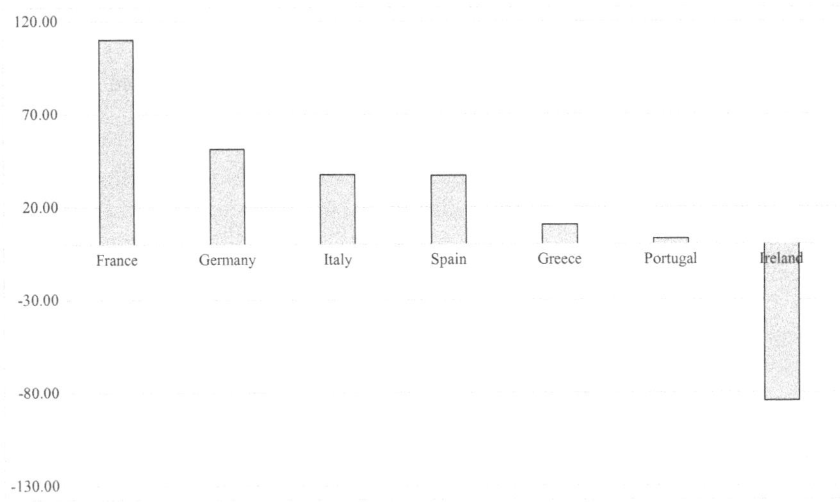

Figure 2.3 Belgium trade balances with top three partners and the periphery: percentage of world surplus, average figures 2003–7

Source: IMF Direction of Trade Statistics

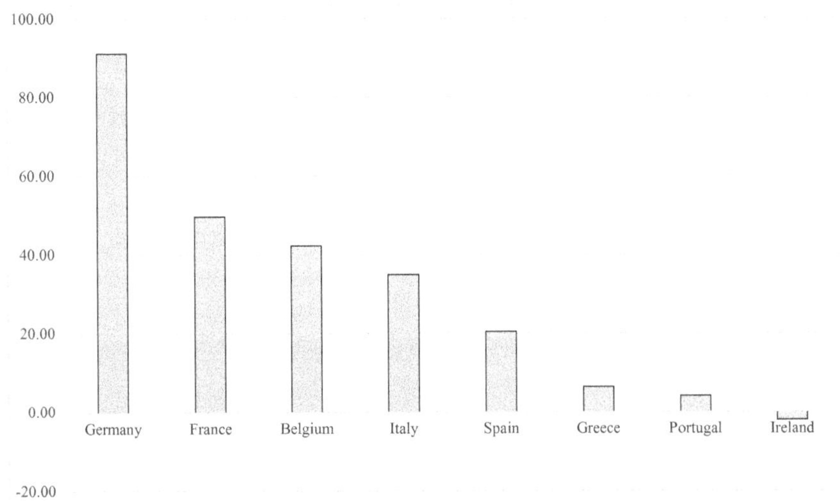

Figure 2.4 Netherlands trade balances with top three partners and the periphery: percentage of world surplus, average figures 2003–7

Source: IMF Direction of Trade Statistics

Italy ($6.87 billion; 37.42 percent). Belgium also runs a substantial trade surplus against Spain ($6.75 billion; 36.75 percent). Greece accounts for 10.5 percent of Belgium's world surplus ($1.93 billion), Portugal for 2.85 percent ($0.52 billion), and Belgium has a relatively huge trade deficit of $15.53 billion with Ireland (or −84.53 percent of its world surplus). The Netherlands (Figure 2.4) has large trade surpluses with Germany ($39.56 billion; 91.23 percent of its world surplus), France ($21.57 billion; 49.75 percent), and Belgium ($18.34 billion; 42.30 percent). Similar to the other three core cases, Italy ($15.15 billion; 34.95 percent) and Spain ($8.86 billion; 20.44 percent) make substantial contributions to the Dutch world surplus. Greece ($2.77 billion; 6.39 percent of its world surplus), Portugal ($1.81 billion; 4.17 percent), and Ireland ($0.89 billion of a trade deficit; −2.06 percent) feature as relatively small in comparison.

In spite of being a deficit country, France is included as part of the 'core' in most core–periphery analysis, including Lapavitsas et al. (2012). Austria and Luxembourg are similar examples of 'Northern' or core deficit countries.[14] As Table 2.1 shows, France's top three positive trade balances are with the UK ($8.58 billion; 1.82 percent of total exports), Spain ($8.55 billion; 1.81 percent of total exports), and the USA ($6.78 billion; 1.44 percent of total exports). France runs a small trade surplus with Greece of $3.32 billion (0.70 percent of total exports), and a smaller surplus with Portugal of $1.08 billion (0.23 percent). France has trade deficits of $3.59 billion (or −0.76 percent of total exports) with Ireland and $1.4 billion (or −0.3 percent of total exports) with Italy. Aside from a relatively large surplus vis-à-vis Spain, France's trade relationship with the periphery is a varied tale of small deficits and smaller surpluses.

Austria's top three positive trade balances (Table 2.1) are with the USA ($4.2 billion; 3.27 percent of total exports), Italy ($2.6 billion; 2.03 percent of total exports), and the UK ($2.5 billion; 1.98 percent of total exports). Austria has a relatively large surplus with Spain of $1.98 billion (1.54 percent of total exports), a smaller surplus with Greece ($0.59 billion; 0.46 percent) and Portugal ($0.27 billion; 0.21 percent of total exports), and – like the other cases – a deficit with Ireland ($0.19 billion; −0.15 percent of total exports). For Luxembourg (Table 2.1), France ($1.01 billion; 5.32 percent of total exports), the UK ($0.95 billion; 5.03 percent of total exports), and Italy ($0.95 billion; 5.0 percent of total exports) are the top three positive trade balances, with Spain close behind

Table 2.1 Core 'deficit countries': top three positive trade balances and trade balances with periphery, percentage of total exports

	1	*2*	*3*	*Portugal*	*Ireland*	*Italy*	*Greece*	*Spain*
France	*UK* 1.82%	*Spain* 1.81%	*USA* 1.44%	0.23%	−0.76%	−0.30%	0.70%	1.81%
Austria	*USA* 3.27%	*Italy* 2.03%	*UK* 1.98%	0.21%	−0.15%	2.03%	0.46%	1.54%
Luxembourg	*France* 5.32%	*UK* 5.03%	*Italy* 5.00%	1.24%	−0.17%	5.00%	0.49%	4.91%

Source: IMF Direction of Trade Statistics

($0.93 billion; 4.91 percent of total exports). Portugal ($0.23 billion; 1.24 percent of total exports) and Greece ($0.09 billion; 0.49 percent of total exports) are again relatively small, and Luxembourg runs a trade deficit against Ireland of $0.03 billion (−0.17 percent of total exports). For these three Northern deficit countries, Italy and Spain tend to contribute relatively significant positive balances (although France runs a deficit with Italy), Portugal and Greece contribute modest or minor positive balances, and Ireland contributes to their deficits. Crucially, for France, Austria, and Belgium there is no overall trade surplus for the periphery to contribute to.

Taking these six cases together reveals a more complex picture than the beggar-thy-neighbour dynamic core–periphery analysis proposes. The core EMU tends to generate substantial trade surpluses vis-à-vis *certain* peripheral countries, namely the large economies of Spain and Italy. However, it is core EMU, non-EMU, and non-EU trading partners that are most important in each case. Crucial 'crisis' countries such as Greece barely feature as source of trade surpluses, or as positive trade balances. The same goes for Portugal, and Ireland generates trade surpluses against each core country. While the figures for Spain and Italy are far from insignificant, in terms of visible balances of trade, it is clearly misleading to argue that peripheral current account deficits are the 'structural mirror' of core 'surpluses'. This is intuitive when it is considered that Germany's balance of trade did not decline from 2009 onwards, as would be expected, based on the premises of the core–periphery thesis and given the collapse of the propensity to consume across the eurozone periphery (Milios and Sotirpoulos 2010, 235). On the contrary, German trade flourished during the crisis, precisely because its trading partners in the core of Europe, and outside the eurozone, are much more important to its current account surplus that the relatively small economies of the eurozone periphery (Reisenbichler and Morgan 2013; Beck 2013).[15] At best, the core–periphery argument can show evidence for a beggar-thy-neighbour dynamic at play in Spain and Italy, but it certainly cannot explain the crucial cases of Greece, Portugal, and Ireland, which were each at the epicentre of the crisis.

Even if core–periphery analysis cannot say that the periphery is of any great importance to the generation of core *surpluses*, another argument could perhaps be developed highlighting the role that Germany and the core play in the generation of *peripheral deficits*. Yet, if we are to look at what percentage of trade deficits of each peripheral country comes from Germany and the core, the evidence for a beggar-thy-neighbour dynamic is much stronger in some countries than it is in others.

For the period 2003–7, almost half of Portugal's trade deficit (Table 2.2) results primarily from trade with the periphery. Spain accounts for 36.62 percent ($8.46 billion) of Portugal's deficit, while Italy accounts for 8.77 percent ($2.03 billion). Germany is highly significant as the second biggest deficit ($3.72 billion or 16.10 percent of the world deficit), but is nevertheless almost 20 percent lower than Spain. Belgium, France, Austria, Luxembourg, and Finland are each relatively marginal. As already mentioned, Ireland (Table 2.2) has an overall trade

Table 2.2 European periphery: top three negative trade balances plus balances with the core, average figures 2003–7

	1	*2*	*3*	*Germany*	*Belgium*	*France*	*Austria*	*Luxembourg*	*Finland*
Portugal (D)	*Spain* 36.62%	*Germany* 16.10%	*Italy* 8.77%	16.10%	1.76%	1.63%	1.09%	0.48%	0.21%
Greece (D)	*Germany* 13.8%	*Italy* 13.38%	*Russia* 8.15%	13.8%	4.66%	6.89%	1.28%	0.63%	1.24%
Italy (D)	*Germany* 178.08%	*Netherlands* 137.14%	*China* 131.31%	178.08%	67.15%	−71.24%	10.28%	9.54%	3.89%
Spain (D)	*Germany* 25.47%	*China* 11.5%	*Italy* 8.37%	25.47%	5.06%	4.77%	1.18%	0.65%	1.10%
Ireland (S)	*UK* −14.9%	*Taiwan* −4.16%	*China* −2.18%	5.07%	35.09%	9.75%	0.76%	0.28%	0.39%

(D = % overall trade deficit; S = % overall trade surplus).

Source: IMF Direction of Trade Statistics

surplus, and trade surpluses with each of the core countries considered here. Of its top three trade deficits, none are in the eurozone and only one (the UK at \$5.84 billion dollars; −14.89 percent of its surplus) is (during the period 2003–7) a member of the EU. However, in the case of Greece (Table 2.2) Germany is a clearly significant source of the former's trade deficit (\$5.86 billion; 13.8 percent of world deficit). Yet, fellow peripheral country Italy is a close second at \$5.68 billion or 13.38 percent of Greece's world deficit, and Russia features prominently also (\$3.46 billion; 8.15 percent). Germany and core Europe make up 35 percent of Greece's overall trade deficit, which is highly significant, but far from the whole story.

As mentioned, Germany does run significant trade surpluses with Spain and Italy. This is reflected in the sources of Italy's and Spain's trade deficits (Table 2.2). Germany represents \$17.32 billion of Italy's deficit (178.08 percent of Italy's world deficit), and the Netherlands (\$13.34 billion; 137.14 percent) and Belgium (\$6.53 billion; 67.15 percent) are highly important to Italy's overall deficit. However, Italy runs a large trade surplus with France of \$6.93 billion (−71.24 percent of the Italian trade deficit). Spain is slightly more ambiguous. Although Germany represents the largest individual portion of Spain's deficit (\$24.23 billion), it nevertheless amounts to 25.47 percent of the overall deficit, which is far less than Italy's trade deficit with Germany. China (\$10.95 billion; 11.5 percent) and Italy (\$7.97 billion; 8.37 percent) are the second largest sources of Spain's deficit and the core accounts for 45.6 percent of Spain's deficit collectively.

Taking all of these deficits together, there is no disputing the importance of Germany and the core in the generation of trade deficits in Spain and especially in Italy. Yet these countries are far less important in the generation of deficits in Portugal and are irrelevant in Ireland. Germany and the core are a significant part of Greece's trade deficit, but so too are Italy, Russia, and a whole host of other countries that account for the substantial remainder of its deficit. Naturally, we might expect the relatively large economies of Germany and the core to feature more prominently in the trade deficits of the periphery than relatively tiny Greece, Portugal, and Ireland would feature in the trade surpluses of the core. What is surprising is just how often Germany and the core *do not* dominate these balances.

Empirical limits II: capital flows

Although the aforementioned raises significant problems for 'Step 2' of the core–periphery analysis, a modified version of the beggar-thy-neighbour argument can still be made by looking at capital account imbalances.[16] Lapavitsas et al. correctly identify that "Germany has been exporting capital on a large scale, while peripheral countries have been importing capital" (2012, 31). Even if Germany and the rest of the core are not generating a current account surplus from trade with the periphery, and even if it is not 'necessary' for the core to direct massive capital flows to the periphery, the fact that it is doing so could still be a major cause of the crisis in the periphery (Cesaratto 2013, 113). Lapavitsas et al. demonstrate that flows from the core to periphery during the period have actually become 'more

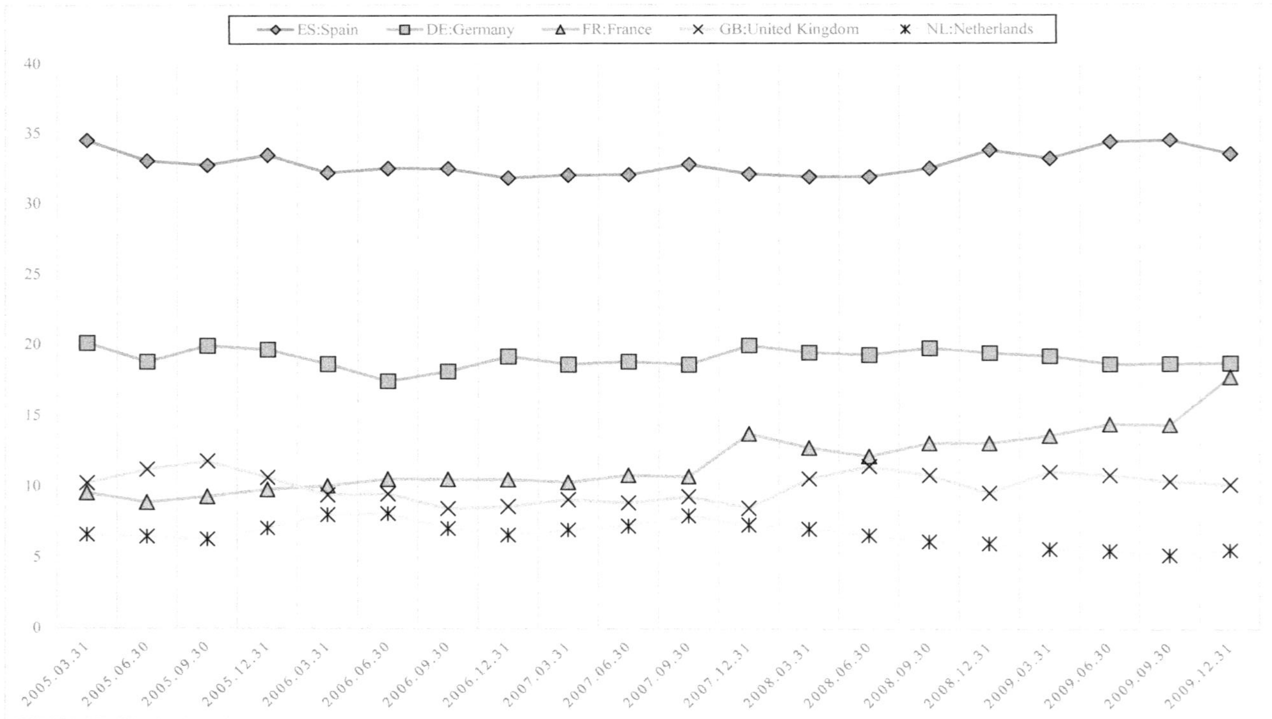

Figure 2.5 Portugal – consolidated foreign claims, percentage of total claims

Source: Bank for International Settlements Consolidated Bank Statistics

important in size' than any other type of capital flows in the eurozone, at least from 2005 to 2009 (2012, 46, 47). However, this argument needs to be unpacked carefully. To highlight the relative importance of core–periphery capital flows, Lapavitsas et al. have grouped the same four countries into the 'core' (Germany, France, Belgium, and the Netherlands) and 'periphery' (Greece, Ireland, Italy, Portugal, and Spain), and it is between these two groups of countries, rather than between specific countries, that the core–periphery relationship, in terms of bank lending and capital flows, has been established (Lapavitsas et al. 2012, 46). As was the case with 'Step 2', the relationship is not so clear-cut if we look at specific country-to-country relations.

As Figures 2.5–2.9 illustrate, the patterns of cross border lending within the eurozone are not so clearly reducible to a German beggar-thy-neighbour dynamic once we examine the countries on a case by case basis.[17] Germany is the most important lender *only in* the case of Spain, but not in Portugal, Ireland, Italy, or Greece. Indeed, as Thompson notes, German exposure is less than France in the case of Greece, and in total (2013, 8). Moreover, once we unpack the complexities of capital flows in each case, while the fact of high German exposure cannot be disputed, the case for German lending being more important to the origins of crisis in the periphery than other countries is seriously undermined.

Disaggregating capital flows from groups of 'core' economies to groups of 'peripheral' economies reveals some important challenges to core–periphery analysis. For example, in the case of Portugal (Figure 2.5), we can see that, although Germany is heavily exposed to the country (meaning that an average of $39,538 million of capital flowed from Germany to Portugal for the period 2005–9, an average of 19.0 percent of total claims), capital inflows from fellow peripheral economy Spain are close to twice as high, at an average of 32.9 percent of total claims, or $68,215 for the same period. Additionally, the combined average capital inflows from France ($25,174 million) and the UK ($20,816 million) exceed the amount from Germany at 21.8 percent of total claims. In the case of Ireland (Figure 2.6), the neighbouring UK is the most important lender (an average of 27 percent of total claims, or $163,774.70 million, for 2005–9), edging ahead of Germany at 26 percent ($159,411.10 million) of total claims for this particular period. Germany is indisputably a major lender to Ireland, and 50 percent of the time, Germany or the UK will be the biggest lender to Ireland for a given quarter during the time frame. Nevertheless, singling out the importance of German rather than UK banks for the case of Ireland is somewhat arbitrary.

In the case of Greece (Figure 2.7), Germany is the second most important lender at an average of 18 percent of total claims ($38,976 million from 2005 to 2009) falling behind France at 20.8 percent ($50,895 million). However, Germany is clearly the most important lender to Spain (Figure 2.8) (average of 27.5 percent of total claims or $223,519 million from 2005 to 2009) with France and the UK as distant, yet still important, second and third (averages of 17.4 percent; $143,073 million and 13.9 percent; $110,697 million respectively). The case of Italy France dwarves Germany as the most important lender (Figure 2.9; average of $341,417 million, or 31.1 percent of total claims – much larger than Germany's $209,615 million or 20.6 percent of total claims).

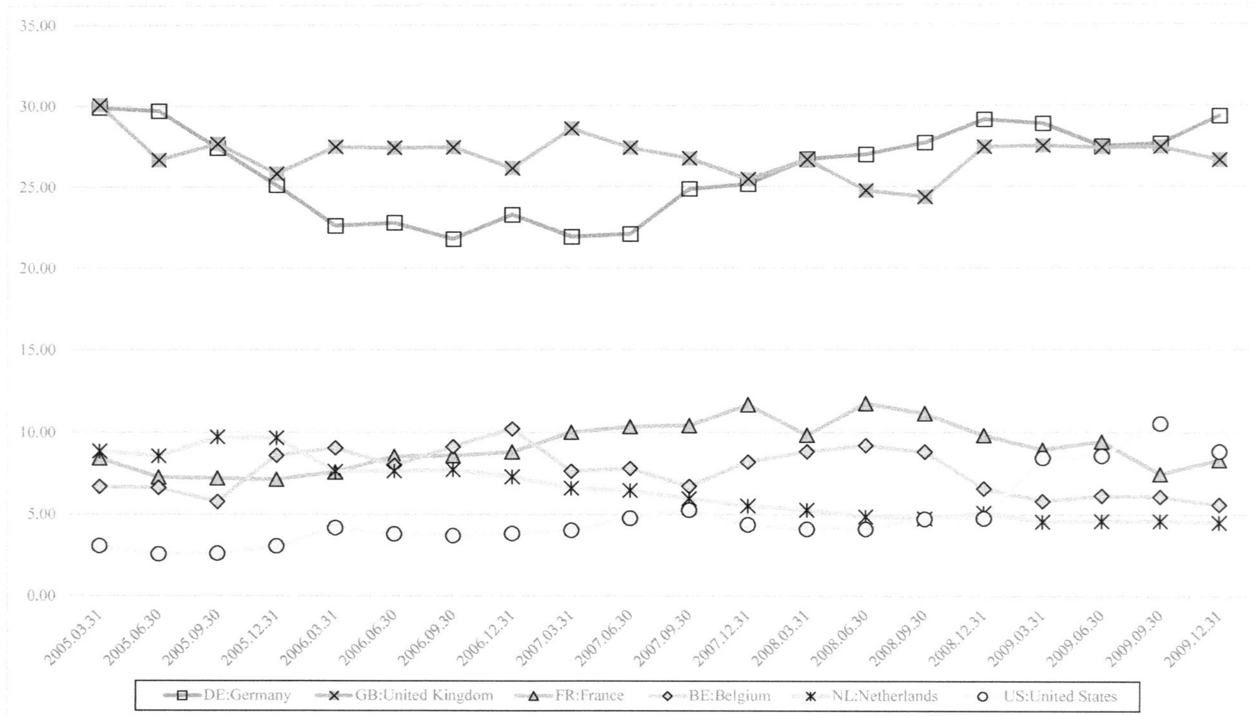

Figure 2.6 Ireland – consolidated foreign claims, percentage of total claims

Source: Bank for International Settlements Consolidated Bank Statistics

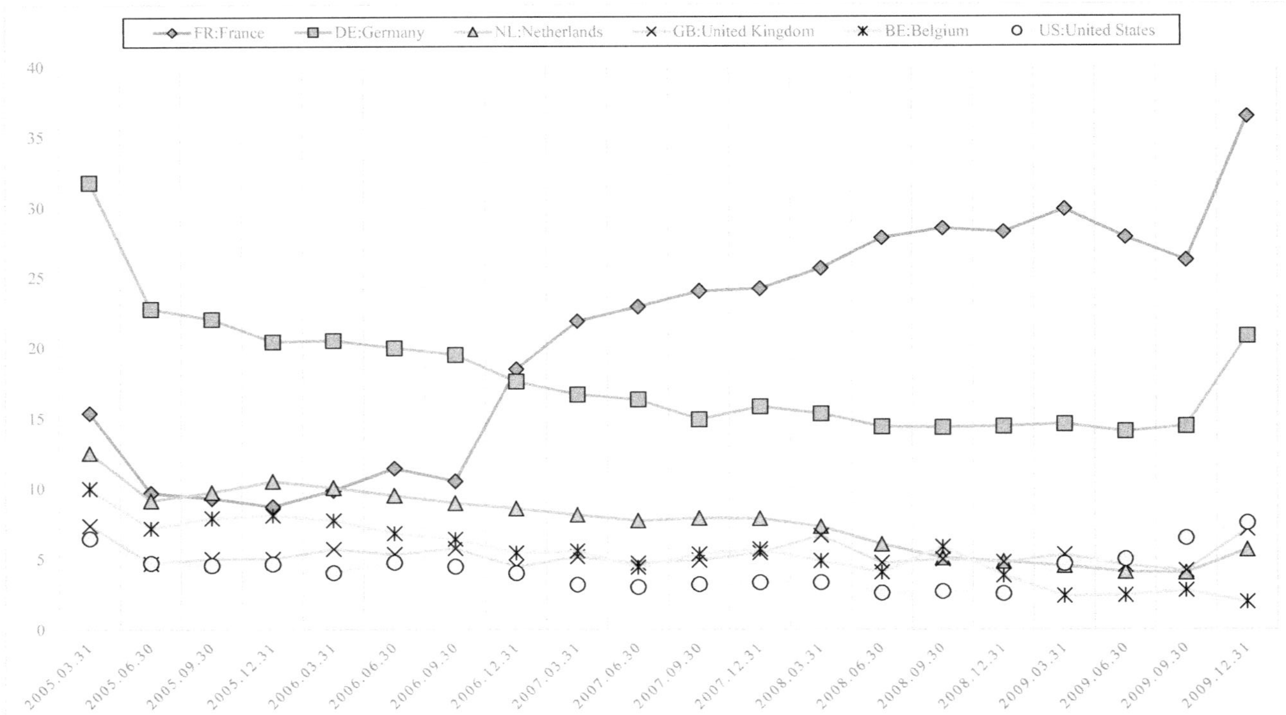

Figure 2.7 Greece – consolidated foreign claims, percentage of total claims

Source: Bank for International Settlements Consolidated Bank Statistics

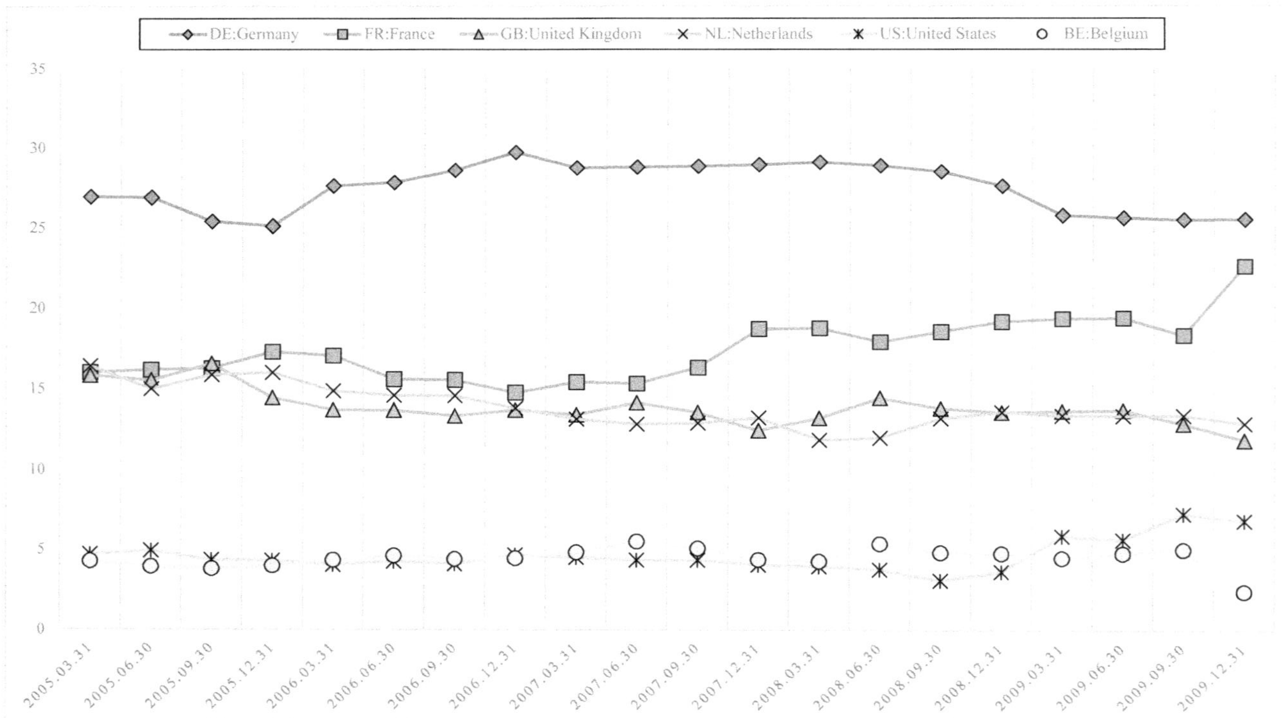

Figure 2.8 Spain – consolidated foreign claims, percentage of total claims

Source: Bank for International Settlements Consolidated Bank Statistics

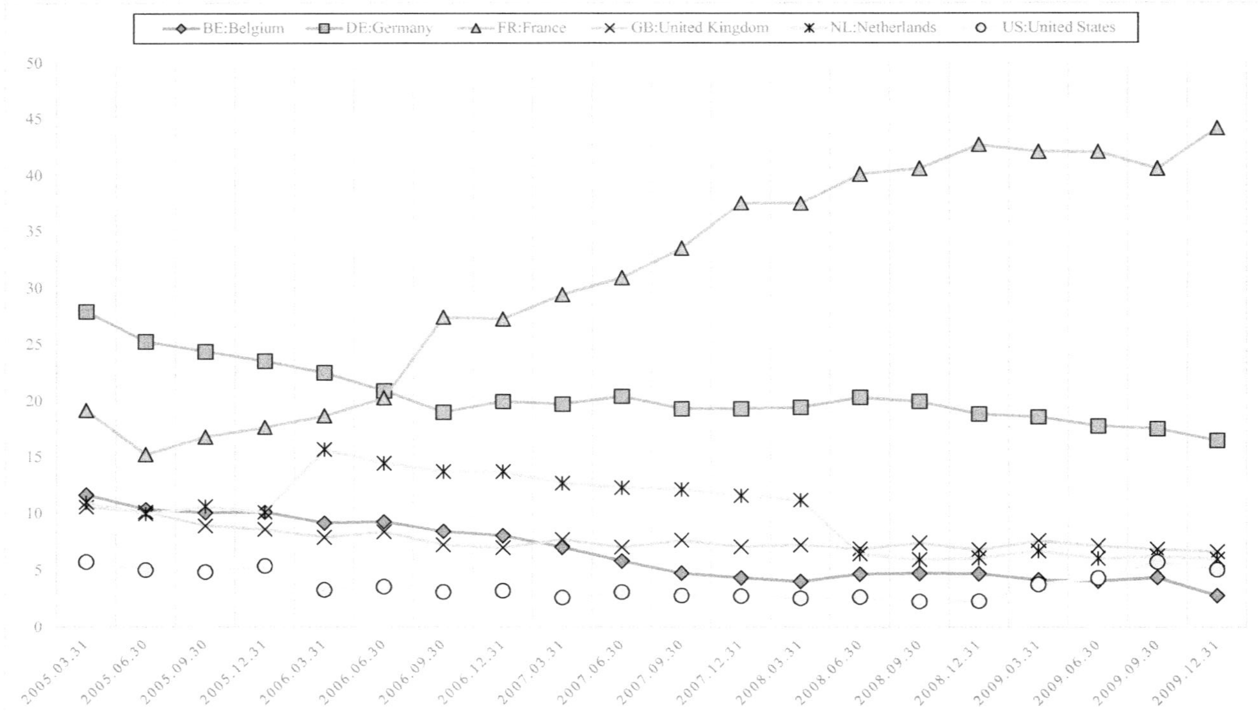

Figure 2.9 Italy – consolidated foreign claims, percentage of total claims

Source: Bank for International Settlements Consolidated Bank Statistics

Naturally, none of this should be seen as denying the significant impact or implications of German or core exposure to the periphery.[18] If Germany, France, the Netherlands, and Belgium are grouped together, Lapavitsas et al.'s claims about the 'core' are absolutely correct. There is no disputing the importance of core flows to the periphery, and it is remarkable that the same core countries seem to feature in each case. Even more clearly, these figures support Thompson' (2013) argument that Germany's problematic *response*, itself a major cause of the eurozone crisis, can be criticised and explained by fears underpinned by the interests of its powerful banking sector over significant exposure to the periphery. Germany's real concern was Italy and Spain, and German actions can be understood as aiming to prevent contagion to those countries (Thompson 2013; 2015). Germany's problematic response to the debt crisis protected German banks at considerable cost to the periphery, and Germany managed to reduce its exposure to the periphery by more than half between 2009 and 2012; a rate unparalleled by any other core economy (Thompson 2015, 859–60). Nothing that is said here disputes this important critique being levelled at Germany.

However, the central point remains that analysing these flows through a core–periphery prism can be limiting, leading to the omission of important specificities in relation to 'peripheral' cases, so as to occasion important blind spots in the understanding of the how crisis has *originated* as being distinct from how it has been *responded* to (Dooley 2014, 945).[19] One such blind spot is the under-appreciated salience of inter-periphery financial flows (such as the importance of Italian lending to Germany, and Spanish lending to Portugal). Another is the importance of exposure to a variety of different countries as illustrated by Figures 2.5–2.9 (especially the UK, the Netherlands, and the USA). Another issue is that while core–periphery lending can be posited as important, there is little reason to single out the role of Germany, as most core–periphery literature does. Only in one case, Spain, is Germany the most important lender to the periphery. Moreover, the systemic approach of core–periphery analysis eschews anything approximating an explanation of the very different kinds of crisis encountered by the periphery, focusing exclusively on core–periphery divergence. It is certainly true that capital flowed from the more developed financial centres of Northern Europe to Portugal, Ireland, Greece, and Italy. It is far less apparent that this fact supports the tale of the German 'big bad wolf', while Spanish, UK, and French banks have all been lending more to these four countries than Germany. Financial and trade imbalances are certainly crucial to any understanding of the crisis in the European periphery, as will be shown in the following chapters. But more is obscured than revealed by contorting these multiple flows into a simplistic core–periphery model.

Core–periphery analysis inverts the immaturity thesis' narrative of blame, and doesn't get us much closer to a convincing explanation of the asymmetry of the crisis. That narratives of blame emerged quickly and prominently as central explanations of the eurozone crisis is hardly surprising. As noted by Bovens and t'Hart (1998), "to explain is to blame". Like the foreign policy fiascos these authors study, the label 'crisis' signals a trespassing or violation of fundamental values and issues. It has been argued that the identification of a crisis and the analysis of its causes tend to also be a part of "a process of accounting and blaming" (Bovens and t'Hart 1998, 129). What is surprising is how the specific narratives of blame, the immaturity and beggar-thy-neighbour theses, echoed earlier political economy debates between modernisation theory and dependency theory. As with dependency theory, core–periphery analysis traded the problematic internalism of the modernisation theory style immaturity thesis for its own equally problematic externalism; thus, reducing the complex and multiple trajectories of political economic change in countries such as Portugal, Ireland, and Greece to a passive function of the interests of their more powerful European neighbours. For core–periphery analysis, the periphery is still represented as the 'other' of the core, except that such frameworks adopt assumptions of dependency; "rather than a failure to act appropriately, the peripheral state is represented with an inability to act efficaciously due to structural constraints" (Dooley 2014, 945). Whereas assumptions of immaturity explain away asymmetry by pathologising different forms of development (rendering them immature, incomplete), core–periphery analysis views peripheral models as 'stunted' modernisations. Tom Young sums up the similarities:

> Modernization theory can see only a failed state to be explained by 'tradition', its explanatory framework allowing only a vacuous teleology or a facile exoticism. Dependency theory is no better, seeing . . . realities only as externally determined by global class forces.
>
> (Young 1999)

The reanimation of the modernisation versus dependency theory likely reflects the use of readily available, heuristically attractive 'off the peg' approaches to respond quickly to a rapidly evolving crisis. While, as will be shown in Chapter 3, the debate on the eurozone crisis moved on from these initial interpretations, the legacy of narratives of blame is clear in ongoing political and media accounts of the crisis (see Münchau 2018). Narratives of immaturity and German/core domination both leave scholarship on the eurozone crisis without an adequate explanation for the dramatically different forms of crisis experienced by the countries of the European periphery. To take the asymmetry of the eurozone crisis seriously, we need to move beyond the safety of the immaturity versus beggar-thy-neighbour debate, itself a reanimation of the modernisation versus dependency theory debates of decades ago – as (Gourgouris 2015) has said – "no matter how dressed up with new terminologies and allegedly new significations".

Conclusion

This chapter highlights the definite need to rethink peripheral immaturity and German beggar-thy-neighbour assumptions in explanations of the asymmetry of the eurozone crisis. The crisis is not best understood as one of peripheral profligacy, misgovernment, or cultural deficit. But neither is it a crisis of German or even core economic domination. I have shown that core–periphery analysis singles out and overstates the role of Germany in the competitiveness and indebtedness problems of the countries of the European periphery, as well as the 'structural role' of the periphery for Germany/the core in its generation of trade surpluses and as a destination for capital outflows. The immaturity thesis, on the other hand, is too preoccupied with 'obstacles to convergence' to explain the very different kinds of crisis across Greece, Ireland, and Portugal.

The empirical case for the immaturity thesis is weakened by what it overlooks, namely the design flaws of EMU, the role of international capital flows, and a narrow conceptualisation of competitiveness as being all about unit labour costs, labour market flexibility, and sound fiscal policy. The empirical case for a beggar-thy-neighbour relationship between the core/Germany and the periphery was similarly exposed as seriously limited, even though it fills in many of the blind spots left by the 'official narrative'. This has important consequences for critical scholarship on the origins of the eurozone crisis because, while it allows us to recognise that notions of peripheral immaturity are little more than typically misleading heuristic devices (Brazys and Hardiman 2013), a genuine critical rethinking of the vulnerabilities of the so-called PIIGS requires more than the addition of a big bad wolf if we are to finally move beyond the fairy tale of the immaturity thesis. In Chapter 3 I show how literature from CPE and Europeanisation can do exactly that.

Notes

1 A version of this chapter appears in *New Political Economy* as Dooley, N. (2017a) "Who's Afraid of the Big Bad Wolf? Rethinking the Core and Periphery in the Eurozone Crisis", *New Political Economy*: http://www.tandfonline.com/doi/full/10.1080/13563467.2017.1417363. It is reprinted here with the permission of Taylor and Francis Ltd., http://www.tandfonline.com.

2 For illustrative examples of this approach see Sinn 2014; Manolopoulos 2011; Diamandouros 2011; and for critical overviews see Papadimitriou and Zartaloudis 2014; Lyberaki and Tsakalotos 2002, 93, 95.

3 Although the three components of the troika are not as equally sold on this narrative: see (Snaith and Nedergaard 2015). See also (Inman 2018) for an account of how the IMF and the European Commission fell out over how to treat Greece during the course of its third bailout programme

4 Refracted through sensationalist media and often political discourse, the 'official narrative' can be mischaracterised as being reductively fiscal. This is not strictly true, it just as often focuses on weak competitiveness and poor political decision making. It is fair to say, however, that there is often a tendency to explain 'competitiveness' issues as the result, at least partially, of immature fiscal policy.

5 See also the large body of literature on Greek 'underdog culture', summarised in Triandafyllidou, Gropas, and Kouki 2013, 4–6; but see in particular Tsoukalas 1995; Clogg and Diamandouros 1993; Diamandouros 2011; and for indispensable critical interventions see Tziovas 2001; 2014; Xenakis 2013.

6 Different typologies of the 'core' exist. For the purposes of this chapter, I adopt Lapavitsas et al.'s list: Germany, France, Belgium, and the Netherlands.

7 An extended version of this section appears as Dooley 2017a.

8 See Dullien and Guérot 2012; Moravcsik 2012; Matthijs and Blyth 2011; Thompson 2013; Bulmer and Paterson 2013; Jacoby 2015; Newman 2015; Matthijs 2016a.

9 See also Bulmer and Paterson 2013; Paterson 2011; Matthijs and Blyth 2015.
10 See Matthijs 2016b; Beck 2013; Goetz and Dyson 2003; Lapavitsas et al. 2012, 3–5.
11 It is also worth noting that while the analysis of Lapavitsas (2012) and colleagues (Flassbeck and Lapavitsas 2016) focuses on the relationship between the core (Germany, France, Belgium, and the Netherlands) and the periphery, it is Germany that ends up being the primary focus. This is evidenced, inter alia, by chapter headings in the most recent work of Flassbeck and Lapavitsas, such as Germany as the Source of the Eurozone Crisis (2015, 21–38), rather than Core EMU as the Source of the Eurozone Crisis, and the preoccupation with German wage moderation in Flassbeck and Lapavitsas' (heated) exchange with Storm (2016). While it would be unfair to say that the distinction between the core and Germany has been imprecise, Germany's role in generating current and capital account imbalances is the one that steals the headlines in this literature. This distinction between the core and Germany matters, as it has implications for how valid it is to blame the German big bad wolf for the eurozone crisis.
12 See Storm 2015, 2016 for a more extensive account of this critique.
13 Lapavitsas et al. (2012) consider Germany, France, Belgium, and the Netherlands as the 'core'. As per the suggestion of an anonymous peer reviewer, I have also included the cases of Austria and Luxembourg. Dooley 2017a also looks at Finland.
14 Because these countries are deficit countries, there is no overall trade surplus for the periphery to contribute to. Accordingly, positive trade balances are represented as percentages of total world exports, rather than as percentages of world surplus.
15 Of course, Germany benefitted from a weakened euro and increased demand from emerging markets. I thank an anonymous peer reviewer for stressing the importance of this point.
16 As Milios and Sotiropoulos (2010) do, in spite of their critique of a beggar-thy-neighbour core–periphery explanation.
17 These figures are calculated using data from the Bank of International Settlements (BIS) consolidated banking statistics. This data set provides information regarding banks on sheet financial claims vis-à-vis the rest of the world and provides a measure of the risk exposures of lenders' national banking systems. This data set was chosen because Lapavitsas et al. (2012, 46–7) and Thompson (2013, 8) use BIS consolidated banking statistics to support their argument regarding the importance of core lending to the periphery. The time frame (2005–9) was selected as BIS consolidated statistics do not contain data for ultimate risk basis before 2005, and Lapavitsas et al. (2012) use the same time period.
18 The case could be made that the ultimate source of Portuguese debt, indirectly, is Germany and France via Spain. However, rather than contort these relationships further into the core–periphery model (why would Germany indirectly lend to some peripheral states while directly lending to others?), I suggest that it makes more sense to take the specificities of financialisation in each state more seriously.
19 Of course, the division between causes and responses is somewhat murky, because the problematic response to the crisis is a big part of the origin story. Nevertheless, we still need an understanding as to why the European periphery got into difficulty in the first instance.

3 Comparative political economy and Europeanisation

In this chapter I outline the analytical framework that I will apply to Greece, Portugal, and Ireland in the following three case study chapters. This framework will account for the asymmetry of the crisis in the European periphery by contributing the concept of 'divergence via Europeanisation'. As shown in Chapter 2, notions that the European periphery were either unwilling or unable to converge economically with Western Europe resonate through existing accounts of the eurozone crisis (Dooley 2017b). The concept of divergence via Europeanisation instead locates one of the key drivers of processes of divergence in the EU project of convergence itself.

The framework I develop critically engages with VoC and brings it into dialogue with Europeanisation. The EU has obstinately promoted a single model of economic integration across a variety of different European economic trajectories. My framing makes it possible to show how Greece, Ireland, and Portugal have been at the centre of the eurozone crisis, because their attempts to converge with their Western European neighbours, *at their most successful*, were generative of brand new patterns of divergence. Recognising this leads to the central claim of this book: it was the periphery's attempt to 'follow the rules' of European integration, rather than their failure or inability to, that explains their current difficulties.

This chapter develops the framework through three sections. First, I critically engage with VoC. This approach is adept at highlighting the central role of *institutional path dependence* (or stickiness) in Greece, Portugal, and Ireland's competitiveness problems. However, it suffers from a number of shortcomings, namely a relatively narrow conception of 'competitiveness' and a difficulty in recognising institutional transformation. Next, I address the limits of VoC by bringing it into dialogue with the literature on Europeanisation. This combination makes it possible to draw out the significant role of *institutional transformation* in the origins of the crises in the periphery. This allows me to highlight the significance of the successful adaptation to projects of European financial integration by Greece, Portugal, and Ireland. This is much overlooked by literature, which emphasises the unwillingness or inability of these countries to introduce other 'painful but necessary' reforms. In contrast, I show how, in different ways, domestic adaptation to European financial integration (Europeanisation) transformed the countries of the

European periphery into debt-led models of growth. Finally, I outline the research framework, which is applied to the subsequent case study chapters. Tracing divergence via Europeanisation requires an inductive, theory-generating research design in order to move beyond analysis of more readily apparent 'obstacles to convergence' in the origins of the eurozone crisis.

Institutional stickiness and the limits to export-led growth in the European periphery

As the debate on the origins of the eurozone crisis has evolved, the 'official narrative' described in Chapter 2 has fallen seriously out of favour, at least within academic circles (see Johnston and Regan 2016, 321). In its place, CPE, especially VoC has emerged as a rich and important body of literature, which studies the asymmetry of the eurozone crisis on the basis of identifying key differences in national institutions. Here, I show how such an approach can form part of an account of the crisis in the European periphery. National institutions matter: different institutional configurations of EMU member states produce different economic capacities and problems, have developed over long periods of time, and are 'sticky' or path dependent (Dooley 2017a, 2017b). EMU certainly advantaged the institutional configurations of the core and disadvantaged those of the periphery in various ways (Dooley 2017b). However, VoC is an incomplete explanation. Like the official narrative, a focus on institutional path dependency under EMU can tell us much that is useful about the *absence* of export-led growth in the periphery, but considerably less about institutional transformation leading to debt-led growth.

To offer a fuller explanation, this section first outlines the core elements of the VoC approach to the eurozone crisis. I show its value in highlighting the role of institutional stickiness for explaining the divergence between the core and periphery in terms of their respective abilities to develop patterns of export-led economic growth. I then outline the limits of VoC. These limits necessitate a dialogue with Europeanisation to draw out the twin role of institutional transformation in the origins of the crises in the periphery. Institutional stickiness matters, but I show that we also need the analytical space to consider the role of institutional transformation.

VoC and export-led growth

VoC has emerged as one of the most influential and prominent explanations of the eurozone crisis (see Hall 2018; Johnston 2016; Hancké 2013). Like core–periphery analysis and to some extent, the official narrative, VoC asks how and why the periphery lost competitiveness vis-à-vis the European core. Although largely positioned as a critique of the official narrative, there is a convergence in their headline argument, which claims that the countries most affected by the eurozone crisis were those that were least competitive:

> either because they had excessive wage growth in the context of irrevocably fixed exchange rates, or because they had rigid labor market institutions that translated even relatively moderate wage growth into excessive relative price differences. The corollary is that those countries most affected by the crisis *will only emerge once they have adjusted to restore their competitiveness*.
>
> (Jones 2016 [italics added])

VoC scholarship tends to focus on how the Mixed Market Economies (MMEs) of the European periphery *lacked* the kinds of institutional complementarities that allow the Liberal Market Economies (LMEs) – such as the UK – and Coordinated Market Economies (CMEs) – such as Germany – of core Europe to act as relatively more sustainable models of capitalism. Nevertheless, there are a number of key differences between VoC and the official narrative. For authors such as Johnston, Hancké, and Pant, the eurozone crisis is decidedly *not* chiefly a fiscal crisis (2014, 1773–5). VoC differs from the official narrative by emphasising the long, path-dependent institutional development of these national political economies, and recognising that it would have been very difficult for these economies to introduce painful but necessary reforms during the 1990s and 2000s. Given the reality of an EMU made up of CMEs, LMEs, and MMEs, VoC can logically argue that the eurozone and Single Market themselves should have reformed in order to be more sensitive to this variation, rather than the other way around. It also tends to set up the aforementioned version of the 'competitiveness thesis' (see Jones 2016 for a summary; see also Belke and Dreger 2011; Bibow 2012; Wihlborg, Willett, and Zhang 2010) as a critique of the official narrative's framing of the crisis as rooted in fiscal profligacy. Rather, the crisis is better explained by the emergence of competitiveness imbalances, which, in turn, led to national imbalances in total borrowing (Johnston et al. 2014). These differences do matter, and get us part of the way towards a theory of eurozone asymmetry.

Specifically, Johnston (2016) and colleagues (Johnston et al. 2014; Hancké 2013) focus on how the MMEs of the European periphery (although excluding Ireland) lacked the capacity to control wage growth in the sheltered sectors of their economy, relative to wage growth in their non-sheltered sectors. During the 1990s, the European periphery largely succeeded in inflation rate convergence with the core, precisely because the criteria for joining EMU required it, and the threat of non-entry, was effectively costly for these countries. However, once in the euro, these constraints vanished. Without these tight fiscal rules at the EU level national, wage negotiators (especially in sheltered sectors) could allow wages to rise (Dooley 2017b; Johnston 2016). Under EMU, MMEs lost important tools such as national central banks that were averse to inflation, and currency devaluations (Johnston 2016; Dooley 2017b). Accordingly, while MMEs have always lacked the institutional capacity to effectively manage inflation, this only became a serious threat while a member of the euro (Johnston 2016).

On the other hand, CMEs (such as Germany) in the European core had coordinated wage bargaining systems, which allowed them to keep wages in both sheltered and non-sheltered sectors down. The result was a divergence of competitiveness between the core and the periphery (Johnston et al. 2014; Johnston 2016). Rising wages in the sheltered sector in MMEs contributed to inflation and, inevitably, to rising wages in the non-sheltered sectors also. Over time, "inflation differentials between the core and periphery created a divergence in relative export market performance and current account imbalances" (Jones 2016). A 'pathological symbiosis' then emerges between the current account surplus countries of the core and the deficit countries of the periphery (Hall 2018). The profits made from the relative export success of the core found their way back to the periphery, recycled as capital lending, allowing the periphery to import more, to widen its current account deficit further, and to continue the cycle. In short, as Hancké puts it, different wage coordinating mechanisms in the core and periphery of Europe contributed to current account imbalances: "Put simply, no current account deficit, no fiscal crisis and/or no banking crisis, and vice versa" (Hancké 2013, cited in Jones 2016, 7). The logic of the VoC argument is that the periphery lacked the correct institutions to flourish under EMU, but also that EMU was unsuitable in its 'one size fits some' (Vermeiren 2017) institutional design to handle the different kinds of economies that made it up.

Limits of VoC

VoC can be viewed as an important revision of the official narrative, jettisoning the 'fiscal recklessness' assumption and greater specifying the link between labour markets and declining competitiveness. It is perfectly capable of highlighting the international dimensions of the crisis, and of paying attention to the role of capital flows (although see Jones 2016; Storm 2016), structural inequalities, and design flaws of EMU. Its focus on path dependency and the pathological symbiosis of EMU means that it does not tend to buy into the assumption that the MMEs of the periphery could have converged their real exchange rates with the CMEs of the core. It is an explicitly comparative approach that highlights differences in specific national institutions, and therefore gets us very close to an explanation of the asymmetry of the crisis in the European periphery, which does not necessitate narratives of blame. However, it suffers from some of its own empirical limitations and even comes close to smuggling in its own version of the immaturity thesis.

First, VoC can be subjected to similar criticisms as those levelled at core–periphery analysis in Chapter 2, in the sense that unit labour costs are not the only component of a country's competitiveness. Export prices are arguably less responsive to changes in unit labour costs, and current account deficits may have much more to do with rising imports than declining export volumes (Dooley 2017a; Storm 2016). Jones (2016) argues that VoC does not pay enough attention to the role of capital flows in generating competitiveness problems for the periphery. Capital flowed into the periphery rapidly and in great quantities in the run up to the crisis, leaving Greece, Portugal, and Ireland seriously vulnerable to a sudden stop following the global financial crash (Jones 2016). Jones demonstrates how current account deficits are linked more closely to indebtedness and import penetration associated with inward capital flows than they are with rising unit labour costs (Dooley 2017a). Nevertheless, other CPE scholars emphasise the role of financialisation in their work. Lapavitsas and Powell (2013), Rodrigues and Reis (2012), and others develop CPE approaches that emphasise the linkages between national VoC, capital flows, and competitiveness (see Dooley 2017a, 19).

Second, although it would be unfair to characterise VoC as an instance of the immaturity thesis, it does carry with it a similar preoccupation with obstacles to convergence. While Johnston et al. can show why it was peripheral countries that fell victim to heavy market speculation while the CMEs of the core remained unscathed, they still cannot explain the asymmetry of the crisis between Greece, Portugal, and Ireland. It may be true that countries with corporatist institutions that tie wage growth in the sheltered sectors to sectors exposed to trade were better able to weather the eurozone crisis than those who allowed sheltered sector wage rises to appreciate national inflation and thus the real exchange rate (Johnston et al. 2014, 1772). Yet this only explains why these countries *lacked* competitiveness and *didn't* develop export-led models of growth. Moreover, it is far better at explaining differences between the core and periphery than it is at explaining differences between peripheral countries themselves. VoC's granular focus on differences between national VoC is most likely the way forward for a theory of the asymmetry of the crisis. But it requires revision in order to focus on the parallel histories of not just declining competitiveness but emerging forms of debt-led growth in Greece, Portugal, and Ireland.

To tie all of this together, VoC has a number of strengths that can be incorporated into this book's analysis, and one major limitation, which requires modification. First, VoC can be applied to the subsequent case studies by focusing on identifying challenges to the historical development of export-led growth (of varying success) in the countries of the European periphery. Chapters 4, 5, and 6 will show how Greece, Portugal, and Ireland each faced unique sets of challenges to their pursuit of export-led growth. VoC has been criticised for its reductive definition of 'competitiveness' as relative unit labour costs. However, Baccaro and Pontusson (2016) as well as Hall (2012, 2014, 2018) have developed VoC analysis to show how countries with different VoC tend to be better or less suited to pursuing 'growth models' oriented towards manufacturing for export. CME economies such as Germany have institutional setups, built up over long periods, which are characterised by high levels of coordination between employers, employees, and the state, which assists wage setting as well as skills and training. These economies are also well able to use fiscal and monetary policies to control inflation, and control wage increases in the public sector, which lower the real effective exchange rate of Germany. MMEs in the periphery are not well structured for operating export-led models of growth. They tend to lack capacity for 'strategic coordination of wages', especially in the sheltered and/or public sectors (Hall 2018). They tend to have powerful trade unions who can demand wage increases, but are nevertheless divided and compete with one another, discouraging coordination. But MMEs also lack capacity for skill formation and tend to be more oriented to low–medium-technology manufacturing for export, products that are much more sensitive to price than the high-technology exports of Germany.[1] In other words, a broader CPE approach can provide a more historical analysis of the different institutional challenges faced by each country in converging with Western Europe in terms of their patterns and levels of economic growth.

The major limitation that requires modification is the exhaustive focus on obstacles to export-led growth, which VoC shares with the official narrative. It is not enough to explain why the periphery did not develop patterns of export-led growth, because this downplays the significant transformations that did occur in Greece, Portugal, and Ireland. To put in another way, the immaturity thesis privileges the *unwillingness* of the periphery to 'follow the rules' in its analysis, while VoC privileges their *inability*. There is a world of difference between these positions, but they are united by their emphasis of stasis; of non-transformation. As I discussed in relation to the immaturity thesis in Chapter 2, this discounts the possibility that something other than an obstacle could have played a pivotal role in the crisis. The problem can be pinpointed as one of focusing on the history of obstacles to convergence, a history of *what was not* done and thereby neglecting possible counter-narratives, or histories of *what was done*. In the next section, I show how this can be addressed.

Institutional transformation: divergence via Europeanisation[2]

Focusing only on the path dependencies of peripheral VoC can cause us to overlook the real and significant institutional transformations that the economies of the European periphery did experience. The problem is not that institutional stickiness or EMU design flaws do not matter. The real problem is that perspectives emphasising this 'perfect storm' of sticky national divergences within an 'unfit-for-purpose' EMU problematically assume that the lack of institutional transformation exhausts the *origins of divergence* in the political economies of Greece, Portugal, and Ireland. The logic is simple – the periphery diverged because it didn't transform. These countries experienced speculative pressure from 2009 onwards because of competitiveness problems in the years before. Yet, as I demonstrate, the very distinctive forms of crisis encountered by Greece, Portugal, and Ireland suggests that something is missing from this formulation.

In this section I draw on the literature on Europeanisation to develop a new account of the origins of the crisis in the periphery, which can complement CPE's sensitivity to path-dependent national VoC under an EMU that is flawed in design. Bringing these two literatures together makes it possible to propose that the economic divergence experienced by the periphery involved not only institutional stickiness, but also institutional transformation. The peripheries crisis is about more than a failed attempt to converge. This approach makes it possible to show how the European periphery's attempt to participate in *projects* of convergence was generative of *processes* of divergence. In other words, Europeanisation was generative of divergence. This is the concept of 'divergence via Europeanisation'. I develop this argument by first showing how CPE and Europeanisation can be brought into a fruitful dialogue with one another. Following this I briefly outline the project of European financial integration, which the periphery attempted to adapt to.

Disentangling 'divergence' from 'institutional stickiness'

Focusing on the resilience of path-dependent institutions can certainly help us explain declining competitiveness of the European periphery under EMU, but it downplays the commensurate importance of institutional transformation in the generation of their debt-led growth (Streeck and Thelen 2005; Streeck 2008). The key strength of CPE more generally is also its major limitation. That is, its meta-theoretical foundations in historical institutionalism, approaches that, as Thelen notes, have quite poor records in explaining institutional change (Thelen 2009). This makes a lot of sense if we consider the origins of the approach. It first emerged as a critique of the hyper-globalist thesis and makes the argument that national models of capitalism can resist transformation in the face of external pressure for convergence (Featherstone 2008). Because institutions are 'sticky', these approaches have a strong tendency to emphasise continuity through time in the basic structure and logic of models of political economy (Thelen 2009). CPE scholars consequently have less to say about institutional change over time because, as Thelen puts it:

> [The] idea of persistence is virtually built into the definition of an institution, it should perhaps not be a surprise that the question of change is a weak spot in the literature as a whole, and indeed across all varieties of institutionalism. (Thelen 2009, 473)

Perspectives emphasising institutional stickiness overlook the fact that simply because a country has 'failed to converge' it does not mean that 'things have stayed the same'. Failing to generate competitive economic growth does not mean a simple persistence of tradition. When Portugal, Greece, and Ireland attempted to reform and modernise during the 1990s and 2000s, their efforts to do so resulted in significant and dramatic changes to their political economies, because transformation was an outcome of the attempt to reform and modernise. Had Greece, Portugal, and Ireland not attempted reform, they would not have transformed in the same way. Ultimately, a theory of institutional stickiness shuts down a myriad of interesting and important questions about the role of institutional change in generating economic divergence in these countries.

This overlooking of institutional change can be addressed by bringing CPE into dialogue with the literature on Europeanisation. Scholars of Europeanisation study a country's "domestic adaptation to European regional integration" (Vink and Graziano 2007) and take the possibility of domestic transformation as a result of adaptation to European regional integration as their starting point. For CPE, external pressure is not likely to lead to domestic change, it will only shed light on and confirm existing national specificities. All meaningful change comes from within, and thus the approach "stress[es] the resilience of the particular market model in interpreting such pressures" (Featherstone 2008).

Similar to CPE, Europeanisation literature has recognised that domestic adaptation to European integration is very unlikely to lead to convergence; as Radaelli puts it: "Diversity of domestic responses – across countries, institutions, and policy domains – has become a key theme in Europeanization research" (Radaelli 2004, 3; Bulmer 2007; Börzel and Risse 2003; Heritier et al. 2001; Knill, Tosun, and Bauer 2009). Existing specific domestic contexts may lead to differential results from the process of Europeanisation (Vink and Graziano 2007, 9). Laffan sees a persistence of diversity across national executives rather than convergence towards a particular model (Laffan 2007). Although European directives are aimed at harmonising national policies, in reality, they leave much room for continued national diversity (Vink and Graziano 2007, 10–11; Wessels 2003, xv).

However, digging a little deeper, the different variants of Europeanisation also tend to be explained as institutional path dependency or, in other words, how nation states can account for the timing, extent, and terms of their adaptation to European integration. Radaelli (2000) notes that Europeanisation is sometimes measured in four ways.[3] The first is accommodation, which indicates a pre-existing closeness of fit (i.e., Germany). The second is transformation, suggesting lack of fit, but leading to fundamental challenges to existing domestic structures. Third is inertia, indicating a dearth of change due to lack of fit and deeply entrenched domestic institutional veto players. Finally, there is retrenchment, which suggests a paradox of negative Europeanisation.

Much like CPE, most research on Europeanisation and the European periphery tends to focus on inertia. This is perhaps because, as of yet, not enough attention has been paid to how transformation due to 'lack of fit' is much more likely to lead to divergence/institutional transformation, rather than convergence. When convergence fails to occur, researchers tend to focus on domestic obstacles to that convergence – leading them to identify institutional, cultural, and political obstacles. Indeed, in cautioning against using the concept of Europeanisation as "yet another way to refer to convergence and homogeneity in Europe", Radaelli and Pasquier recommend that "the prediction to test is about *lack of convergence*, not its presence" (Radaelli and Pasquier 2007, 39 [italics added]). Much recent scholarship on Europeanisation therefore emerges as a critique of earlier studies in the field, which tended to expect convergence as a result of domestic adaptation to European integration. Framing their positions in this way has led them to emphasise the resilience/persistence of national differences just as VoC scholarship tends to (and as Wessels (2003) and Heritier et al. (2001) do). This similarity is precisely the reason that Featherstone (2008) also advocates the combination of these two approaches for the study of the eurozone crisis – they complement each other, with each offering a different perspective while both emphasising domestic institutional resilience in the face of international pressure for transformation.

However, as will be shown in the subsequent case study chapters, there is an implicit third option other than 'convergence' or 'non-convergence' available within the Europeanisation framework: the possibility that domestic adaptation to

European integration can lead to profound institutional transformation of existing domestic structures. It is possible to conceive of Europeanisation leading to the emergence of radically new hybrid domestic structures and patterns of growth. Divergence is conceptualised here as more than the resilience of national differences. It is (at the same time) the possibility of the emergence of entirely new kinds of national differences. Combining CPE with a Europeanisation framework makes it possible to show that the European project did not simply fail to manage a diverse range of VoC. It is actively implicated in generating brand new patterns of fragility through transforming existing varieties, over time, into something new.

Europeanisation of banking and finance

In the following case studies, a particular aspect of the European project is identified as being pivotal to the emergence of debt-led growth in the countries of the European periphery. Each case study emphasises the key role played by the 're-launched' project of European integration since the late 1980s. European integration had placed pressures on member states to adapt before this period. But the 'one market, one money' project of the mid-1980s – comprising the Single Market and preparations for EMU (Emerson, Gros, and Italianer 1992) – provided Greece, Portugal, and Ireland with a relatively explicit and extensive 'blueprint' for their adaptation to Europe. Preparations to join both of these acted as relatively strong imperatives for reform in the countries of the European periphery between the 1980s and 2000s (Featherstone, Kazamias, and Papadimitriou 2001, 462), in a way that they could not be after these countries succeeded in becoming members of the Single Market and euro. As such, these 1990s reforms are identified as particularly important drivers of transformation for each of the case studies. These imperatives constitute a project of convergence, which the periphery participated in. But it did not lead to the processes of convergence that may have been hoped for. As will be shown in the case study chapters, it was the attempt to adjust to these imperatives that acted as an important catalyst of divergence in the European periphery.

By the 1980s, economic integration in Europe was considered to have failed to reach its potential. Europe was 're-launched' with the Single European Act (SEA) and the first Delors Commission's plan to 'complete the Single Market', create the EU, and introduce EMU soon after (Giordano and Persaud 1998, 8). "One market, one money" (Emerson et al. 1992); an integrated Single Market, that was free from all barriers to the free movement of trade, capital, and labour, and a single currency for that market were seen as the cornerstones of a new vision for a European economy that could gain a competitive edge in global export markets and adapt to the perceived challenges of globalisation; namely rival economies and internationally mobile capital (see Laffan 1998, 235–6; Buch-Hansen and Wigger 2011; Wigger 2015). Although competitiveness agendas have been essential aspects of the European project from the outset, they only acquired heightened agenda status with the acceleration of the Single Market project following the signing of the SEA (Wigger 2015, 119; Deeg 2012, 79).

The Single Market was to be achieved through a number of reforms intended to stimulate trade, increase competition, and promote European-wide economies of scale by dismantling a variety of nontariff trade barriers, which included national differences in taxes, regulations, and health and safety standards (Fligstein and Mara-Drita 1996, 9). During the period from 1986 to 1992, the EU adopted approximately 280 pieces of legislation. In many areas, twelve sets of national regulations from the then twelve member states were replaced by one common European law (European Commission 2012b). Every member state was required to transpose European directives relating to everything from harmonisation of manufacturing standards to banking and capital market liberalisation. The Single Market was successfully 'completed' on the 1st of January 1993.[4] With all of these new pressures for adaptation to EU rules, it is no coincidence that it is during this period that the literature on Europeanisation began to develop (Bache et al. 2015, 3).

The particular significance of EU developments relating to banking and finance in stimulating debt-led patterns of growth in the European periphery from the late 1980s onwards is apparent in the following chapters. Completing the Single Market resulted in a dramatic shifting of the landscape of European banking and finance (Deeg 2012; Abdelal 2007, 79; Bieling 2003, 208). A Single Market for banking, together with European financial integration were viewed by their proponents as the backbone of the strategy of transforming Europe into, as it was later put in the Lisbon Agenda, the "most dynamic and competitive knowledge based economy in the world" (Bieling 2003, 213). Specific EU directives on the dismantling of barriers, capital standards, and deposit protection were issued in 1989, 1992, and 1994 (Murphy 2000). The idea was that if European banks could conduct business anywhere in the EU, increased economies of scale, competition, and capital availability would result in benefits to businesses and consumers (Murphy 2000, 2). As the Presidency Conclusions to the Lisbon European Council in March 2000 put it:

> [e]fficient and transparent financial markets foster growth and employment by better allocation of capital and reducing its cost. They therefore play an essential role in fuelling new ideas, supporting entrepreneurial culture and promoting access to and use of new technologies. It is essential to exploit the potential of the euro to push forward the integration of EU financial markets. Furthermore, efficient risk capital markets play a major role in innovative high-growth SMEs and the creation of new and sustainable jobs.
>
> (European Council 2000)

New developments in European banking and finance proceeded in various ways. Minimum standards for banking conduct are set out in various EU directives. The cornerstone of the EU's policy at the time was the 'Second Banking Directive', which was adopted in 1989 and by 1992 all member states were required to have in place laws and regulations consistent with it. Murphy (2000, 3) outlines the basic principles of the directive. The first was the highly important principle of mutual recognition. This entailed that a host nation must allow any foreign bank to do whatever is permitted in that bank's domestic environment. This implies that foreign banks may initially have different powers and capabilities over domestic banks. Mutual recognition, accordingly, has the potential to provide foreign banks with a competitive edge over domestic banks, driving the adjustment and transformation of the latter if they are to compete with foreign entrants (Murphy 2000, 3). Secondly, banking activities were explicitly defined by the EU, and all member states were required to address any differences in existing practices so that they were in line with the principle of 'universal banking' by 1993. Concretely this entailed, inter alia, a considerable degree of dismantling of regulations, interest rate and capital controls, and harmonisation of solvency ratios. The third principle was the 'single passport' for banking in Europe. This authorised any bank licensed in an EU country to do business in any other EU nation as well, free from any barriers to such action (Murphy 2000, 4). As will be seen in the subsequent chapters, each of these principles had dramatic effects on domestic banking across the periphery and beyond (see Murphy 2000; Deeg 2012, 79; Bieling 2003, 209; Cockfield 1994; Pérez-Caldentey and Vernengo 2012, 10, 11). They introduced new competitive pressures, new forms of banking activity, and greater inflows of cheaper capital to these countries in ways that had never been the case before.

Beyond the Single Market, financial integration was pursued clearly and extensively during the 1990s and 2000s, both through the Lisbon Agenda and the introduction of the euro. Yet, following EMU membership, the hard edge of these EU pressures was absent, and adaptation to Europe through such mechanisms as the Lisbon Agenda's 'Open Method of Coordination' attempted to achieve transformation through more voluntary or persuasive means (Smith 2012b; Vink and Graziano 2007, 10; Umbach and Wessels 2008, 63–6). Nevertheless, the 2000s entailed dramatic changes in providing the Single Market for banking with a deep, easily accessible source of capital. Developments such as the 1999 Financial Services Action Plan (FSAP) represented a programmatic and operative platform for financial market integration in Europe (Bieling 2003, 211, 212). The headline goal of the Lisbon Agenda was to achieve investment in research and development across Europe, and in order to do this financiers needed to be encouraged to invest in more risk-oriented capital to finance innovation projects (Deeg 2012, 74). Yet, Deeg notes that this development was associated with the shareholder value ideology in financial markets – which has led to an increased focus on short-term profitability (Deeg 2012, 75) – so while cheap capital became readily available, it did not tend to flow to so-called 'productive sectors'. As is well known, the euro itself led to a deepening of financial market integration and liberalisation (Papadimitriou and Wray 2012, 2; Noeth and Sengupta 2012, 466; Bieling 2003, 211). With the removal of exchange rate risk, cross-border banking activity became much easier and liquidity became more abundant as domestic banks had easier access to interbank loans from banks in other euro area countries. The introduction of the euro also brought with it a historic reduction in interest rates: because the ECB effectively adopted the Deutschemark interest rate levels, countries such as Portugal, Ireland, and Greece witnessed their own interest rates fall sharply (Koo 2011, 1; de Grauwe 2013, 6–7).

Specifically, in relation to banking and finance, the 'blueprint' of the 'one market, one money' strategy provided the European periphery with very specific pressures to adapt from the late 1980s onwards. From the brief historical background provided here, we can note that since the 1980s the European project has become a supranational internal market and monetary union that aims to promote policies of market efficiencies, capital market liberalisation, competitiveness, and convergence (van Apeldoorn, Drahokoupil, and Horn 2009). Financial market liberalisation, monetary integration, and national competitiveness strategies based on 'knowledge-based' innovation and 'sound finance' have underpinned the European project since the 1980s (Featherstone 1998, 23–4; Bieling 2003, 207; see also van Apeldoorn et al. 2009). The one market, one money project was expected to unleash "unprecedented potential for accelerated growth and enhanced competitiveness across Europe" (Pellegrin 2001, 1). Leaving aside its more or less evident failure in achieving these aims (Pisani-Ferry and Sapir 2006; Jessop 2006; Copeland and Papadimitriou 2012), it presented a clear vision of the type of modernisation that should be aspired to and, more than this, provided concrete mechanisms for member states to reshape themselves.

It is of great significance that each of the countries considered in this study successfully adapted to the various directives discussed; which is often overlooked by focusing on the more readily apparent ways in which the periphery failed to introduce other structural reforms. As will be discussed in more detail in the following chapters, domestic adaptation to these EU-driven reforms helped catalyse patterns of domestic demand and debt-led growth in Greece and Portugal during the 1990s, and helped set the scene for a credit-fuelled property boom in Ireland during the 2000s.

The significance of recognising debt-led growth as an outcome of Europeanisation in this way is that it can take a domestic-level approach while telling a very different story to that of the immaturity thesis. By paying attention to the consequences of domestic adaptation to European integration, it is possible to overcome the internalism of existing domestic-level analyses without resorting to the externalism of the German beggar-thy-neighbour thesis. Similarly, by taking on board the insights of the CPE literature on capitalist diversity, the case studies can shed light on how supposedly 'non-immature' practices of Europeanisation have been generative of divergence, while outlining the role of European developments in banking and finance in particular. Attempting to participate in an EU *project* of convergence contributed to *processes* of divergence (in terms of patterns of economic growth) in each country. In this way, the three case studies can deflate the central premise of the immaturity thesis – because they posit a narrative wherein non-exceptional processes are recognised as the problem, rather than purely considering the 'exceptional' character of the Greek, Portuguese, and Irish crises.

In this respect, I will show in the following case studies that the eurozone crisis has never simply been about the failure or the inability of the periphery to introduce 'painful but necessary' reforms, because many of the reforms they successfully adopted will be shown to have been responsible for the emergence of the crisis. Significantly, the *divergence* of the European periphery is shown to be an outcome of *Europeanisation.*

Research framework

The combination of Europeanisation and CPE guides the research framework of the following case study chapters in two main ways. First, I adopt an historicist, multiple case study approach to reinterpret the asymmetry of the eurozone crisis. This is set up as an inductive and theory-generating approach, in contrast to the deductive search for obstacles to convergence in other accounts. Second, the multiple case study approach will be 'structured', in the sense that I will study the evolution of export-led growth, and the development of debt-led growth across each of the three cases. This makes it possible to draw out the common presence of 'divergence via Europeanisation' in the origins of the Greek, Portuguese, and Irish crisis.

So far, this book has highlighted the problems inherent in approaches that focus on identifying obstacles to convergence. These approaches tend to employ deductive research designs where they look for a series of impediments that will have stopped the European periphery in their tracks on their respective roads to an arbitrary yardstick of 'competitive development'. In doing so they overlook and neglect the transformative effects of Europeanisation as a catalyst for *divergence* – precisely because they have been preoccupied with identifying 'obstacles' to an assumed trajectory of 'convergence'. Its strengths notwithstanding, deductive approaches like VoC involve the use and abuse of ideal types, and tend to always be in danger of forcing the "square peg of empirical reality into the round hole of the conceptual ideal type" (Clift 2014, 209).

In contrast, addressing this limitation implies a historicist, multiple case study research design to trace processes of divergence via Europeanisation. The following case study chapters inductively trace the relatively successful adjustment of the periphery to projects of European financial integration, and link this to their respective paths to crisis. This approach makes it possible to overcome the central limitation of VoC and the immaturity thesis in that it is theory generating, rather than hypothesis testing; inductive, rather than deductive. Naturally, not knowing in advance which obstacles to look for implies a broader historical research approach, and the leaving behind of the 'ideal types' of VoC. While it is a truism that each political economy can be treated as sui generis and not as representative as cases of a broader category (Goodin 2003, 203), if we are to gain a deeper understanding of the very different paths to crisis followed by Greece, Portugal, and Ireland it is important to keep the historical specificity of these political economies front and centre in the analysis. Labels such as 'MME' and 'CME' can obscure important distinctions between Greece and Portugal, and simply don't apply to Ireland. A historicist approach does not necessarily generate generalisable claims, but this approach can tell us something new and important about the asymmetric origins of the eurozone crisis in these three key countries.

Second, because an inductive, theory-generating approach can't focus on every aspect of the economic history of each country, the multiple case studies will be structured in the sense that, similar to a "comparative structured-focused research design [the researcher poses general questions] . . . that reflect the research objective and that these questions are asked of each case under study to guide and standardise data collection, thereby making systematic comparison and cumulation of the findings of the cases possible" (George and Bennett 2005, cited in Hardiman forthcoming). Specifically, I pose two general questions, which will be put to each of the case studies. First, what were the circumstances surrounding the development (or lack thereof) of export-led patterns of economic growth in each case? To answer this, I will use a CPE approach to identify the role of institutional path dependency and historically trace the evolution of export-led patterns of growth in each case. Second, how did debt-led patterns of growth emerge and develop differently in each case? In order to answer this, I will study the domestic adaptation to EU reforms (Europeanisation) of banking and finance in each case. A structured approach makes it possible to organise the research-gathering stage around answering these two questions.[5]

Finally, a note on case selection. The countries that were worst hit by the crisis were chosen, and these were deemed to be those countries that faced pressure to agree to IMF–ECB–EU bailout agreements. Of course, this relates to five countries: Greece, Ireland, Portugal, Spain, and Cyprus (and there is certainly a strong case to include Italy on this list also). For reasons of space, three countries were chosen, and in the interests of maximising the diversity that needed to be accounted for, Cyprus and Spain were left out because – important differences notwithstanding – the crises of Spain and Cyprus were very similar to the Irish case in that they both stemmed from banking crises due to housing bubbles (not to mention that Cyprus was heavily exposed to the Greek crisis). Portugal, Ireland, and Greece on the other hand represent well the different kinds of crises that occurred across the European periphery, that is, stagnation and recession, banking crisis, and a public debt and fiscal crisis respectively.

In sum, the combination of CPE and Europeanisation involves adopting an inductive, theory-generating, historicist, multiple case study approach. This approach has potential to deepen existing critical debates on the origins of the eurozone crisis. It makes it possible, across a multiple case study analysis, to account for the specific paths to crisis followed by the periphery. It avoids the limits of the immaturity thesis by focusing on the ways in which putatively 'mature' processes of Europeanisation may have been generative of divergence. In addition, by bringing the insights of CPE together with those of Europeanisation, issues highlighted by narratives of German economic domination can be dealt with in a way that existing domestic-level approaches tend to avoid. Studying 'domestic adaptation' to European integration makes it possible to consider the role of the latter in catalysing peripheral divergence in a way that does not posit the periphery as being 'passively reshaped'.

Conclusion

This chapter has outlined the analytical framework that will underpin the three case studies in Chapters 4, 5, and 6. By shedding light on how Europeanisation has been generative of brand new trajectories of debt-led growth, rather than simply leaving existing national path dependencies behind, it has shown the real potential of Europeanisation studies to inform CPE theories of capitalist diversity. It by no means suggests that declining competitiveness and institutional stickiness do not matter. Even if the periphery's banking and finance sectors had not transformed so dramatically (as the following chapters will show), it still would have likely encountered the problems of competitiveness highlighted by CPE scholarship. Thus, the Europeanisation approach proposed here should be seen as complementing CPE, in the sense that it makes it possible to account for the dual importance of debt-led growth and declining competitiveness in the origins of the periphery's ongoing difficulties. The challenge for Greek, Portuguese, Irish, and EU crisis management involves addressing each of these aspects.

This novel reading of the origins of the eurozone crisis has important consequences for how existing political responses to the eurozone crisis should be evaluated. The official EU response has been marked by measures designed to correct the divergences of the peripheral states; to drive convergence more extensively and systematically – to prevent the periphery from endangering the rest of the eurozone through its failure to converge. Yet, if adaptation to new developments at the level of the EU is understood as central to emergence of crisis-prone trajectories of economic development, it suggests that a lack of convergence is not the main problem facing the eurozone. In fact, the following case studies show that quite the opposite is true. The relative severity of the crisis in the periphery is explained by the EU's commitment to the promotion of a single model of convergence across a variety of different European economic trajectories. It follows that any response to the eurozone crisis will produce similar tensions unless it is recognised that any project of European integration is likely to produce multiple models of development. The challenge is not to heedlessly push for future convergence, but to envision ways in which virtuous patterns of divergence can be cultivated within a project of integration. This argument will be explored in detail over three case studies, beginning with Greece.

Notes

1 This is a summary of the discussion in Hall (2018).
2 This section, together with the conclusion, is reproduced from Dooley, N. (2017b) "Divergence via Europeanisation: Rethinking the Origins of the Portuguese Debt Crisis". *Third World Thematics: A TWQ Journal* 0 (0): 1–22. It is reproduced here with the kind permission of Taylor & Francis.
3 Specifically, in this case, Radaelli looks at European nation states' adaptation to EMU, but the four criteria are widely used.
4 Although, as some noted upon its 20-year anniversary, in many respects the Single Market remains 'incomplete' (Egan 2012; de Bois 2014).
5 Throughout the case study chapters I draw on a range of different sources of evidence to develop the concept of 'divergence via Europeanisation'. For instance, in order to study credit expansion and credit allocation (debt-led growth), I draw on annual reports from the Bank of Greece and the Banco de Portugal, and annual reports and quarterly bulletins from the Central Bank of Ireland, as well as a range of secondary academic and

policy material, especially country-specific literature on the banking and finance sectors. To trace the evolution of export-led growth I draw on a broad range of sources from secondary country-specific economic history and political economy literature, as well as central bank annual reports, IMF country reports, European Commission reports, and – where relevant – macroeconomic data from a range of sources. Dealing with these types of sources has the benefit of making it possible to conduct theory-generating research while dealing with three cases over multiple decades. Although the aim of this project is not to generate new primary data, through engaging with the aforementioned sources I develop a new interpretation of the crisis that addresses existing shortcomings and can thus potentially set new agendas and better direct the collection of new primary research.

4 Greece

This chapter provides the first of three case studies. Greece is the epicentre of the eurozone crisis and 'patient zero' for the immaturity thesis. The country is often, as Greek Minister for Finance Euclid Tsakalotos (2014) has observed, conceived of as 'exceptional' to a purported European norm of fiscal responsibility, and thereby cast as the principal architect of its own downfall. The origins of the Greek crisis are typically presented as a salacious mix of chronic and misreported public finances, political corruption, widespread tax evasion, and a bloated, inefficient public sector.

Yet the Greek crisis has never been purely fiscal. Explanations that over-rely on notions of immaturity in the guise of 'Greek exceptionalism' have proved inadequate to the task of accounting for the deeper structural problems facing the Greek economy. In this chapter I apply the analytical framework outlined in Chapter 3 and show that the Greek crisis of 2009 is linked to the country's divergence via Europeanisation. It is a twin crisis; a crisis of competitiveness as evidenced by its widening current account deficit, and a crisis of public finances as evidenced by its debt and deficit to GDP levels. These twin crises are linked, to different extents, by Greece's attempt to adapt to a 'one size fits all' project of European integration.

I will develop this argument over three sections. Section one engages with perspectives that emphasise how particular 'exceptional' national and political traits are primarily responsible for the country's fiscal crisis. I take many of these insights on board by focusing on how long-standing problems relating to tax collection, welfare provision, and poor reform capacity do indeed have an important role in Greece's fiscal crisis. Yet, I also outline two important limitations. First, perspectives in this vein have misleadingly explained the origins of these problems as stemming primarily from processes of clientelism and fiscal irresponsibility. Second, they have problematically conflated the fiscal crisis with the causes of the competitiveness crisis.

These limits are addressed in the second section, by showing how the skyrocketing of public debt in 1980s Greece should be understood as partially bound up in a process of state directed investment in a project of industrialisation, with a specific focus on the high-technology sector. This strategy was undoubtedly a failure, but it is important to understand that this failure is indicative of the challenges faced by a small, newly democratised peripheral 'latecomer' economy attempting to realise a rather typical modern European vision of economic growth based on the exporting of "products of specialised labour and high technology" (Bank of Greece 2006, 40). In addition, I establish the link between EMU, capital flows, and the changing dynamics of Greek public debt and deficits.

The third section traces Greece's divergence via Europeanisation. Chiefly, I show how the emergence of a brand new pattern of debt-led growth emerged during the 1990s and 2000s in Greece as a result of the country's adaptation to the European Single Market and the euro. It was during this period that the Greek economy started to exhibit strong economic growth for the first time in decades. Greece's banking sector underwent dramatic transformations through processes of deregulation, privatisation, and liberalisation. Considerable credit growth occurred in relation to housing and consumer credit. Consumers ended up with higher levels of disposable income, which fuelled a growth in imports. Despite a modest increase in export competitiveness, growing imports widened Greece's current account deficit and helped ignite a recession following the global financial crash. This helped make Greece a target for international speculation in 2009.

The central contribution of this case study is to shed light on the much overlooked 'non-exceptional' causes of the Greek crisis and, in doing so, establish the crucial role played by Europeanisation in the country's economic crisis. The Greek crisis was catalysed just as much by non-exceptional attempts to adapt to European integration as it was by putative exceptional 'obstacles to convergence'.

Contesting the 'exceptionalism' of the Greek crisis

Greece is often represented in mainstream scholarly, political, and media narratives as 'exceptional' and as the antithesis of 'advanced' Northern European economies. As shown in the previous chapters, existing 'domestic-level' approaches tend to emphasise the ways in which Greece failed to 'play by the rules' befitting a modern, mature member of the European project. On the other hand, critical and 'systemic' literature on the Greek sovereign debt crisis has had difficulty in 'explaining away' Greek immaturity, as Kevin Featherstone's response during a debate with Costas Lapavitsas demonstrates:

> [you say that it] has "nothing to do with state profligacy." Sorry, I had understood that the debt to GDP ratio since 1993 has been consistently around 100% of Gross Domestic Product. How could a state sustain those levels of debt and not be vulnerable?
>
> (in Lapavitsas 2010)

Clientelism, corruption, and tax evasion have played important roles in Greece's crisis. However, in this chapter I show that these well-documented, supposedly 'exceptional' aspects of Greece's political economy do not tell the whole story. This section sketches the most important claims of the exceptionalism thesis,[1] before identifying some important limitations. Crucially, I show that while notions of exceptionalism may capture important aspects of the historical character of Greece's fiscal crisis, they are inadequate in accounting for the origins of Greece's competitiveness crisis.

Debt-fuelled clientelism: the 'exceptional' origins of the Greek crisis

The story of Greece's crisis typically begins with the foundation of a new party, the Panhellenic Socialist Movement (PASOK) in 1974 under the leadership of Andreas Papandreou. PASOK secured an overall majority in the 1981 elections at the expense of New Democracy (ND). As Figures 4.1 and 4.2 show, public deficits and debt rose significantly from the late 1970s, and particularly from 1981 to 1989. Most of the debt was accrued by PASOK governments in the 1980s, through socioeconomic policies aiming to expand the public sector and increase social spending, and raising wages by borrowing. For many, the electoral success of Papandreou and PASOK can be explained through skill, party organisation, and ingenuity on the one hand, and personal charisma and the inherent emotive appeal of populist rhetoric on the other. In this narrative, Papandreou and PASOK effectively 'seduced' the masses, and then consolidated this support once in power through patronage, at the expense of Greek public finances and macroeconomic sustainability.

According to this perspective, the public debt of the 1980s is the primarily the result of reckless short-term political power consolidation by PASOK and their supporters.[2] PASOK's strategy of political power consolidation in the 1980s is understood to have catalysed a 'Greek Tragedy of the Commons', or in other words, in tandem with rising deficits and debt, PASOK transformed the Greek

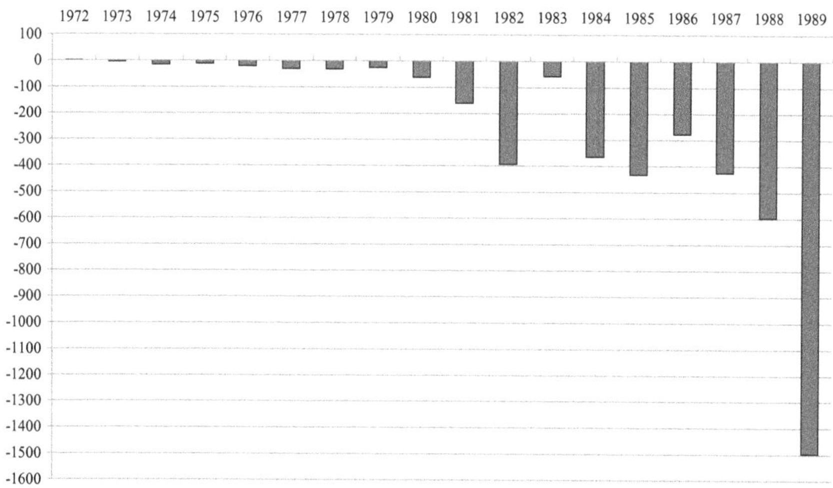

Figure 4.1 Greek government deficit/surplus in millions of national currency (drachma)

Source: IMF, Government Finance Statistics

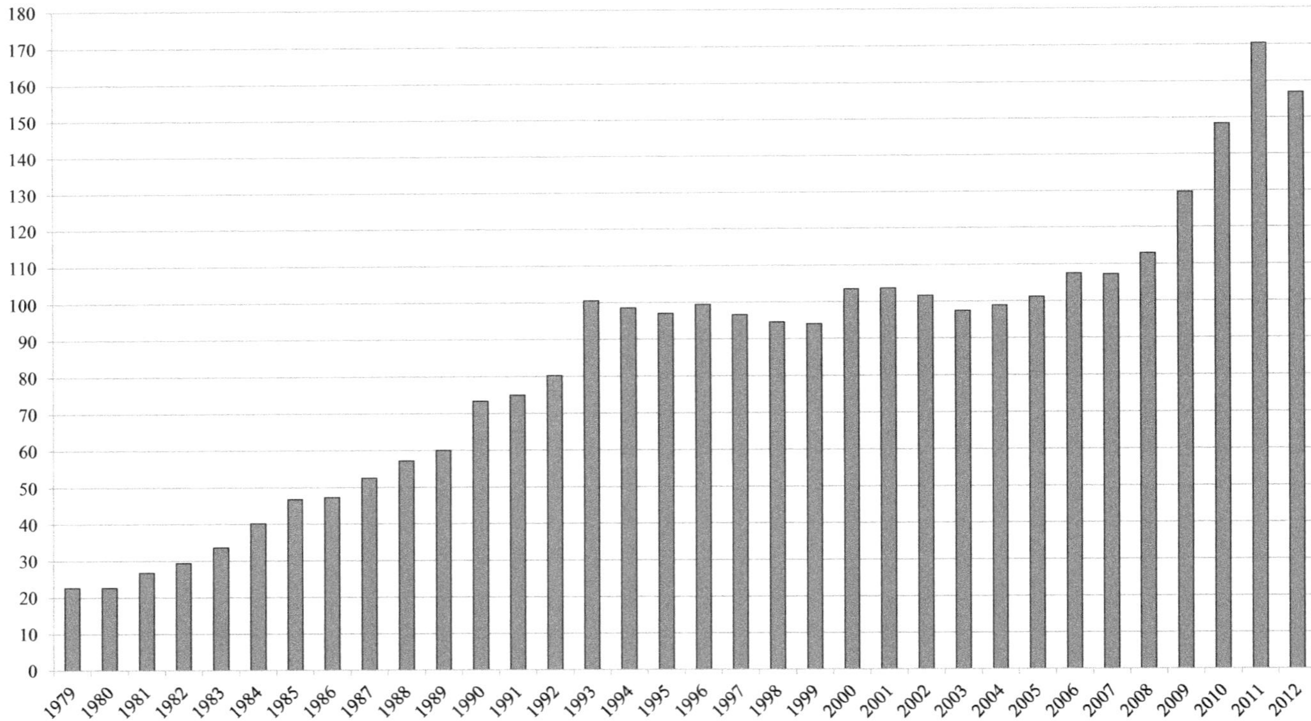

Figure 4.2 Greek public debt as percentage of GDP, 1979–2012

Source: IMF, Historical Public Debt Database

state into a complex system of clientelism/patronage, the upshot being that major sections of society became dependent upon the state for favours, employment, and a particular lifestyle, in return for electoral support. The absence of the state governance in this regard was just as important, as tax evasion became a common and widely practiced phenomenon. Bribery and corruption in the everyday provision of public services became a 'national pastime' (Manolopoulos 2011, 103–4). Put very simply, Greek society became bound up and complicit in the debt-fuelled clientelism of PASOK's state during the 1980s; as PASOKs power became consolidated, so did a widespread 'culture of entitlement' (see Triandafyllidou, Gropas, and Kouki 2013 for a summary of this argument).

Thereafter, despite wide ranging reform efforts, this system of debt-fuelled clientelism proved impossible to supplant. In such analysis, the 1980s emerges as a 'big bang' moment for Greece. It gave rise, in a once and for all fashion, to static and immovable political and economic pathologies that would, in due course, lead Greece to inevitable fiscal and sovereign debt crisis (Diamandouros 2011). Although this literature has produced important scholarship, which recognises, evaluates, and takes seriously the emergence of modernising forces in Greek politics and civil society from as early as the 1980s (but mainly in the 1990s and 2000s), the battle between 'modernity' and 'tradition' in Greece is analysed as a losing one for modernisation.

As a result, much of the debate concerns discussions of the causes and dynamics of 'poor reform capacity' in Greece.[3] The upshot of this argument is that few meaningful and necessary structural reforms were made during the 1990s and 2000s (see Diamandouros 2011) because debt-fuelled clientelism had become endemic and impossible to supplant; the state's growth, and the interests of society at large, not to mention powerful interest groups, were all too dependent on the 'Greek' model.[4]

The limits of emphasising Greek exceptionalism

This approach has key strengths in terms of its ability to account for several central causes of Greece's fiscal and public debt crises. For instance, tax evasion in Greece is pervasive and a practice that has significant effects on its economy. It has been suggested that as much as 64 percent of eligible taxpayers in Greece did not pay any tax in 2009 (Oltheten et al. 2013, 332).[5] In addition, Greece has one of the largest 'shadow economies' in Europe, amounting to about 30 percent of GDP – implying an annual loss in taxes of about €8–10 billion (Oltheten et al. 2013, 332). Moreover, as Featherstone and others have argued (Featherstone and Papadimitriou 2008; Featherstone 2008), problems of state efficiency cannot be ignored, even if Greece's fiscal difficulties are more to do with revenue shortfalls than overspending (contrary to common misconceptions). State spending on social provision compares favourably with other EU states, but the coverage is relatively limited. For example, unemployment benefit is relatively low and limited in scope and duration, while that spent on pensions is notoriously high. The weakness of the welfare state and social provision in turn contributes to widespread tax evasion (Featherstone 2008, 24).

Despite these important contributions to our understanding of the historical character of the Greek political economy, there are two key limitations to the ability of accounts that emphasise Greek exceptionalism to explain the contemporary problematique. First, they tend to neglect of the ways in which Greece's economic trajectory dramatically transformed over the course of the 1990s and 2000s. In clarifying his own position on this debate, Nikos Diamandouros neatly outlines this manoeuvre:

> Let me immediately clarify that my argument is not that the dominant paradigm has remained entirely unchanged or frozen in time for more than a century. Such an assertion would be clearly untenable, both theoretically and empirically. It is, rather, that, notwithstanding significant evolution, notable improvements, important modifications, and occasionally substantive reforms, the *fundamental logic* underpinning and informing the dominant paradigm has, in fact, retained its integrity throughout this period.
>
> ([original italics] Diamandouros 2011, 2)

Emphasising the stubborn path dependence of obstacles to modernisation posits an unbroken continuity in how the Greek economic trajectory is conceptualised from the 1980s onwards. In doing so, it provides a framework that is not well suited to accounting for the important changes that took place during the 1990s and 2000s, which I show contribute to the emergence of brand new and unanticipated trajectory of Greek economic development.

A second limitation is the disproportionate focus on the fiscal dimension of Greece's crisis, which is by now widely recognised as simply one part of the twin crisis facing the country, comprising also of a competitiveness dimension (Wihlborg, Willett, and Zhang 2010; Fouskas and Dimoulas 2012; Lapavitsas 2010). This is not simply a problem of emphasis; the causes of the fiscal crisis have actually been used to also account for the competitiveness crisis. As Oltheten et al. (2013) argue, the reason that Greece has underperformed and lost competitiveness in past decades is because "the education system is ineffective, the government is incompetent, the tax system is corrupt, and the system of justice is dysfunctional" (330). This diagnosis is evident across the Memoranda of Understanding (European Commission 2010) and other policy analyses of the Greek crisis (e.g., Bank of Greece 2010). All of this supposedly culminates to make Greece a deeply unattractive country in which to do business. "The private sector, normally a source of entrepreneurship and growth is so weighted down that it can no longer overcome the burden of its own government" (Oltheten et al. 2013, 330–1). Featherstone similarly writes about corruption as a cultural phenomenon and claims that it is "anti-competitive: it imposes costs and distorts the market, whilst offering privileged contact via enclosed networks. It is evident at all levels and across sectors" (Featherstone 2008, 19).

Eliding the causes of these twin crises appears somewhat misleading. Even if Greece had tackled the aforementioned 'exceptional' traits via structural reforms aimed at convergence, its failure to succeed in tackling them does not automatically explain the unique path of debt-led growth Greece diverged onto. In fact, as I show in the following sections, beginning with the period of PASOK's first governments, precisely that period in which Greece is conventionally considered to have diverged most significantly from modern European norms, Greece's road to crisis was paved with good, non-exceptional intentions.

The Greek fiscal crisis: limits to export-led growth at Europe's periphery

Greece's exorbitant public debt, persistent public deficits, and pervasive corruption and clientelism can all be traced back to the late 1970s and 1980s. During this critical period, Greek policy aimed at 'modernising' the economy. However, this agenda was shaped by both the pathological features identified by the 'exceptionalism' thesis, and further factors that are conventionally understood as non-exceptional. The importance of the latter has hitherto tended to be overlooked by literature on the contemporary Greek crisis. As I show in this section, Greek policymaking in the 1980s was aimed at modernising the economy. But this agenda was operationalised within the parameters set by political, economic, and at times geopolitical imperatives. Greece's, in many important respects, non-exceptional attempt to develop an export-led model of growth during the 1980s was just as important as its embrace of corruption and clientelism in sowing the seeds for its eventual fiscal crisis. Accordingly, without denying the role of the well-documented emerging 'dysfunctions' of this period, I show that running parallel were dynamic and complex patterns of policymaking that contained a distinctly 'modern' vision for Greece, which were in turn subject to and limited by various constraints, challenges, and imperatives. In this section, I provide a revisionist historical narrative of the origins of the Greek crisis in the 1980s, which reveals the ways in which distinctly non-exceptional patterns of Greek agency may be seen to have been equally as generative of divergence as those that may be identified as exceptional.

The era of 'Metapolitefsi': challenges to Greek modernisation, 1974–89

Like so many other peripheral European countries, Greece in the 1970s and 1980s was clearly an 'economic latecomer', attempting to 'catch up' with its Western European neighbours in terms of economic growth, living standards, and by developing an export-led model of growth. Greece attempted this project of catching up in the face of a number of urgent challenges during this period. Following the Turkish invasion of Cyprus, the first oil crash, and mounting social unrest, the seven-year right-wing authoritarian Regime of the Colonels collapsed in 1974, beginning the period of Metapolitefsi[6] in Greece (see Clogg 2002; Fouskas and Dimoulas 2013, 109–34). In 1974 Constantine Karamanlis and his ND party formed a conservative government which began the process of 'de-juntafication', which carried on throughout the 1980s, in the context of the international economic crisis, and where, as Clogg (2002) argues, "the overriding priority of this new government was to defuse risk of war with Turkey" (166). Hence, the newly established Third Hellenic Republic began a process of converging with Western Europe's growth rates, per capita income, and growth models in the middle of unprecedented and severe international economic and geopolitical crises.

By 1980 per capita GDP was just 68 percent of the EU average, higher only than that of fellow peripheral country Ireland (Oltheten et al. 2013, 319). Greece remained predominately agricultural, de-industrialisation had generated serious economic difficulty for the country from as early as 1973, and these difficulties were accelerated by the oil shocks of that decade.[7] Although it had witnessed some industrialisation in the post-war period (the so-called 'Golden era' – see Mavroudeas 2010, 5), by the 1970s this had already begun to decline; and as Louri and Minoglou (2002) put it, Greece "never fully completed the transition from a backward mercantile/agricultural economy to an advanced capitalist economy" (324, 337). Even at its peak, industrial employment in Greece was 30 percent as opposed to roughly 47 percent for other Western economies. The trend was set to continue; by 1994 the share of manufacturing output in GDP was 15 percent, down from 19.8 percent in 1951 (these figures are provided by Louri and Minoglou 2002, 338). Foreign Direct Investment (FDI) also fell sharply and technology-intensive sectors stopped increasing, remaining basically static from the mid-1970s onwards. Following the second oil crisis and European Economic Community (EEC) membership, Greece became increasingly exposed to import penetration and declining export competitiveness into the 1980s.

In addition to the aforementioned economic crisis, the processes of democratization and dejuntafication required a new urgency on the part of the Greek state to respond to the demands of those who had been excluded not just under the authoritarian regime of Colonels but via the various repressive tendencies of the post-war Greek state.[8] Concretely, various imperatives aligned during the 1970s and 1980s, which led to the (comparatively late, especially compared to the UK and Western Europe) necessity to begin the establishment of a welfare state. This is crucially important to note: Greece found itself in a position of having to respond to an unprecedented economic crisis, while also having to begin the construction of a welfare state. Modernisation, stabilisation, and the establishment of the welfare state were pursued *all at once* (Markantonatou 2012, 422).

Adding insult to injury, the (seemingly legitimate) prospect of a war with Turkey made Greece one of the world's highest per capita military spenders' during this period and right up until the present day (Pappas 2013, 34). Precipitated by the 1974 Cyprus emergency, tensions between Greece and Turkey continued from 1974 to 1990 and beyond. Massive expenditures on military hardware meant that "infrastructural reforms, e.g. in education and health care, that demanded urgent attention received a low priority" (Clogg 2002, 173), something that fell to the 1980s PASOK governments to rectify. Although there is not the space here to provide a more detailed account, suffice to say, tensions regarding Turkey continued to be significant from 1974 to 2009, and this translated into persistently high defence spending for Greece, something that had a clear and direct effect on public finances.

As such, Greek governments in the 1980s found themselves compelled to tackle a triple challenge; an economic crisis, a welfare crisis, and a potential geopolitical crisis. This triple crisis contributed to a particular strategy of economic development, one that attempted to meet the welfare and economic crisis together through fostering economic growth. Conventional accounts that highlight corruption and clientelism tend to downplay this aspect of 1980s Greece. The goal of economic "stabilisation through development" (Tsakalotos 1991, 179) is an important part of the transformation of the Greek political economy at this time, to which I now turn.

Stabilisation through development: Greek modernisation strategy in the 1980s

'Stabilisation through development' refers to PASOK's attempt to meet this triple challenge through an early programme of modernisation. It aimed to manage the economic crisis while at the same time attempting to restructure the public sector, modernise the banking system, and harness the private sector for developmental purposes (Lavdas 1997, 149). Specifically, PASOK made use of an inherited post-war *dirigiste* strategy of development, which hinged on publicly financing a national project of industrialisation. It was a strategy that suffered from serious limitations and ended in outright failure by the end of the decade. Specifically, it contributed detrimentally to the accumulation of public debt and deficits and to rising inflation; it also had little success in modernising the Greek economy in the way it intended. This strategy failed because, aside from being constrained by the political, economic, and social imperatives outlined earlier, the strategy was caught between a specific vision of Greece's future and a particular institutional framework inherited from Greece's past that was to prove no longer effective.[9] Nevertheless, in this respect, we can re-interpret the dysfunctions of the 1980s as a product not simply of the exceptionalism noted in the first section, but as a product of the limitations of an ambitious project of modernisation, that nevertheless could not escape the imperatives that shaped its attempted implementation.

Turning to the strategy itself, Euclid Tsakalotos argues that PASOK's strategy was based on its structural analysis of the problems facing the Greek economy at the time. In particular, PASOK wished to reverse deindustrialisation in Greece through coordinated national development plans and public investment (Tsakalotos 1991, 136). It was widely perceived by PASOK elites at the time that existing state investment was ad-hoc and that no previous government had ever effectively integrated the "financial sector into any specific strategy for development" (Tsakalotos 1991, 137) and furthermore, the deteriorating economic performance of the Greek economy by 1981 represented the failure of the private sector to invest in industry (Tsakalotos 1991, 152). PASOK's national development plan, in contrast, assigned a clear role for a reformed public sector along with various supervisory councils to direct the financial sector towards national development goals.

A key element of PASOK's new development agenda, particularly in its first term (1981–5) involved a policy of 'sectoral targeting'. Law 1262/1982 was introduced (Lavdas 1997, 152; see also Tsakalotos 1991, 154) to explicitly target 'high end' 'export' manufacturing sectors – and so public investment was concentrated in what were perceived as "a number of dynamic areas (electronics, IT related branches, biotechnology and precision instruments" (Lavdas 1997, 152). This strategy is widely agreed to have had limited success, partly to do with poor implementation and planning, but also because the sector targeting policies failed to consider that some of the traditional sectors in Greece (cement, food and beverages, textiles, clothing, etc.) were more likely to be areas where Greece had a comparative advantage, while the manufacturing sectors were declining (Lavdas 1997, 152). It was also aggravated by Greece's entry into the EEC in 1981, which led to an increase in import penetration and poor export performance (Tsakalotos 1991, 154). Eventually, this policy helped a majority from the traditional sectors.

This strategy was also expected to tackle the much-prolonged issue of welfare provision. As Markantonatou (2012) notes, during the post-war period, an authoritarian state "undertook an active ideological role in the perpetuation of the division between the losers and the winners of the [Civil] war, by offering jobs and state subsidies to the latter, repudiating and purging the former, long after the end of the hostilities" (418). A particular form of economy emerged during this period, one that was characterised, inter alia, by low wages and little to no welfare state (Markantonatou 2012, 418, 419). The 1980s represented an attempt to rectify this in various ways. Papandreou introduced a number of reforms, including the establishment of a National Health Service, the building of hospitals and clinics, the raising of salaries in the public sector, and other measures (see Clogg 2002 181–6). Yet, as Clogg argues, any hope of creating a modern welfare state "hinged critically on putting the economy on a sounder footing and in particular, on improving productivity" (2002, 181). The limited success achieved through this strategy by the end of the 1980s meant that Greece never really ended up with a modern welfare state, which was to have consequences for tax evasion and fiscal policy going into the 1990s and 2000s.

In spite of its failure, it is important to note that the PASOK governments' pursuit of 'high-technology' industrialised growth was a distinctly 'modern' vision for Greece that should be understood as a not unusual example of a 'late developing' economy catch up or converge with its Western neighbours. Indeed, in aspiring towards a 'smart' and high-technology economy, it anticipated many aspects of the Single Market and the Lisbon Agenda that emerged years later, as Lavdas notes:

> In business circles, the perception of the PASOK strategy was that the Papandreou government wished to achieve a dominant role for the public sector supported by clusters of 'smart' SMEs in areas that were new or almost new for Greece.
>
> (Lavdas 1997, 152)

This is true, even if the means by which this vision were pursued were somewhat out of step with the abandonment of domestic demand-led growth strategies in most European countries at the time. Because the PASOK strategy resulted in nationalisations and enormous public spending and investment, it goes without saying that the pursuit of this modernisation strategy was to be politically and economically costly for Greece. Numerous advisory bodies were also set up to function as "channels for the flow of information and proposals between public and private agencies" (Lavdas 1997, 153). The infamous OAE[10] was established during this period also to deal with ailing firms' problems, to restructure them in line with this modernising vision. The OAE, a public sector organization set up by Law 1386/1983 to take over bankrupt or overburdened firms in order to reduce unemployment, was justified as being in the public interests with reference to unacceptable levels of employment and by 1985 had obtained control of 41 industrial firms with a total debt of Dr350 billion (Lavdas 1997, 162). Of course, the restructuring of these firms proved ineffective, and many of these problematic companies remained on the public balance sheet for years to come.

If high-technology modernisation was a vision of Greece's future, it was to be implemented using an institutional framework inherited from Greece's recent past. The dirigiste model was an inheritance from the so-called golden years of Greek economic growth, which took place in a context where the USA was imposing and directly dictating policy in Greece. Accordingly, the 1980s in Greece do not represent an 'abrupt discontinuity' (Louri and Minoglou 2002, 323; see also Alogoskoufis 2000) with the post-war model, but an appropriation of it to continue a project of modernisation (Pagoulatos 2003). The first PASOK government's economic plan made use of this existing state–bank–industrial investment infrastructure to tackle the economic and employment crisis that had emerged since the 1970s, but also to restructure the Greek economy away from traditional towards advanced and semi-advanced industrial production – partially stimulated by domestic demand.

However, it was becoming clear that a dirigiste industrial model was no longer appropriate for Greece post-1974. For one thing, the repressive political mechanisms of the post-war Greek state were no longer available. Previously marginalised groups, especially labour, were now able to demand and receive economic benefits previously denied to them. These demands, however, partially translated into an attempt to protect the 'industrial model' as a way of maintaining employment over the course of the 1970s and 1980s, which explains why the industrial sector continued to receive state support during the period (Pagoulatos 2003, 88–9). As such, Greek democratisation took place using the tools available from the pre-existing pre-1974 'developmentalist' or dirigisme model. Pagoulatos (2003) describes such measures as "[the] last ditch effort of what remained of a developmental state seeking to prop up industrial growth amidst a highly adverse economic environment" (96). Indeed, joining the EEC can be actually be seen as an initial post 1974 attempt to rescue, *not* dismantle the pre-1974 model, and the Karamanlis government attempted to prop up the Greek manufacturing sector though exports and direct investment towards heavy industry (Pagoulatos 2003, 88).

These attempts by PASOK governments to 'catch up' by pursuing a 'modern' developmental agenda during the 1980s while continuing to utilise the pre-existing infrastructure of the post-war dirigiste model generated a number of key contradictions in the Greek economy, which have had major significance for the contemporary conjuncture.[11] Firstly this bank-based institutional model contributed heavily to the accrual of public debt in Greece during the period. Secondly, the expansion of the public sector and the raising of salaries can be seen as an attempt to develop a form of welfare provision.

It is important to recognise that using this model was a necessary and immediate decision of both ND in the 1970s and PASOK in the 1980s. There wasn't another model that was readily available or 'waiting in the wings'. Crucially, PASOK's policy agenda during its second term in office was shaped by the evident failures of its first term, and represented something of a radical shift in policy. PASOK knew that it needed to control inflation, tackle the deficit, and confront the problem of falling private investments, the decline of which since 1979 (two years before PASOK took office) had reached a record low in 1985 (Lavdas 1997, 174–5). Indeed, as the next section shows, as Greece prepared for the European Single Market and the euro, a new trajectory of economic growth resulted in the gradual supplanting of the old dirigisme model.

The changing dynamics of Greek debt: financialisation and externalisation

The 1980s bequeathed Greece with enormous levels of public debt that it never managed to meaningfully recover from. Nevertheless, Greece had some success in improving its public finances in the decades to follow. During the 1990s, reforms aimed at preparing Greece for EMU membership succeeded in reducing deficit to GDP levels to 1.2 percent of GDP by 2002. Greek public debt, having risen from about 20 percent of GDP in the early 1980s to almost 100 percent of GDP in the 1990s, stabilised at around 100 percent in 2000, and displayed a weak downward trend until 2007 (Alogoskoufis 2012; Bank of Greece, various years).[12]

Yet, expansionary policies returned after the meaningful threat of exclusion from EMU was absent and the constraints of the stability and growth pact did little to dis-incentivise negative developments in public finances (Johnston 2016). Extraordinary costs such as the 2004 Olympic Games accelerated public spending, but costs relating to grants, civil service staff costs, and other aspects of primary expenditure proved persistent over the 2000s. Greece activated the EU's Excessive Deficit Procedure (EDP) twice before the eurozone crisis, first in 2004 as total government expenditure rose substantially – largely due to run of the mill expenditure on public salaries, pensions, and other primary expenditure – and again in 2008 as a result of the global economic crisis. Problems with tax collection continued throughout the 2000s, and Greece persistently held the highest or second highest ratio of public debt to GDP in the euro area. These public finance problems came to a head, as is well known, when revised data released to Eurostat revealed Greece's budget deficit to have widened to 12.9 percent of GDP in 2009, over four times higher than the 3 percent EU rule, while public debt climbed to 115.1 percent of GDP (Bank of Greece 2010).

The acceleration of public debt during the 1980s, in other words, remained as a structural vulnerability for Greece right up until the crisis. However, Greece's levels of public debt (as a percentage of GDP) fluctuated, but did not grow significantly until after 2008. It is worth emphasising, as Figure 4.3 shows, that joining the euro did not result in an 'explosion of debt' for Greece. In fact, as a percentage of GDP, it exhibited a slight downward trend.

What did change as a result of EU directed reforms to banking and finance (see the following section) was that Greece's public debt became mostly held by external lenders. For example, in 2009, Italy only had 50 percent of its public debt held abroad, contrary to 80 percent of Greece's (Pagoulatos and Quaglia 2013, 190–1). During the 1990s, most of the public debt in Greece was domestic, held by the Greek banking system – most of which was state controlled (see Manolopoulos 2011, 137). Manolopoulos (2011) notes that in 1994, 85 percent of Greek government debt was held by domestic financial institutions, and by 2007 this had been practically inverted with 75 percent held by foreign investors (Pagoulatos and Quaglia 2013, 190–1; see Manolopoulos 2011, 137). Membership of the euro had transformed Greece as a source of risk to international bond holders – and this externalisation of debt, in addition to its high level, can be argued to be fundamental to understanding the 2009 crisis.

The public debt conversion from domestic to foreign was accelerated into the 2000s. The euro made it much easier for Greece to push its debt-servicing burden to the future while becoming highly exposed to global debt market fluctuations' (Pagoualtos and Quaglia 2013, 190–1). Once Greece adopted the euro in 2001, it experienced a sharp reduction in interest rates. The nominal interest rate on ten-year

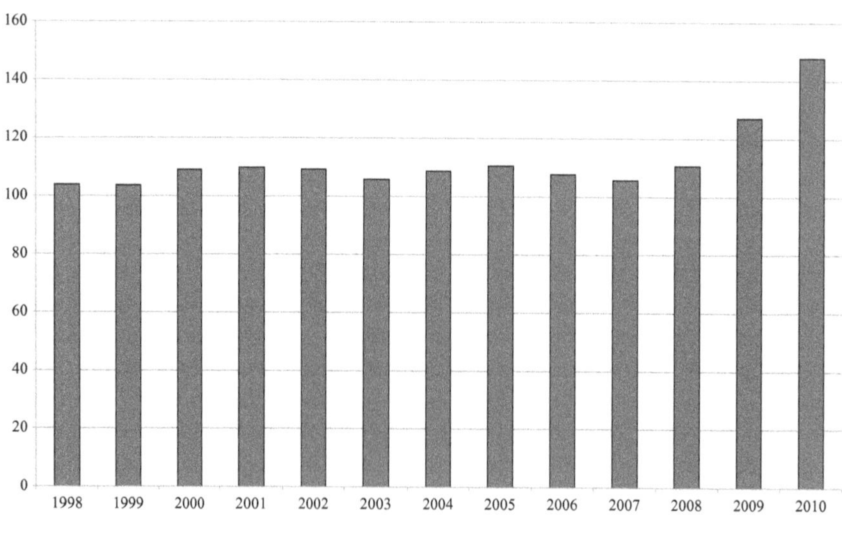

Figure 4.3 Total Greek central government debt, percentage of GDP, 1998–2010
Source: OECD

Greek government bonds declined from 20 percent to 3.5 percent by 2005 (Kouretas and Vlamis 2010, 391–3). Low inflation and low interest rates led to an increase in private investment and robust real growth rates of 3.9 percent per year over the period 2001–8 (Kouretas and Vlamis 2010, 391–3). "Greece's adoption of the euro in 2001 provided sharply-reduced interest rates. Nominal interest rates declined from about 20% in 1994, at the time when Greece announced its intention to join the eurozone, to less than 3.5% in early 2005" (Panageotou 2011). For the Greek government itself, debt repayments had been consuming 12 percent of government revenues in 1994, but by 2006 this figure had dropped to just 4 percent of revenues (Lynn 2010, 115). Joining the euro entailed a significant change in the dynamics of Greek public debt, in that the low interest rates lowered the costs of servicing public sector debt (Kouretas and Vlamis 2010, 391–3).

To conclude this section, it is certainly impossible to ignore the unprecedented growth of public debt and budget deficits that emerged during this period and it would be unwise to downplay their impact in Greece's current crisis. It would also be imprudent to fully discount the importance of new modes of corruption and clientelism that emerged during this period, and their constitutive role in Greek debt and deficits. However, the 'big bang' moment of the 1980s, as I have shown, cannot be understood *solely* as an abandonment of a sound project of modernisation in favour of a nefarious project of political power consolidation. Rather, the problems of the 1980s are better understood as stemming also from the imperatives of pursuing economic development, within the context of an international economic crisis, geopolitical turbulence in the Aegean, achieving legitimate democratisation, and the desire to transform into an export-led economy using the inherited dirigisme institutional structures of the post-war period, all at the same time as trying to develop a welfare state.

These were the real imperatives that Greek modernisers had to negotiate. PASOK governments of the 1980s faced nothing less than the complex problematique of a late developing peripheral European state attempting to catch up with its Western European neighbours (Dooley 2018, 88). The debt that was accumulated remained a persistent problem in the years to come, but the changing dynamics associated with the Single Market and the euro contributed to the growing riskiness of that debt. It is to these EU reforms, and their relationship to Greece's competitiveness crisis, that I now turn.

Greece adapts to Europe: debt-led growth via Europeanisation

If the 1980s were characterised by early, failed, attempts by the newly formed Greek democracy to mark a rupture with its past, the following two decades saw Greek governments succeed in doing just that. Yet, transformation was not achieved through enhanced export competitiveness or high-technology industrialisation as was hoped. Rather, Greece transformed into an economy that was driven by domestic demand and debt-led growth. This section shows how this transformation was made possible by the country's Europeanisation.

I analyse Bank of Greece annual reports data,[13] together with supplementary material, relating to credit development, current account balance, and GDP to show that that while Greek 'exceptionalism' or resistance to European style convergence may account to an important (although not exhaustive) extent for Greece's fiscal problems, *at the same time*, successful adaptation to the European Single Market and the euro resulted in the transformation of the Greek economy into a fragile and non-competitive model of growth.

I trace Greece's divergence via Europeanisation in four main ways. First, I introduce the major changes to occur to the Greek banking and financial system in the decades before the eurozone crisis. Second, I analyse credit developments to outline the key aspects of a new pattern of growth for Greece: one based predominantly on debt-led domestic demand. Third, I make explicit the link between this new pattern of growth and the crisis of competitiveness, which came to a head in 2009. Finally, I emphasise the role of path dependency in keeping the Greek banking sector relatively underdeveloped, which sets the Greek crisis apart from the kinds of banking crises that occurred elsewhere in the periphery, such as Spain and Ireland.

The Europeanisation of Greek banking

From 1998 to 2008 Greece experienced a decade of above average GDP growth (Figure 4.4) and converging living standards with its Western European neighbours. By 2006, the last year before Greece started to be impacted by the global financial crisis, the country celebrated a decade of GDP growth rates that were among the highest in the EU, and living standards that were finally converging towards the EU average (Bank of Greece 2007, 43). But all was not well. Greece's unprecedented period of prosperity was underpinned by a brand new and precarious growth regime. This new growth regime was founded on institutional transformations, driven by processes of European integration. Specifically, the Greek banking sector underwent a wholesale transformation due to its attempts to adapt to the EU requirements of the Single Market and the euro.[14]

Prior to the emergence of the Single Market, the Greek banking sector was among the most heavily regulated and tightly controlled in Europe. Interest rates were highly regulated, and banks had limits set on their lending to so-called 'non-productive' sectors, including to construction, mortgage lending, and consumption. The banking sector was largely state controlled and set up to fund public enterprise and services (see Gorstos 2002, 142). The sector was highly specialised, and there were restrictions in place for what services and products different kinds of financial institutions could provide. This was all to change with the preparations for the Single Market. Greece was expected to make reforms relating to the banking and financial sectors as part of its accession to the EEC and due to its participation in the Single Market project. Capital movements were liberalised, interest rates deregulated and ultimately reduced, and the financial sector was deregulated and strengthened through various reforms, legislature, and directives associated with deepening European integration from the late 1980s onwards (Pasiouras 2012, 1; Deeg 2012; Bakker 1996).

Initial steps towards deregulation were taken in the 1980s, and picked up speed throughout the 1990s. The Greek Parliament passed the Second Banking Directive into law in 1992 (Kosmidou 2008, 146). Three major consequences are worth emphasising. The first was the deregulation of the Greek banking system, which had been characterised by high levels of specialisation up until this point. Credit and interest rate policy had been used as a policy tool by successive Greek governments to promote public enterprises and pursue export strategies. SMEs, inter alia, had special interest rates, which they could avail of from specialised credit institutions. After the EU's Second Banking Directive, specialised credit institutions were now allowed to provide services previously reserved for commercial banks, and vice versa (Hondroyiannis, Lolos, and Papapetrou 1999, 379). This increased competition between banks for new products and services, especially consumer and housing credit.

A second and related consequence was that banks were now allowed to set their lending rates on their own terms, and had to provide new financial products, including products related to housing and consumer finance. This set new competitive dynamics between banks in motion. Requirements were abolished over time for Greek banks to purchase government treasury bills. A fateful consequence of this was the shift in government borrowing from its own banks to market financing, typically from abroad (Eichengreen and Gibson 2001, 28; Hondroyiannis et al. 1999, 379).

Third, with the Single Market, but especially with EMU, Greek banks had easier access to a deep pool of European credit as capital movements were

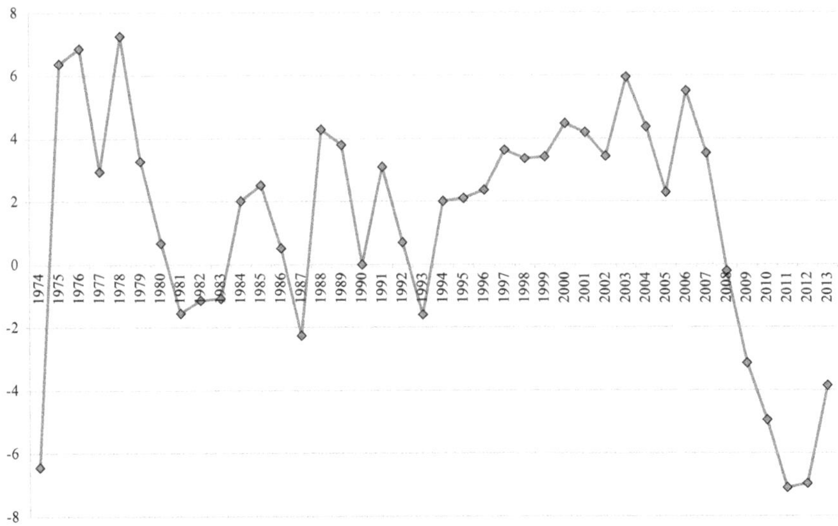

Figure 4.4 Annual percentage growth rate of GDP in Greece at market prices based on constant local currency (US$)

Source: World Bank national accounts data, and OECD National Accounts data files

liberalised by 1994 and free from currency exchange risk by the advent of the euro. Liberalisation also allowed the entrance of new banks, even if the largest domestic banks in the system maintained a dominant market share, and Greece remained relatively untouched by foreign entrants.[15]

These transformations continued and deepened as Greece joined the euro. Lingering controls on credit allocation were dismantled, specifically for the consumer loan and housing loan sectors. Economic stability, lower (initially) inflation and a considerable decline in interest rates increased supply and demand for credit in Greece, which further intensified competition. On average, the lending rate decreased by over 10 percent between 1998 and 2005, and credit expanded considerably.

Debt-led growth as a consequence of Europeanisation of banking

Because of these EU-led reforms, Greece entered a decade of financial boom (Pagoulatos 2014). Loans for housing and consumption expanded as a share of total lending and, in parallel, the share of credit to the industrial sector and to trade declined substantially over the 2000s (Pagoulatos 2014). The growth of these two sectors left the Greek growth regime dangerously unstable in the context of the 2008 financial crisis, and expanded the current account deficit.

This transformation did not occur over night. Anti-inflation policies dominated economic policymaking in Greece during the 1990s, and there was a real (and warranted, as it turned out) concern that credit expansion would lead to rising inflation. In April 1999 the Bank of Greece took steps to combat inflation by constraining credit expansion to consumer credit.[16] Total credit to the private sector fluctuated over 1999, but overall increased by 14 percent in 1999, compared to 15 percent in 1998. The effects of credit-containing restrictions persisted and were strengthened through 1999, until mid-2000 (Bank of Greece 2000, 138). Once these restrictions were lifted in March 2000, total credit to private sector doubled in growth from the previous year, growing by 28.5 percent (Bank of Greece 2000, 123). Credit was growing to most sectors, but credit to manufacturing was more modest than to housing and consumer credit.[17] Consumer credit expanded especially sharply (a 46.5 percent rise in 2000, Bank of Greece 2001).

From 2000 to 2006, competition intensified between Greek banks to meet growing demand for housing and consumer loans. Reflecting this heightened competition, as well as falling interest rates following Greece's accession to the euro, by 2002 credit expansion to households absorbed 61.4 percent of total credit expansion, up from 34.7 percent in 2000 (Bank of Greece 2003, 44; Markantonatou 2012, 423). By 2004 loans to households were 71.4 percent of total credit expansion to households and enterprises, which was far above the EU average of 59.3 percent in 2003. Housing credit continued to be high, but decelerated in 2004 slightly, before picking up again in 2005 (Bank of Greece 2005, 2006). By 2005, Greek households were coming closer to the average levels of indebtedness in the euro area, reaching 38.0 percent of GDP in 2005 compared with a corresponding euro area average of 52.6 percent (Bank of Greece 2006, 55).

2006 was the last year before Greece felt the first ripples of the economic crisis to come. By this point, the impact of Greece's adaptation to the Single Market and the euro were abundantly clear on its model of growth (Fouskas 2012, 35). The year 2006 marked a decade of above average (4.1 percent) growth and rising living standards. This was driven by increased domestic demand and investment, and a Bank of Greece report published in 2007 notes the pivotal role of dramatically declining interest rates, a deregulated banking and finance system, and membership of the euro in driving investment and consumption (Bank of Greece 2007, 23).

Total household liabilities against banks rose to 44 percent of GDP by the end of 2006, compared to a euro area average of 54.3 percent. By 2006 private consumption contributed 2.7 percentage points to a 4.1 percent increase of GDP in 2006, or approximately two thirds of the total increase (Bank of Greece 2007). With growth rates so dependent on consumer and housing credit, Greece's economic stability was highly vulnerable to a credit crunch. By 2008 Greece was hit head on by the global financial crisis. Banks tightened lending, which dried up the supply of loans. In parallel, households and enterprises lost confidence and found their propensity to consume weaken, causing a decline in the demand for credit (Bank of Greece 2009, 18). As the Bank of Greece noted, by 2008:

> The favourable factors that had supported growth rates for a number of years, fostering complacency with regard to the economic outlook, have lost their momentum.
>
> (Bank of Greece 2009, 18)

In the four-month period from November 2008 to February 2008, net flow of financing declined by 72 percent compared to the same period a year earlier (Bank of Greece 2008). For the first time since becoming a member of the euro, domestic final demand decreased in Greece, shaving −0.7 percent off of the GDP growth rate, which fell to 2.9 percent in 2008, from a 4 percent rise in 2007 (Bank of Greece 2009, 18, 56). Residential investment shrank by a massive 29.1 percent in 2008 (Bank of Greece 2009, 56). Greece reached the limits of debt-led growth with an abrupt stop.

The role of debt-led growth in the 2009 crisis

Greece's transformation into an economy reliant almost exclusively on credit-fuelled domestic demand to underpin high annual GDP growth rates is central to the origins of its crisis, in two ways. First, the global financial crisis led to a credit crunch in Greece as well as elsewhere, meaning that there was less credit to fuel domestic demand, igniting a recession. Second, Greece became an economy that was characterised by limited saving, credit-fuelled consumption, and high import penetration. This trajectory of growth directly contributed to Greece's widening current account deficit.

First, Greece's debt-led model of domestic demand growth suddenly collapsed in 2007–9, igniting a deep recession. When credit was no longer available to fuel demand, the growth rate accordingly plummeted, turning negative and freefalling by 20.1 percent between 2008 and 2012 and beyond, as the impact of austerity further dampened domestic demand (Bank of Greece 2013). The sudden stop of credit halted domestic demand in Greece, and the recession to follow was primarily due to this decline (Bank of Greece 2013, 51).

For approximately a decade, private consumption had driven GDP growth (see Table 4.1), and post-2007 the decline in domestic demand and investment was the biggest contributor to declining GDP rates (Bank of Greece 2012, 41). Between 2004 and 2008, private consumption accounted for an average of 72 percent of Greek GDP (Bank of Greece 2010, 21). As the recession continued, job losses, wage cuts, and extremely low confidence on future employment and income added to declining private consumption, which had begun with the sudden end to easy credit in 2007–8. The above average growth rates Greece enjoyed during its euro membership were precarious, and once credit dissipated in 2008, Greece's growth rates went with it. As the Bank of Greece notes in 2010:

> These developments have made it imperative . . . to develop an alternative growth model, not based exclusively on private consumption (with a high import content and excessive reliance on strong credit expansion) or on private residential investment.
>
> (Bank of Greece 2010, 28)

Naturally, the recession put further strain on Greek public finances from 2007 onwards, not least because tax revenue from consumption-related economic activity slowed, from VAT, car registration tax, excise tax on fuel, and all sorts of other taxes (Bank of Greece 2009).

Second, Greece's debt-led model of growth contributed to the widening of its current account deficit (see Figure 4.5). High levels of private consumption, fuelled by borrowing but also by wages, contributed to rising inflation and an appreciation of Greece's Real Effective Exchange Rate (REER). Between 2001 and 2009 average inflation in Greece exceeded the euro area rate by approximately 1.1 percent, and the REER weighted against Greece's major trading partners increased by 18.6 percent (Bank of Greece 2010, 28).

Table 4.1 Private consumption and its contribution to domestic demand (Greece)

	2001	*2002*	*2003*	*2004*	*2005*	*2006*	*2007*	*2008*	*2009*	*2010*	*2011*
Contribution of private consumption to GDP change (percentage points)	3.3	3.5	2.4	2.6	3.3	2.99	2.6	2.8	−0.9	−2.7	−5.6
GDP at market prices (annual percentage changes)	4.5	3.4	5.9	4.6	2.2	5.5	3.0	−0.2	−3.2	−3.5	−7.1

Source: Bank of Greece annual reports (various years)

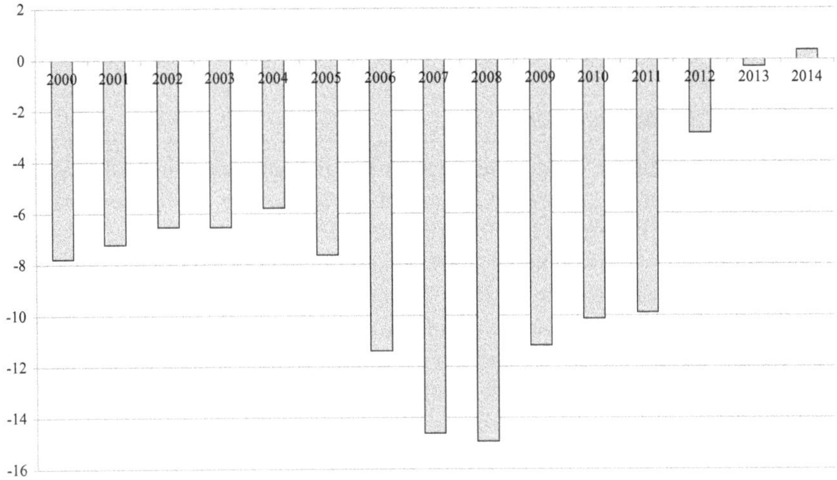

Figure 4.5 Current account balance of Greece (percentage of GDP)

Source: IMF Balance of Payments Statistics

Greece's trade deficit was affected by this model of growth through growing import penetration. Greek exporters actually performed relatively well during euro membership. Greece added manufacturing workers between 2000 and 2008, and retained its (admittedly tiny) share of world export markets while moving up the value chain to export pharmaceutical products, plastics, metal, machinery, and so on (Jones 2015). Greece pivoted to new markets and built up trading links with the Balkans especially. However, Greece's modest successes in exports were dwarfed by its import bill. In 2001 Greece's import bill rose by 50 percent, largely because of imports of consumer durables and non-durables, clearly associated with the growing rate of disposable income and (mostly borrowed) resources in Greek households during the 2000s (Bank of Greece 2002, 212). From 2001 to 2005, Greece's current account balance benefitted from lower oil costs, but the deficit continued to expand, partially due to higher inflation and higher REER, but also due to increased imports, which in 2002 were almost three times the volume of exports (Bank of Greece 2003, 251).

In 2005 the current account deficit widened substantially and was to continue a steep downward trend. From 2000 to 2003 the deficit had been high, at an average of 6.3 percent between 2000 and 2003. The rise in the deficit in 2005 was reflected in the return of high oil prices, purchases of ships, low price competitiveness, and especially by the very low savings in the Greek economy – which were only 14.6 percent of GDP in 2005. High public deficits and the rapid increase in household borrowing help account for this (Pagoulatos and Quaglia 2013, 188). By 2006, private consumption was responsible for a 9.8 percent rise in imports. Despite increased market share of Greek exports in 2006, private consumption, driven by debt, boosted imports 'drastically', which is a major driver of trade deficits (Bank of Greece 2007, 31).

The limits of Europeanisation

Credit-fuelled domestic demand-led growth is a fundamental driver of Greece's competitiveness crisis. However, even during its decade of financial boom, Greece had one of the lowest levels of private and household debt in the eurozone (see Pagoulatos and Triantopoulos 2009; Pasiouras 2012). In fact, household leverage ratios in Greece rose from 35 to 70 percent in 2003–9, compared with the 80–90 percent for the eurozone (Pagoulatos and Quaglia 2013, 188–98). Unlike Ireland and Spain, the case of Greece was quite clearly *not* a banking crisis. This is partially due to the relatively late continuation of credit controls by the Bank of Greece, which were in place much later than anything similar in Ireland, which was a more straightforward banking crisis (see Chapter 6), and the fact that during the 1990s real interest rates in Greece remained relatively high, delaying household indebtedness in a way that was not the case in Portugal (see Chapter 5). Until 2000, Greek households had relatively limited access to mortgage and consumer credit because of high interest rates and tight regulation of mortgage and consumer credit (Pagoulatos 2003, 133). The rapid expansion of indebtedness from 2000 to 2008 was accordingly from a very low base.

The Greek banking system was traditionally dominated by the state, and an oligarchical structure largely persisted during the 1990s and 2000s (Pagoulatos 2003, 145). Banking liberalisation and deregulation transformed the relationship between the states and banks, but what emerged was equally oligopolistic in terms of the very small number of players (Pagoulatos 2003, 147). In fact, between 1997 and 2007 the five largest banks in Greece grew their market share from 56 percent to 68 percent. Overall, the Greek banking system remained underdeveloped relative to the rest of Europe (Pagoualatos 2014, 467). Greek banks actually maintained relatively conservative credit policy stances and had a comparatively limited integration of the Greek banking system with international financial markets (Pagoulatos 2014; Pagoulatos and Triantopoulos 2009).

The Greek banking sector grew from a very low base, and EU reforms made it possible for the sector to fuel a debt-led boom. Yet, the low entry of foreign banks, relatively low levels of competition due to an oligopolistic structure, and fairly conservative credit stances meant that because the Greek banking sector didn't reach the heights expected from the Single Market reforms, it was in a much more stable position than the troubled banks of Ireland and Spain (Pagoulatos and Triantopoulos 2009). Competition and the integration of the Greek banking system with the European market was strikingly low. Interest rates of many categories of loans remained higher relative to the rest of Europe, and the Greek banking sector remained concentrated (Pagoulatos and Triantopoulos 2009 39). Almost paradoxically, the limits of Europeanisation in Greek banking spared the country from a banking, and therefore a triple, crisis in 2009 (as Pagoulatos and Triantopoulos 2009 have shown). This shows the importance of recognising domestic adaptation to European integration as an uneven and divergent process across the European periphery.

This section has shown the link between following the rules of European financial and banking integration, and Greece's competitiveness crisis. Greece's participation in the integration process was, as former Prime Minister Costas Simitis put it, intended as the "strongest lever for our exit from a reality of economic and social retardation" (quoted in Featherstone and Papadimitriou 2008, 190). Instead, European integration created new sources of tension and instability for Greece's political economy that were analytically separate to the fiscal dimensions of Greece's crisis. As sections one and two noted, Greece's fiscal difficulties emerged in the 1980s, and persisted beyond the 2009 crisis. However, in this section, I have shown that the 1990s and 2000s witnessed the emergence of new, parallel fragilities, as EU driven reforms catalysed a competitiveness crisis through creating a trajectory of debt-led growth. In this way, Greece's successful admission to EMU did not represent culmination of its drive for economic convergence with the core of Europe. Instead, it helped drive Greece down a path of unanticipated and historically specific divergence.

Conclusion

As the first eurozone member country to encounter a sovereign debt crisis, Greece has borne the brunt of the charges of the immaturity thesis. It has been understood as responsible, not only for its own difficulties, but for triggering a crisis of systemic proportions, threatening the supposedly 'mature' economies who were not 'living beyond their means'. The Greek immaturity or 'exceptionalism' thesis traces the origins of the country's sovereign debt crisis back to 1981, when the fiscally expansionary socioeconomic policies of the PASOK governments created a corrupt and clientelistic state, heavily reliant upon debt to fund an overstaffed and inefficient public sector. This debt-fuelled clientelism is understood to have persisted throughout the 1990s and 2000s, apparently immune to the efforts of the 'modernisers'. Greece, in this analysis, is 'exceptional', and the 2009 crisis was "predictable . . . [and] a long time coming, one that was to expected from a country that did not quite modernize" (Triandafyllidou, Gropas, and Kouki 2013, 1–2).

In response to this, I provide an alternative narrative of the Greek crisis. By locating it in the longer history of the Greek economy and in the context of critical international dynamics associated with European integration, I have sought to uncover the various ways in which 'non-exceptional' processes of Greek agency contributed to its fiscal and particularly its competitiveness crises. The modern Greek Republic has been attempting to catch up with Europe since the 1970s, and has introduced ambitious projects of economic development in order to do so. It has overcome various economic crises and aimed to move beyond its historic economic role as an agrarian, 'relatively backward' economy. However, it was only during the 1990s that Greece began to follow a fairly clear blueprint of 'European style' economic policy, in order to ensure its participation in the EU, the Single

Market, and EMU. Adapting to European integration, in spite of clear instances of 'poor reform capacity', nevertheless dramatically transformed Greece's economy into one characterised by domestic demand debt-led growth. By neglecting these processes, in favour of the more readily apparent pathological features of the Greek political economy, conventional accounts do not adequately capture the limits to the capacity of Greek policymakers to transcend the parameters within which they operated, which were, as I have shown, bequeathed by, inter alia, a long and complex history of indebtedness and geopolitical competition. Contrary to this, I argue that Greek attempts to modernise according to the European blueprint are the key causal factor in the genesis of the political economic features that the immaturity thesis has identified as exceptional and backward. Integration with Europe has, as I have shown, played a critical role in catalysing the crisis of 2009.

As such, Greece's weaknesses cannot be solely explained with reference to its exceptional national and political traits. Because just as crucial were the non-exceptional patterns of Greek agency that were generative of its divergence. Paying attention to the putatively 'mature' causes of the Greek crisis has highlighted the important role played by European integration in that country's ongoing crisis. Chapter 5 will turn to Portugal, and also identify the pivotal role of divergence via Europeanisation in its crisis.

Notes

1 In the case of Greece, notions of 'exceptionalism' can be seen as synonymous with ideas of 'immaturity'. It is precisely the various aspects of political and social life wherein Greece is viewed as 'immature' that account for its 'exceptionalism'. As such, in this chapter I use the 'immaturity thesis' and the 'exceptionalism' thesis interchangeably.
2 See various chapters in Clogg (1993, 2002 (173–209); see discussion on 'Hellenic Peronism' in Manolopoulos 2011 (1–13).
3 For contributions to the literature on Greece's 'poor reform capacity', see Featherstone and Papadimitriou 2008 and various chapters in Mitsos and Mossialos 2000. See also various chapters in Kalyvas, Pagoulatos, and Tsoukas 2013, and for more critical contributions see Lyberaki and Tsakalotos 2002 and Monastiriotis and Antoniades 2009.
4 For literature on the persistence of clientelism through the decades, the discussion in Triandafyllidou, Gropas, and Kouki 2013. See also Manolopoulos 2011 (1–13, 81–109); Diamandouros 2011, 1994; Tsoukalas 1995.
5 Although there is good reason to be sceptical of these widely reported figures. A recent article in BBC News notes that although Greece has a 'massive' tax collection problem, such exorbitant figures are likely a product of accounting anomalies (BBC News 2015).
6 Democratisation; for the purposes of this chapter, this refers to the period from 1974 to 1989.
7 On de-industrialisation, see Louri and Minoglou 2002; Sapelli 1995; Fouskas and Dimoulas 2012, 2013; Markantonatou 2012.
8 For more on this see Clogg 1993; Fouskas and Dimoulas 2013 (80–109); Draenos 2009; Gerakis and Wald 1964; Botsiou 2009; Michaelides, Papageorgiou, and Vouldis 2013; Kornetis 2010; Michael-Matsas 2010.
9 See Pagoulatos 2003 for a detailed version of this argument.
10 The Organismos Anasygkrotiseos Epicheiriseon (Business Reconstruction Organization).

11 See Tsakolotos 1991 for a comparison between the PASOK strategy and the contemporaneous model of the French Socialists under Mitterrand before the 'U Turn' (43–50).

12 Greek public debt exploded in the aftermath of the 2008 crisis. From 2008 until 2011 it rose to more than 150 percent of GDP. In the aftermath of the 2008 crisis, the average fiscal deficit in the euro area rose from just 0.7 percent of GDP to 6.3 percent of GDP in 2009. Public debt also rose, from 66.2 percent in 2007, to 88.5 percent in 2012. Greece made significant adjustment during the 1990s and 2000s – for example, the general government deficit declined from 7.5 percent of GDP in 2004 to 3.6 percent in 2006 – but the situation deteriorated again in 2007. In 2009, the deficit exploded to 13.6 percent (these figures are all taken from Alogokoufis 2012, 5, 17, 26–7).

13 See Bank of Greece, various years.

14 For more, see Christodoulais 2013; Pagoulatos 2005; Pagoulatos and Triantopoulos 2009; Pasiouras 2012.

15 For more on this, see Hondroyiannis et al. 1999; Pagoulatos and Triantopoulos 2009; see also Pasiouras 2012; Pagoulatos 2005, 360; Christodoulais 2013, 94–5; OECD 1994.

16 Specifically, if the rate of lending exceeded 12 percent, an amount equal to the overrun would have to be deposited in a six-month non-interest-bearing account with the Bank of Greece. This strategy didn't work initially as consumer loans were increasing over 40 percent in the first half of 1999 (Bank of Greece 2000, 138). In July 1999 the Bank of Greece specifically targeted consumer loans. If such loans increased over 2 per cent in the July-September period, an amount twice as much as the overrun would have to be deposited. More on this in (Bank of Greece 2000, 138).

17 This is partially because enterprises were tending to look to the stock exchange instead of banks for funding (Bank of Greece 2001).

5 Portugal[1]

This chapter explores the case of Portugal's economic crisis. Portugal's 2011 bailout occurred amid severe instability in Europe. To an important extent, the country was a victim of contagion. Portuguese elites have been quick to insist that they are not Greece nor, for that matter, are they Ireland (Vossole 2016, 12). If Greece is the epicentre of the crisis, Portugal is perhaps the aftershock. Yet, this contagion fed off the longer-term structural vulnerabilities of the Portuguese economy (Dooley 2018, 87). In this chapter I show that the origins of the Portuguese crisis can be traced by examining its divergence via Europeanisation in the years before the eurozone crisis hit. As it turns out, Portugal is like Greece, in the sense that its adaptation to the European project during this period resulted in the critical transformation of its patterns of economic growth.

I advance this argument in three main ways. The first section highlights the specificities of the Portuguese case, showing how the economic crisis in the EU's westernmost state differs markedly from Greece and Ireland. Portugal had public finance problems, but these never reached Greek proportions. Portugal exhibited signs of overheating while a member of the euro, but without any of the accelerated growth experienced by Ireland or Greece. Private indebtedness rose to among the highest levels in the eurozone, but Portugal's crisis did not originate in its banks. The second section emphasises the role of institutional stickiness as a central cause of the Portuguese crisis. As a small, open 'economic latecomer', Portugal struggled to overcome long-standing institutional weaknesses. A CPE approach identifies various path dependencies that help explain the limits to export-led growth in Portugal. However, these institutional obstacles are far from the whole story. The third section emphasises the importance of institutional transformation. I trace Portugal's Europeanisation and show how its variety of capitalism did not simply persist following EMU membership. Rather, Europeanisation of banking and finance during the 1980s and 1990s transformed the Portuguese economy into a brand new and unanticipated debt-led growth regime, leaving the economy in a particularly vulnerable position upon entering EMU.

Echoing Greece, the story of Portugal's economic crisis is one of it largely following the rules of European integration, while being unable or unwilling to follow others. Even though there are many respects in which Portugal's trajectory was very different to that of Greece, I show that the important turning points occurred for Portugal when it was most successful in following the rules of European integration.

Portugal: an exceptional case?

The eurozone had never seemed so likely to break apart as it did during late 2010 and 2011. Ireland followed Greece in officially applying for bailout funds in November 2010, causing bond yields to soar across Greece, Spain, Italy, and Portugal. European leaders continued to muddle through in their responses to the Greek crisis, leading to countless debacles and escalations. The 'PIIGS' acronym had come to be widely used by international media, capturing an apparent shared economic vulnerability across the European periphery, and contributing, in a kind of self-fulfilling prophecy, to market anxiety (Brazys and Hardiman 2013, 8–10). Fears of exit, sovereign default, banking insolvency, and break up propelled the EU from one emergency summit to another. It was within this broader tumultuous context that the Portuguese bailout occurred. By 2010, Portugal's cost of borrowing skyrocketed, its credit rating plummeted, and the country had little choice but to seek help (Dooley 2018, 74).

As shown in Chapter 2, the 'official narrative' of Portugal's crisis identifies familiar 'obstacles to convergence' as central causes of its crisis. Many have emphasised fiscal mismanagement and productivity problems in signalling vulnerability to international markets in 2010 (e.g., Royo 2012a; Pereira and Wemans 2012; OECD 2013). Yet, Portugal's path to crisis differs in important ways from the rest of the periphery. Several divergences are worth noting initially. First, in stark contrast to the overheating of the Irish and Spanish economies during EMU membership, Portugal experienced anaemic rates of growth (see Figure 5.1) (Arnold 2015; Blanchard 2007; Brazys and Hardiman 2013).

Second, Figure 5.2 shows that Portugal failed to converge in terms of GDP per capita with neither its euro area partners nor its fellow so-called 'cohesion countries' (Giavazzi and Spaventa 2010).

Third, Portugal certainly had fiscal problems. It first breached the EDP in 2001, 2005, and 2009 and consistently ran large fiscal deficits throughout the 2000s, yet its public debt to GDP ratios tended to be around 10 percent over that of Germany, never approaching Greek proportions (see Figure 5.3).

Fourth, as Figure 5.4 shows, Portugal began to experience a widening current account deficit much earlier than the other peripheral countries. As early as 1995, Portugal's current account deficit began to widen dramatically, which sets it very much apart, not just from Germany, but also from Spain, Greece, and Italy.

In the following sections I explain this seemingly 'exceptional' crisis using the Europeanisation and CPE framework applied to Greece. This makes it possible to emphasise the twin roles of institutional stickiness and institutional transformation in Portugal's crisis. Europeanisation may have generated debt-led patterns of growth, as I show in the third section. Yet, just like Greece,

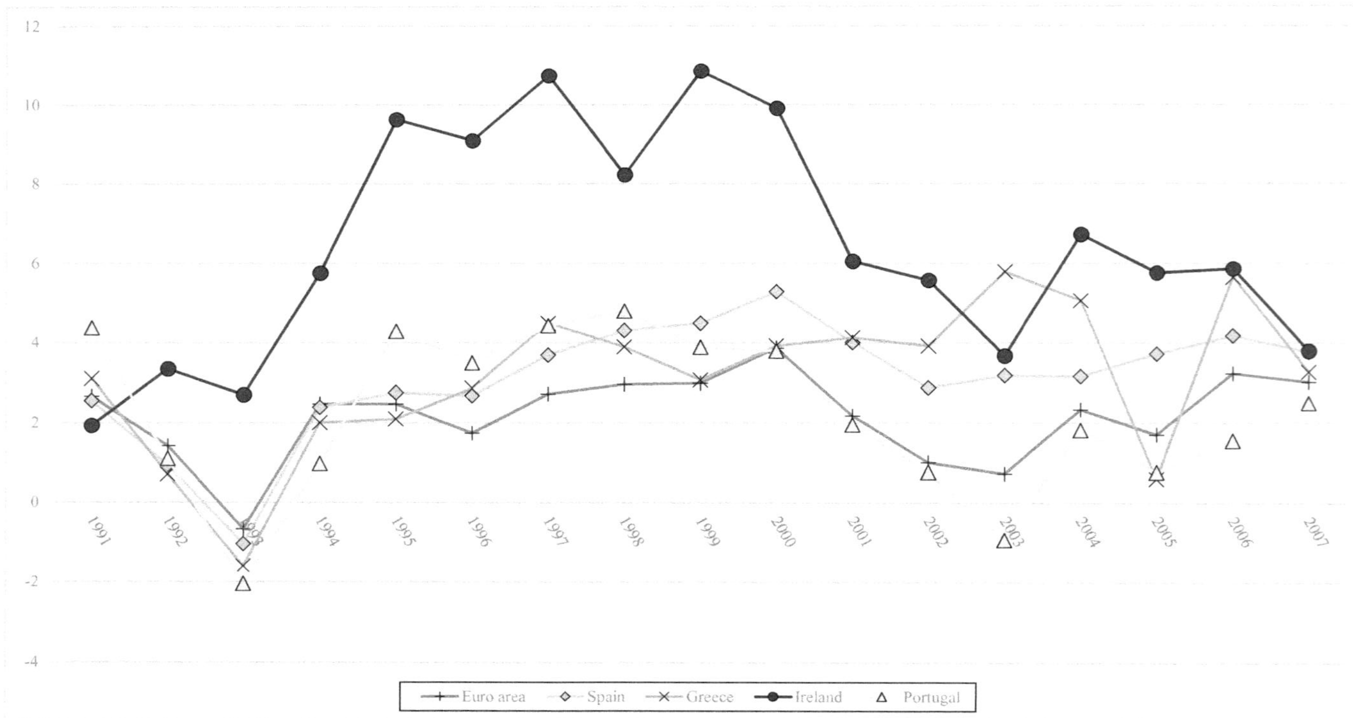

Figure 5.1 GDP growth rate for euro area, Spain, Greece, Ireland, and Portugal (annual percentage)

Source: World Bank World Development Indicators

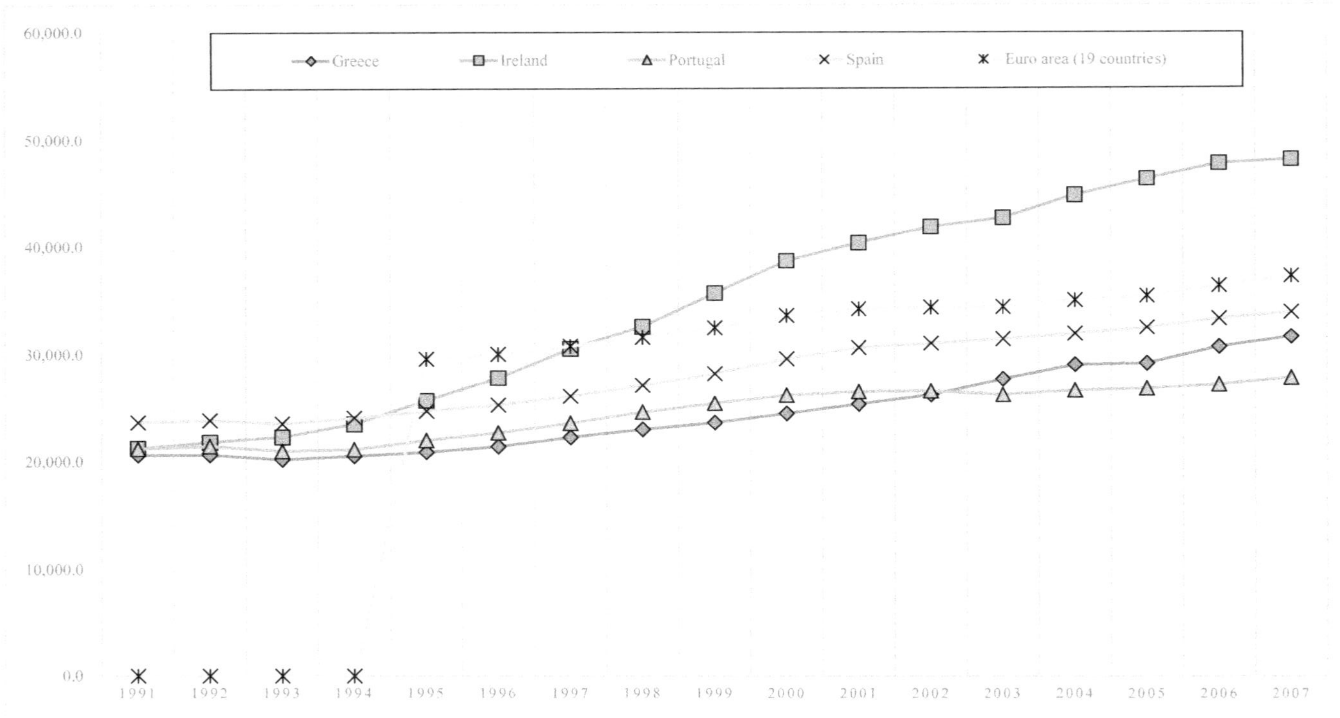

Figure 5.2 GDP per capita (US$, constant prices, 2010 PPPs) for Greece, Ireland, Portugal, Spain, and euro area

Source: OECD

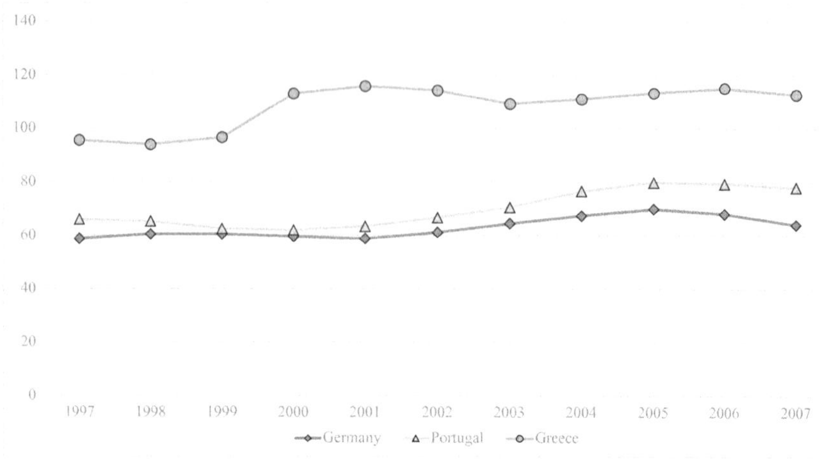

Figure 5.3 General government debt (total, percentage of GDP), 1997–2007 for Germany, Portugal, and Greece

Source: OECD National Accounts at a Glance

as a small, open, peripheral economy, Portugal found it difficult to generate export-led growth. The role of institutional stickiness in the limits to Portugal's export-led growth are now explored.

Portugal's competitiveness crisis: limits to export-led growth at Europe's periphery

Participating in the euro and the Single Market tended to be viewed by the periphery as a 'challenge for development' (Antoniades 2010, 69) wherein Greece, Ireland, and Portugal could each leave their peripheral pasts behind and converge, in terms of their competitiveness, levels, and patterns of economic development, with their advanced Western European neighbours. As the late former Prime Minister and President of Portugal Mário Soares put it in a 1985 interview with *Le Monde*:

> "No if we did not want to miss out on the end-of-the-century technological revolution, we absolutely had to join Europe. Now is the time!"
>
> (Clerc 1985)

This section shows how convergence in terms of competitiveness vis-à-vis the European core was always unlikely, if not impossible, for Portugal because of the specificities of its 'sticky' national institutions. Portugal experienced considerable difficulties in generating export-led patterns of growth in the years before the eurozone crisis. I demonstrate this in two main ways. First, I outline the evolution

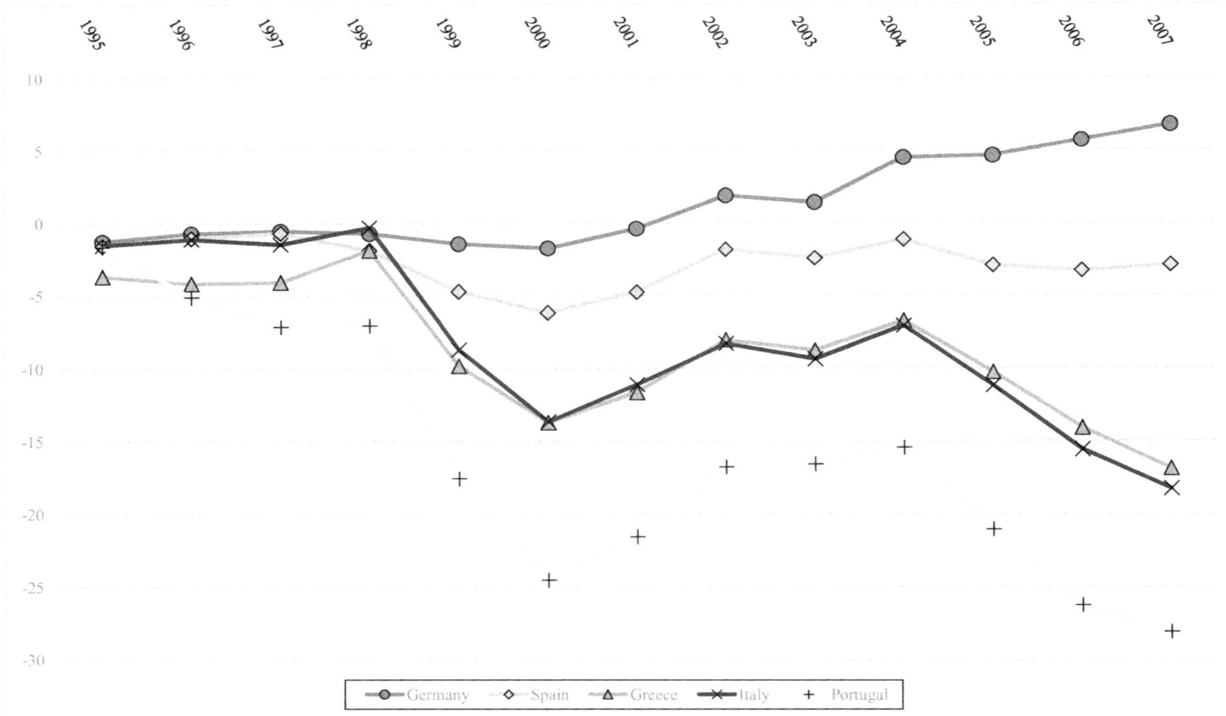

Figure 5.4 Current account balances for Germany, Spain, Greece, Italy, and Portugal (percentage of GDP)

Source: World Bank: Data Source indicated as IMF, Balance of Payments Statistics Yearbook and data files, and World Bank and OECD GDP estimates

of Portugal's export performance since its accession to the EC in 1986, and show how this performance is especially sensitive to fluctuations in world demand and the emergence of new competitors. Second, I apply a CPE framework to explore the role of institutional stickiness in placing limits on Portugal's ability to achieve sustainable patterns of export-led economic growth. This section emphasises the real imperatives that Portugal needed to negotiate to participate in the 'end of the century technological revolution' of which Mário Soares (2012) spoke. National institutions matter. Different institutional configurations of EMU member states produce different economic capacities and problems, develop over long periods of time, and are sticky or path dependent. Just like Greece, Portugal faced the challenges of being a late developing peripheral European state attempting to catch up with Western Europe.

Developments in Portuguese export performance: 1986–2011

It the latter half of the 1990s, Portugal went through a remarkable improvement in its economic conditions, registering some of the highest rates of growth in Europe. The country was even held up by the EC institutions as a model for Central and Eastern Europe (CEE) candidate countries, due to the apparent success achieved during the 1990s (Soares 2012, 121). This growth occurred as Portugal incorporated the *acquis communautaire* into its domestic law, opened its frontiers to the Single Market, and completed the process of nominal convergence, successfully participating in the euro straight away in 1999 (Soares 2012, 121).

Yet, Portugal was not achieving these growth rates in the spirit of what Soares would have hoped, by narrowing "the gap which still separates us from the more developed European countries, by creating for the Portuguese people genuinely European patterns of life and welfare" (Soares 2012). Specifically, Portugal was struggling to maintain its competitiveness and to exhibit strong export-led growth.

Between 1986 and 1994, Portugal's current account was roughly in balance. During this period Portuguese exports benefitted from EC accession and access to the Single Market. Portugal secured nominal export market share gains of over 45 percent cumulatively (Banco de Portugal 2005, 48) during this time. From the mid-1990s onwards, however, Portugal began to record large trade deficits. As a small open economy, Portugal tends to be highly vulnerable to external shocks. Exports of merchandise slowed gradually over the 2000s, responding in part to fluctuations in demand from the rest of the Europe, where most of Portuguese exports typically go (Banco de Portugal various years). Portuguese exports mostly recorded year on year growth from the mid-1990s onwards, but this growth tended to be anaemic and easily overwhelmed by high levels of imports in terms of the trade balance. Low levels of growth can be explained by losses in market share relating to so-called traditional goods exports, especially clothing, footwear, and textiles. European markets saw their demand for these kinds of products grow at meagre levels, while at the same time Portugal was facing competition from emerging markets in East Asia and CEE with lower wage costs (Banco de Portugal various years). From 1997 to 2000 Portugal's economic growth was mainly sustained by domestic demand, as exports struggled and market shares were lost.

From 2000 to 2006 Portugal entered a protracted period of stagnant growth. In 2001 export growth slowed to 3.3 percent growth, compared to 8.5 percent in 2000. Traditional products were behind this slowdown, but exports of vehicles decelerated to 3.5 percent growth in 2001, after 13.4 percent growth in 2000, due to the closing down of a large automobile plant (Banco de Portugal 2002, 9). Exports had moderately more favourable performance between 2001 and 2005, but came nowhere close to recovering their lost market share in the previous years (Banco de Portugal 2005, 48). Portugal experienced stronger levels of export growth in 2006 and 2007, because sales of machinery and appliances went up as more traditional goods continued to decline, and the country expanded into new markets. Exports of services were relatively buoyant during these two years, especially tourism, but also transport and technical and professional services (Banco de Portugal 2008a, 6). This promising new development in Portuguese trade performance was quickly reversed in 2008 as the global financial crisis led to a collapse in worldwide demand and a subsequent widening of Portugal's trade deficit.

Much like Greece, the Portuguese export sector faced serious challenges in the decades before the eurozone crisis hit. Portugal struggled as a small open peripheral country, specialising in so-called 'traditional' and medium-technology exports, and with competition from emerging economies. Like Greece, a number of path dependencies of Portugal's political economy are worth highlighting to explain the limits to Portugal developing an export-led pattern of growth.

The institutional limits to export-led growth in Portugal

A CPE approach can shed light on the limits to export-led growth in Portugal in the following ways. First, CPE approaches focus primarily on identifying the specificities of wage bargaining systems wherein peripheral economies such as Portugal diverge in important ways from the EMU core. Portugal has a specific history of institution building, associated with the Southern European MME variety of capitalism, which sets it apart from the CMEs and LMEs of core Europe (Hall 2014; Nölke 2016, 7–8). As Höpner and Lutter (2014) put it, given the stickiness of wage bargaining systems, which have been "established over many decades, with coordinated wage systems being particularly difficult to emulate", the German case is a "relic of a historical stroke of luck" (cited in Nölke 2016, 9). Interestingly, in the case of Portugal, Royo – among others – observes strong corporatist tendencies (Royo 2012b, 163–71). It is worth noting that during the 1980s, centre–right governments set up systems of social dialogue and concertation at the macro level and succeeded in establishing the Standing Committee for Social Concertation (CPCS), which enabled social dialogue at the national level between trade union confederations, employers' associations, and the state. The CPCS has led to the signing of several tripartite agreements and has made it possible, especially during the 1980s and 1990s, for successive governments to ensure public support for wage bargains linked to important macroeconomic goals such as accession to the EC and membership of the euro (Távora and González 2014, 324).

However, it has also been noted that this corporatist style system is marked by the twin legacies of Portugal's recent authoritarian past and a polarising democratisation process, each of which have resulted in a lack of coordination and trust (Royo 2012b, 139; Távora and González 2014). The institutional character of post-revolution Portugal leaned towards the radical left during the late 1970s, but has certainly been watered down in the decades since. Nevertheless, opposition from trade union confederations has tended to lead Portuguese governments to abandon plans dealing with employers' demands for greater flexibility on dismissals and the reduction of the associated costs, greater working time flexibility, and lower overtime pay (Royo 2012b, 139; Távora and González 2014, 326). This has been inclined to lead to negotiation stalemates, especially during the 2000s, and organised labour's political influence is comparatively stronger than organised business (Royo 2012b, 176; Távora and González 2014, 327).

Yet in many respects, trade unions in Portugal are relatively weak. Royo (2012b) notes that, since democratisation, Portugal's trade union structure has evolved as highly fragmented and union membership has been in decline (153). There are no representation criteria in Portuguese law, which effectively means that all trade unions in Portugal are considered representative, regardless of their actual membership levels (Royo 2012b, 159). This means that employers can bypass the strongest unions in a workplace and instead reach agreement with the unions that may be more accommodating (Royo 2012b, 160). In addition, collective agreements effectively apply to all workers, not just those who are members of the union doing the negotiating. This lowers the incentive to join a trade union, as workers will benefit from agreements anyway (160). The result is a lack of uniform conditions nationally and significant variations in wage levels across different sectors (Royo 2012b, 161).

The second observation recognises that such specificities of Portugal's national specific institutions are by no means the whole story. As shown in Chapter 3, CPE approaches link these different national institutions to the design flaws of EMU. Johnston (2016) focuses on the link between different wage bargaining systems and the instability of the euro. She shows that while institutional differences long predate the euro, they became existential threats under EMU. As the argument goes, EMU transformed sectoral labour market governance in the European periphery and prompted a steady rise in the relative prices of sheltered/non-tradable sectors, vis-à-vis the core (Johnston 2016, 22). There are three broad reasons for this. First, CMEs such as Germany with coordinated wage bargaining systems have the institutional resources to control wage growth in sheltered and non-sheltered sectors, while MMEs like Portugal tend to only achieve some wage moderation in non-sheltered, export-oriented sectors (Johnston 2016, 22). Second, Johnston recognises that despite this institutional asymmetry, during the 1990s, the EU provided political and economic costs to rising inflation across all countries. However, having joined the euro, the institutions and constraints no longer existed. Without these tight fiscal rules at the EU level national wage negotiators (especially in sheltered sectors) could allow wages to rise. Finally, countries like Portugal also lost important tools to manage declining competitiveness, such as national central banks that were averse to inflation, and currency devaluations. MMEs tend to lack the institutions necessary to produce low inflation, and thus ended up with higher real exchange rates and relatively declining competitiveness (Johnston 2016, 5).

Reis notes that it is often cited that unit labour costs in Portugal rose almost 20 percent relative to those in Germany during the period 2000–7 (Reis 2013).[2] Portugal actually achieved a slowdown in the growth of relative real unit labour costs after the introduction of the euro, yet what is important is that they still continued to rise. Relative increases in the cost of labour in Portugal were not associated with higher productivity, in fact, according to Blanchard, it nearly vanished (Blanchard 2007, 7). Blanchard also notes that productivity growth in the business sector fell to around 1 percent between 2004 and 2005 (it was 3 percent in the 1990s) (Blanchard 2007, 7) and Jones observes that total factor productivity grinds to a halt (Jones 2016, 93). This meant that as even nominal wage growth decreased over the 2000s, any competitive advantage that could have been gained was offset by continued increase in relative labour costs and a decline in productivity growth (Blanchard 2007, 7). As the argument goes, this contributed to Portugal's widening current account deficit.

Third, and finally, Nölke (2016) shows how CPE approaches can explain institutional sources of declining competitiveness beyond a narrow focus on relative unit labour costs. CMEs or export-oriented economies such as Germany have an institutional advantage in building up incremental innovations in high-quality manufacturing, "based on a sophisticated system of skill formation, in particular through vocational training" but also through relative job security and traditions in long-term investment practices (Nölke 2016, 10). Peripheral economies typically have more of an advantage in the production of low- to medium-quality goods, which rest on a more uneven system of skill formation. This has a number of consequences, not least of which is the vulnerability to competition from emerging economies outside of the EU Single Market (Nölke 2016, 10).

Portugal's economy has been characterised by a historic lack of large firms, a predominance of SMEs, and a high prominence of low- to medium-technology manufacturing exports. While SMEs employ 66.5 percent of workers in the EU 27, in Portugal the figure is 76.9 percent. Of these, employment is concentrated in micro firms more than it is in the rest of the EU (44.3 percent and 33.5 percent respectively) (Távora and González 2014, 324). Although Portugal's merchandise exports became progressively more diversified and its exports have by now moved into higher value products, during the 1990s and early 2000s traditional, low-technology goods featured prominently in Portugal's exports. These sectors proved extremely vulnerable to international competition from East Asia and CEE over the 1990s and 2000s (Arnold 2015; Corkill 1999, 158–64). As the Banco de Portugal (2008b) notes, although Portuguese exports (excluding energy) grew

5.4 percent between 1997 and 2006, market share declined −2.1 percent over the same period. In particular, Portugal experienced declines in the textiles, textile products, leather and footwear sector for the period 1997–2006, mainly in favour of China and East Asia following the ending of the Multi-Fibre Agreement, which had placed restrictions on the quantities of textiles and clothing that could be exported from developing countries to developed countries. Following the 2004 EU enlargement, Portugal also lost market share in the export of motor vehicles, trailers and semi-trailers over the period 2002–2006, in favour of the relatively highly skilled, low wage labour markets of CEE (Banco de Portugal 2008b).

Although critical of this so-called 'competitiveness hypothesis', Jones (2016) argues that a CPE account should be able to identify divergence of the periphery from the core in terms of five factors: an acceleration in the relative growth of unit labour costs, rising inflation, deceleration in productivity growth, deterioration in export performance, and a deterioration of the current account. As shown, and as Jones (2016) recognises, the Portuguese case reflects all of these divergences. First, although Portugal experiences a slowdown in the growth of relative real unit labour costs after joining EMU (see Figure 5.5), and a slowdown in the appreciation of the real effective exchange rate, both indicators of relative cost competitiveness continue to worsen relative to Germany, just at a slower pace.

Second, domestic price inflation also worsens and labour productivity grinds to a halt. Third, Portugal's labour productivity is stagnant during the 2000s. Fourth, Portugal's export performance deteriorates between 1999 and 2007. Finally, as Figure 5.4 shows, this all appears in Portugal's widening current account deficit. These economic divergences faced by Portugal shed some light on the limits to

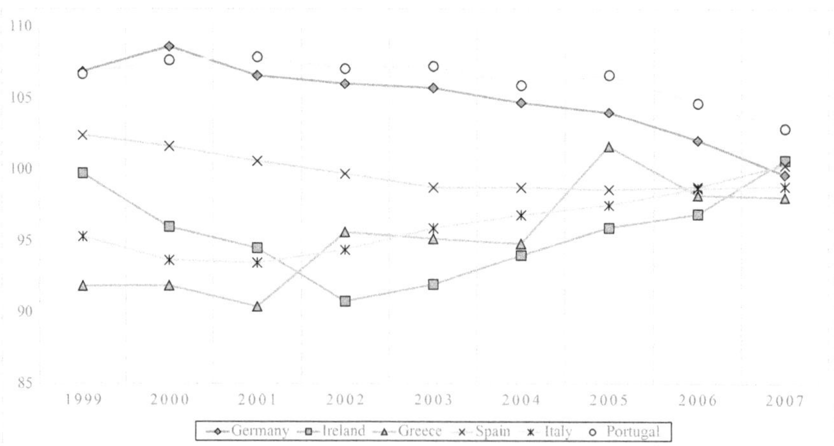

Figure 5.5 Real unit labour costs (total economy: performance relative to the rest of the former EU 15: double export weights (ratio of compensation per employee to nominal GDP per person employed) (QLCDQ))

Source: European Commission, AMECO

export-led growth in Portugal. Central to the emergence of these divergences is that Portuguese institutions proved resistant to change in the context of the Single Market and EMU. Yet, compelling as this CPE account is, tracing the lack of institutional transformation is far from exhaustive. As I will show in the following section, this account is incomplete, even misleading, without considering the role played by *institutional transformation* in the emergence of debt-led growth in the Portuguese economy.

Portugal adapts to Europe: debt-led growth via Europeanisation

As I argued in Chapter 3, focusing only on the obstacles to the development of export-led growth in Portugal can cause us to overlook the real and significant institutional transformations that the country did experience. In this section I will show that consequential institutional *transformations* occurred in Portugal during the 1990s and 2000s that cannot be captured by mere 'persistence' or continuations of existing trajectories. Rather, 'when Europe hit home', it led Portugal's economic development in new and unexpected directions. Specifically, I will show how Portugal's adaptation to EU-driven reforms relating to banking and finance contributed to institutional transformation leading to increasing private indebtedness and a precarious debt-led pattern of growth.

In this section I trace Portuguese divergence via Europeanisation in four parts. First, the major changes to occur to the Portuguese banking and financial system are outlined. Second, I draw on Banco de Portugal Annual Reports and other sources to analyse credit developments, showing the key aspects of a new pattern of growth for Portugal, one based almost exclusively on debt-led domestic demand. Third, I make explicit the link between this new growth pattern and Portugal's contemporary economic crisis. Finally, I emphasise the specificity of Portugal's Europeanisation. Portugal adapted to Europe fast and deep during the 1990s, which was a central cause of its eventual crisis, but also a key reason why Portugal's crisis did not originate as a banking crisis.

The Europeanisation of Portuguese banking

Prior to the Single Market, Portugal's banking and financial sectors were firmly regulated and protected to a level that surpassed even the situation in Greece. Such high levels of control have their roots in Portugal's recent history of revolution. In 1974, the 'Carnation Revolution' brought the forty-year-old dictatorship of Olivier Salazar's *Estado Novo* to an end. Years of political uncertainty and change were to follow (Dooley 2018, 75; Morrison 1981, 19–20; Maxwell 1995, 135–7). The socialist character of the revolutionary period led to the emergence of institutional structures, which included constitutionally 'irreversible' nationalisations of banking and industry (Macedo 1990, 311; Dooley 2018, 75–6). The period was characterised by political and economic crises, including a severe deterioration of public finances, runaway inflation, and balance of payments crises. A period of austerity and two IMF bailouts later, and there was strong public demand for a new, non-socialist political settlement for the newly democratised Portugal from the early 1980s onwards (Dooley 2018, 76; Maxwell 1995, 164). This alternative vision was to be the 'European option'.

Portugal joined the EC in 1986. EC membership was expected to promote the modernisation and economic development of the country by introducing structural reforms that would modernise and improve the competitiveness of the economy (Corkill 1999). Portugal's European accession "represented a strong commitment towards the liberalisation of the Portuguese economy" (Banco de Portugal 1998, 192). This goal was strongly motivated by a view of the integration process as "the only way to keep a peripheral country at the heart of the EU's decision making process" (Teixeira 2012, 18, 19). As a strategy, Portugal very swiftly adopted legislative changes that were outlined in various EC/EU treaties, earning the country the nickname of the 'good student' of European integration (Teixeira 2012, 18–19).

The challenge for reform was a daunting one. A consequence of the Carnation Revolution was that, by 1975, virtually all of Portugal's banks were nationalised. New entrants were not permitted to the market, interest rates were administratively fixed, and if a bank wished to set up a new branch, it had to apply to the Banco de Portugal for permission (Pinho 2002, 230). Much like Greece during the 1980s, Portuguese governments placed pressure on banks to fund their borrowing requirements while rationing out lending to business, the largest of which were state owned anyway. Consumer lending was effectively banned. Some reforms were introduced during the 1980s, but interest rate regulation was still in place during the early 1990s as were numerous credit controls. By as late as mid-1989, banks accounting for 85 percent of market share in Portugal were state owned (see Soares de Pinho 2002 for more detail).

In its integration with Europe, Portugal committed to a reform agenda underscored by privatisation, deregulation, and liberalisation. Because of such high levels of protection and regulation, Portugal's banking sector had to privatise, liberalise, and deregulate deep and quickly if it was going to be on track for the completion of the Single Market in 1992. The fast pace of transformation was to be of major consequence for Portugal's economy and, without the need to comply with EU rules, it is likely that Portuguese governments would have adopted a slower pace (Pinho 2002, 232). As Pinho puts it:

> in less than ten years [Portugal] evolved from a highly protected framework to complete integration in the Single European Market for financial services. Therefore it comes as no surprise that . . . Portugal [is] the country where the impact of the new [EC/EU] legislation was ranked highest.
>
> (Soares de Pinho 2003, 232)

From the mid-1980s onwards, key reforms were implemented, which began the process of institutional transformation. In 1984 the banking system was opened to private, foreign, and domestic entry for the first time since the revolution (Rodrigues,

Santos, and Teles 2016). Following accession, there was a wide-ranging overhaul of the financial system propelled by various EU banking directives, including the Second Banking Directive and other important measures (Decressin and Mauro 1998; Dooley 2018).[3] Portuguese banks could now take on more risk, access new sources of financing and sell new products. Interest rates were deregulated, and credit ceilings were abolished. All restrictions in consumer credit were abolished in 1995 following the completion of the Single Market.

Three main aspects of this EU-driven institutional transformation can be highlighted. First, it resulted in the 'consecration' of universal banking in Portugal in late 1992 (Banco de Portugal 1998). All explicit restrictions to the composition of assets and to banks' activity were lifted. Portuguese banks were no longer required to invest in public debt securities, and the legally enforced segmentation of credit institutions were gradually dismantled, meaning that all credit institutions had common competitive conditions. Second, competition between banks intensified. Banks were no longer controlled directly through credit controls and the administrative regulation of interest rates was abolished. Furthermore, barriers to the establishment of new banks and the expansion of banks branches were lifted. Banks also had their reserve requirements reduced sharply in 1994, from 17 to 2 percent. Finally, capital flows were liberalised within the EC/EU between 1986 and 1992. This provided new sources of credit across the Portuguese banking sector (Banco de Portugal 1998, 193). By the 1990s, as a result of adhering to the requirements from the EC/EU, the banking system in Portugal had completely transformed (Dooley 2018, 79; Honohan 1999; Decressin and Mauro 1998). By 1997, the market share of public banks had been reduced to below 30 percent, from close to 96 percent in 1984 (Banco de Portugal 1998, 193). The gradual dismantling of administratively set banking interest rates was completed in May 1992 and credit ceilings were replaced by a liquidity control regime based upon market mechanisms (Banco de Portugal 1998, 193). The impact of this rapidly transformed banking sector on the Portuguese economy was to be profound.

Debt-led growth as a consequence of Europeanisation of banking

The Europeanisation of Portuguese banking resulted in significant credit expansion leading to above average GDP growth rates in the late 1990s. Portugal exhibited sustained GDP growth between 1997 and 2000, which was above the euro area average. During this period the economy grew by an average of approximately 3.8 percent each year, having risen by only 0.4 percent in 1996 (see Figure 5.1). As changes to the financial sector started to take effect, domestic demand began to overtake all other components of GDP growth. Lagoa et al. (2014) note that private consumption was responsible for 70 percent of GDP growth in the period (7). Real private consumption continued to respond to falling interest rates and the ready availability of credit, growing consistently above the euro area average between 1997 and 2000 (by 5.6 percent in 1998, up from 3.3 percent in 1997) (Banco de Portugal 1999, 20). Household indebtedness grew to well above the euro area average of 80 percent and credit growth accelerated considerably from a virtually non-existent base (European Commission 2004). Although credit for consumption was on the rise during the late 1990s, most of this increase in household indebtedness was through loans for housing, which accounted for 74 percent of total household debt in 1999 (Banco de Portugal 2000, 211). The increased demand for housing during this period was a response to competition among banks for mortgage market share, as well as rising income and falling interest rates (Banco de Portugal 2000, 211).

In addition to the Single Market reforms, the favourable conditions associated with the prospect of joining the euro encouraged households to increase their borrowing at high rates. Consumers responded to disinflation and higher income levels, but especially to lower nominal and real interest rates (European Commission 2004, 57). Historically low interest rates were perceived as permanent, and there tended to be a very close link between the interest rates provided by Portuguese banks to the private sector and the money market interest rates they borrow on. This meant that households and firms were highly exposed to interest rate hikes when they did occur (Banco de Portugal 2001, 7). Interest rates fell more sharply in Portugal during the late 1990s and early 2000s period than in most euro area countries, reflecting the rapid and wholesale transformation of Portugal's banking sector from one with highly controlled interest rates less than a decade before the reforms of the Single Market (Banco de Portugal 1999, 77). In these different ways, EU reforms are strongly implicated in the transformation of Portugal into a 'debt-led domestic demand' model of economic growth during the 1990s (Lagoa et al. 2014).

Bank credit to Non-Financial Companies (NFCs) accelerated strongly during the period 1997–2000 also. Bank credit to NFCs grew at a rate of 21.8 percent in 1997, compared to just 6.6 percent in 1996 and 4 percent in 1995 (Banco de Portugal 1998). Because, on average, Portuguese NFCs are relatively small in size, they tend to rely much more on bank rather than market financing. This would have consequences for their indebtedness at the turn of the century (Banco de Portugal 1998, 209). In 2000, NFC indebtedness was around 83 percent of GDP, compared to 57 percent in 1995 and 74 percent in 1999 (Banco de Portugal 1999, 25; 2001, 12).

Domestic demand decelerated gradually and then considerably during the period 2000–6. The ECB raised interest rates during the latter half of 1999 and throughout 2000 to combat eurozone inflation. By 2000 Portugal was still registering high, albeit slightly decelerating, GDP growth rates. The contribution of domestic demand to GDP had been 7.5 percent in 1998 and 5.7 percent in 1999. By 2000 this had dropped sharply to 3.2 percent. Private consumption grew by 2.8 percent in 2000, 2.4 percent less than in 1999 and 4.4 percent less than 1998 (Banco de Portugal, various years).

Households and firms were confronted with the impermanence of low interest rates and, in a context of high indebtedness, debt servicing payments became more expensive, leading to a slowdown in investment and in consumption (Banco de Portugal 2001, 8). Construction began to contract during the 2000s, in stark contrast to Ireland and other peripheral countries like Spain. GDP growth stagnated in 2001 and 2002, before turning negative in 2003. Even as interest rates began to decline again in 2001, GDP growth reflected low domestic demand. Domestic demand made a negative contribution to GDP growth in 2002 and 2003, after being virtually zero in 2001 (Banco de Portugal 2004). As GDP growth dropped, unemployment rose, eventually reaching historic highs, which further compounded pessimistic attitudes towards future economic prospects. The growth rate of credit to households declined from 21.2 percent in 2000 to 10.4 percent in 2001, and from 24.1 percent to 16.4 percent respectively to NFCs (Banco de Portugal 2001, 184), continuing to decelerate as the decade went on. The drop-in construction activity was the biggest contributor to the declining growth of the Portuguese economy.

However, although the Portuguese economy stagnated during the 2000s, private indebtedness was on the rise. Once Portugal joined the euro, Portuguese banks had access to a deep pool of funds and continued to expand credit to households and the NFC sector, albeit at a decelerating rate (Banco de Portugal, various years). Although credit expansion didn't return to the high growth rates of the late 1990s, and while banks tightened their lending practices for long-term NFC loans and some consumer loans, it still grew steadily enough to increase private sector indebtedness. Mortgage lending remained an area of fierce competition and maintained a steady year on year rise in credit expansion, even if loans to NFCs and consumer credit increased less (Banco de Portugal, various years). Interest rates had fluctuated over the early 2000s but remained at historic lows, which created relatively consistent demand for mortgages. Banks, eager to corner market share for this robust area of credit growth, created new products during the 2000s, especially loans with longer maturities, in a successful effort to attract borrowers (Banco de Portugal 2003; various years). By 2005 Portuguese households were indebted to the tune of 117 percent of disposable income, one of the highest levels in the eurozone (Banco de Portugal 2006, 4).

Debt-led domestic demand-led growth crashed during the 2000s, bringing the entire Portuguese economy with it. Private consumption was no longer translating into above average GDP growth. Yet consumers continued to become indebted as interest rates for housing remained at low levels and fell at key points during the 2000s. The Portuguese economy was overheating in the 2000s, but not accelerating (Deutsche Bank 2010).

From debt-led growth to crisis

This pattern of debt-led growth and stagnation contributed to Portugal's' 2011 bailout in clearly identifiable ways. First, debt-led growth during the 1990s, and to a lesser extent during the 2000s, contributed to a widening of Portugal's current account deficit. Second, relatively high levels of private indebtedness contributed to the stagnation of Portugal's economy throughout the 2000s. Finally, the rejuvenated banking sector tended to allocate credit to the non-productive sectors of the economy, further damaging competitiveness. When Portugal looked structurally weak to international investors circa 2010, these are the reasons why.

First, debt-led growth was a major contributor to Portugal's current account deficits. Net external demand was regularly a negative contributor to GDP growth and to Portugal's widening trade deficit. Debt-led domestic demand (Lagoa et al. 2014) and private consumption were strongly oriented towards investment goods and durable consumer goods, both of which tend to have a high import content. In 1998 the import of goods and services accelerated from 12.3 percent in 1997 to 14.7 percent (Banco de Portugal 1999, 20). The trade balance rose to 11.3 percent of GDP in 1998 (Banco de Portugal 1999, 22). The current account deficit reached 8.5 percent of GDP in 2000, up from 4.8 percent in 1998, reflecting, almost entirely, the goods balance and its high import content (Banco de Portugal various years). As domestic demand petered out between 2000 and 2006, we can see the current account deficit decrease slightly, even as export performance showed negative growth – as was the case in 2002 when the deficit decreased to 7.3 percent of GDP (Banco de Portugal 2003, 152) – before rising again reflecting weak export performance and a modest return to domestic demand.

As I have shown in the previous section, Portugal's trade balance experienced problems beyond those related to its debt-led pattern of growth. Portugal's export performance was consistently disappointing, but even on those occasions when exports exhibited modest growth over the 1990s and 2000s, the trade balance tended to be overwhelmed by high levels of imports from debt-led domestic demand (Banco de Portugal various years).

Second, during the 1990s, the banking sector in Portugal appears to have been relatively more vigorous in fuelling credit led growth than it was in Ireland and Greece at the same time (Dooley 2018, 82; Lourtie 2011; and see Figure 5.6). This is important because Portuguese consumers were overleveraged and worried about future income at the same moment as they joined the euro. This, as well as a falling confidence in the Portuguese economy, contributed to a marked decline in consumption (Cardoso 2005). As Figure 5.6 shows, Portugal's private indebtedness diverged with the rest of the EMU during both the 1990s and 2000s.

High private indebtedness at the end of the 1990s contributed to stagnant growth rates in several other ways. Portuguese non-financial firms were highly indebted to banks at the turn of the century. This further damaged Portuguese growth by the 2000s (IMF 2013). As the IMF (2013) notes, "excess leverage may . . . have had a negative impact on investment, as over-indebted firms tend to pass up on new investment opportunities, particularly those with limited short-term benefits but higher long-term productivity gains" (9). Investment growth in Portugal peaked in 1997 and then gradually declined to turn negative, in line with increasing leverage (IMF, 9 2013). In other words, debt was so great in the corporate sector that it served as a barrier to accessing further debt, stalling productivity (Selassie 2012). Portuguese households and firms were also especially vulnerable to ECB interest rate rises. The ECB raised its key interest rate from 0.25 percent in early 1999 to 4.5 percent in late 2000 (Lagoa et al. 2014, 12). This further dampened domestic demand and made public debt more expensive to service, leading to a breach of the EDP in 2001. The EDP breach committed Portugal to a procyclical, contractionary fiscal policy, which further contributed to falling GDP

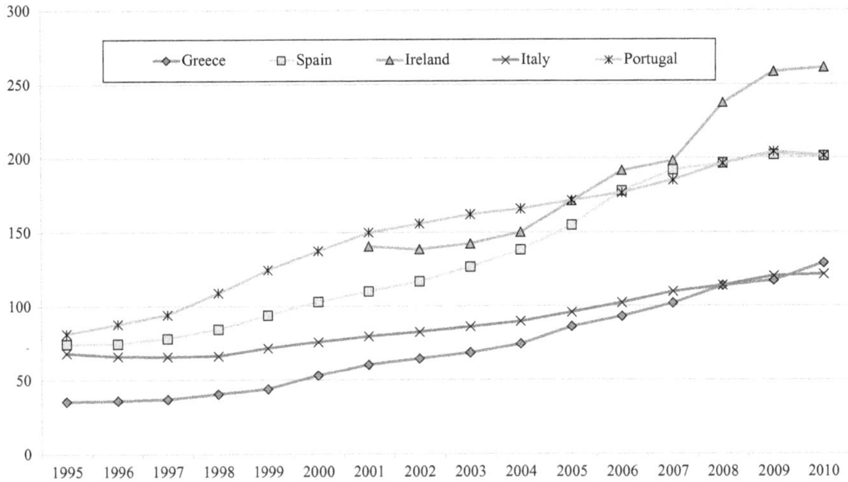

Figure 5.6 Private sector debt, consolidated: percentage of GDP for Greece, Spain, Ireland, Italy, and Portugal

Source: Eurostat

(Lagoa et al 2014; Dooley 2018). In sum, high private indebtedness helped put the brakes on debt-led domestic demand in the early 2000s, a pattern of economic activity that the country's growth rates were overly reliant upon.

Third, the incentives provided by the structural reforms geared investment and capital inflows to the newly profitable non-tradable sectors, including construction, retail, and privatised utilities, which were less exposed to foreign competition (Rodrigues and Reis 2012, 197). During the 1990s, non-tradable sectors, where productivity lagged, attracted far more investment from banking and finance than the vulnerable manufacturing sector (IMF 2013, 8). As manufacturing became perceived as being higher risk due to its exposure to international competition, newly privatised and liberalised banks began to direct credit to real estate, construction, and other non-tradable activities (Leão, et al. 2013; Decressin and Mauro 1998).[4] As manufacturing became increasingly threatened, the inward looking non-tradable sector grew, intensifying declining competitiveness and widening current account deficits.

A key example of this is the construction sector, which, during the 1990s, grew at four times the rate of the rest of the economy (Corkill 1999, 43). These sectors were in turn financed through the pivotal role of the newly invigorated, liberalised, and privatised banking sector. At the beginning of the 1990s 40 percent of bank loans to non-financial firms went to manufacturing firms and this declined to 20 percent in the 2000s (Rodrigues et al. 2016). However, the percentage of the construction and real estate sectors in total business debt rose from 10 percent in 1992 to almost 40 percent in 2008 (Rodrigues et al. 2016, 496). As a result of lower interest rates, an increased credit supply, and growing bank competition to direct a surge in capital flows into the non-tradable sector, macroeconomic imbalances grew (IMF 2013, 8). This contributed to the stagnation in the 2000s as the construction sector saw its share in value added as a percentage of GDP fall from 7.6 percent to 6.6 percent, in stark contrast with Ireland and Spain (Reis 2013, 156). In fact, Portugal was the only European country to register an annual decline in investment in construction every single year from 2002 until 2011 (Lourtie 2011, 6). As such, while the loss in market share for Portuguese exports played a role in the stagnation of the 2000s, the context of Portugal's declining export competitiveness is linked to the growth and decline of these non-productive inward-looking sectors.

The Portuguese crisis can thus be understood as follows. During the 1990s a process of institutional transformation, facilitated by the EU, contributed to the expansion of economic growth in the non-tradable sector via the banking and financial sectors. Secondly, the limits of this new model became evident in the early 2000s when declining export competitiveness was not counterbalanced by domestic demand-led growth, because of over-indebtedness. Tracing the transformation of the Portuguese economic trajectory has highlighted the importance of recognising institutional stickiness in the face of an unfit for purpose EMU. But it has also emphasised the pivotal role of Europeanisation of banking and finance. Through an attempt to prepare for the Single Market and the transposition of associated directives, banking and finance in Portugal dramatically transformed and drove brand new patterns of divergence, ultimately damaging economic growth.

Limits to Europeanisation

As a case study, Portugal illustrates the damage caused by a small, peripheral European economy's attempt to pursue an agenda of economic convergence by endeavouring to adapt to a 'one size fits all' model of European integration. Portugal's divergence from the EMU core (and much of the periphery) is to an important extent generated by institutional change catalysed by Europeanisation, leading to brand new patterns of debt-led growth. Portugal's experience of divergence via Europeanisation is different in important ways to that of Greece. Due to the legacy of the revolutionary period, Portugal had a wide gap to bridge in order to prepare for the Single Market and EMU. Portugal swiftly adopted numerous legislative changes relating to banking and finance, which contributed to the country earning the nickname of the good student of European integration (Teixeira 2012). However, Portugal illustrates that bad things can happen to good pupils (Dooley 2015a). Portugal's relatively rapid Europeanisation of banking and finance in the 1980s and 1990s created a situation where private indebtedness rose and debt-led growth emerged at a much earlier stage than in Greece, or, as Chapter 6 will show, Ireland. Lagoa et al. note the peculiar timing of Portuguese private indebtedness:

> [W]hile in other countries the levels of indebtedness grew slowly until the turn of the century, accelerating only after 2000, in the Portuguese case the reverse happened – private sector debt in percentage of GDP grew most rapidly in the second half of the 1990s, growing slowly thereafter.
>
> (Lagoa et al. 2014, 11)

Accordingly, Portugal exhausted its domestic demand-led growth at a much earlier stage than the rest of the periphery (Lagoa et al. 2014, 66).

However, this chapter has shown that Portugal's crisis is one of institutional stickiness, as well as institutional transformation. Portugal certainly developed a fragile and crisis-prone trajectory of economic growth through its Europeanisation. As I have shown, the deceleration of domestic demand in the 2000s was a major factor in Portugal's structural vulnerabilities. But stagnant economic growth in the 2000s was also clearly linked to Portugal's long-standing institutional difficulties and its specialisation in the exporting of low- to- medium-technology goods. Like Greece, Portugal faced limits to its development of export-led growth, and the declining fortunes of this sector contributed to reduction in employment and domestic demand, widening of trade deficits, and a negative economic outlook throughout the 2000s. It is fair to say that Portugal's crisis is characterised by its experience of following some of the rules of European integration, while finding itself unable to, due to institutional path dependency, follow those that would have supposedly allowed it to develop patterns of export-led growth.

Conclusion

This chapter has shown that Portugal's path to crisis was, to an important extent, catalysed by its attempt to participate in a project of European convergence. Rather than focusing on the ways in which EMU was incapable of handling the resilience of particular varieties of capitalism, I have shown that the real 'design flaw' was the promotion of a specific project of convergence relating specifically to banking and finance. Implementing a 'one size fits all' project of economic convergence across uneven levels and types of economies was always unlikely to produce homogeneity of models (Smith 2012b). Yet, this chapter has developed a different critique of the integration process. I have shown that, in the case of Portugal, the attempt to mitigate these differences through some important and compulsory measures aimed at a specific type European convergence actually contributed to the emergence of brand new and perilous patterns of divergence. Had Portugal's banking and finance sectors not transformed so dramatically, it still would have likely encountered the problems of competitiveness highlighted by CPE scholarship. It has been suggested that "without the need for alignment with single market legislation, the deregulation of the banks would have been much slower and probably less extensive" (Pinho 2002, quoted in Rodrigues et al. 2016). In Chapter 6 I depart from Southern Europe and head to the North Atlantic to explore the origins of this book's final case study, the

Irish financial crisis. Ireland followed an equally distinct path to its own crisis. Nevertheless, like Portugal and Greece, Ireland experienced processes of divergence via Europeanisation that contributed to its own crisis.

Notes

1 A version of this chapter appears in Dooley, Neil (2017b) "Divergence via Europeanisation: Rethinking the Origins of the Portuguese Debt Crisis". *Third World Thematics: A TWQ Journal* 0 (0): 1–22 ISSN 2380–2014. It is reproduced here with the kind permission of Taylor & Francis.
2 Although Reis cautions that the case of Germany is not representative.
3 See Decressin and Mauro (1998) for a detailed summary of these measures.
4 As Leão, et al. (2013) note, from 1993 to 2007.

6 Ireland

This final case study chapter examines the origins of the Irish banking crisis. In the two decades before the eurozone crisis, Ireland was the poster child of European integration and a "showpiece of Globalisation" (Kirby 2010, 3). From the mid-1990s onwards, its economy grew at rates that eclipsed the EU average, per capita income converged with EU levels, and close to full employment was achieved. This growth was well balanced by domestic demand and export performance (Central Bank of Ireland 1996, 7) and achieved with some of the lowest levels of public spending in the EU. However, by 2008 Ireland faced a banking crisis that the IMF claimed to be among "the most severe in world economic history" (quoted in Ó Riain 2014, 240; Dooley 2015c). Irish public debt soared from 25 percent to 110 percent as a consequence of the state issuing a blanket guarantee of bank liabilities in 2008 to the tune of €440 billion (Cooper 2012; Hendrikse 2013, 192). Over the next three years, bond yields on Irish sovereign debt reached unsustainable levels. Unemployment levels approached 15 percent in 2012 and an unprecedented fiscal crisis developed as Ireland had become overly reliant on property related taxes, which had collapsed following the end of the property boom (Dellepiane and Hardiman 2012). In November 2010, just over fifteen years after a Morgan Stanley report drew world attention to Ireland's miracle 'Celtic Tiger' economy (O'Hearn 1998, 1) the Irish government found itself responding to the most severe economic crisis the country had faced since gaining independence. It was forced to negotiate a financial assistance package with the ECB, EU, and IMF totalling €85 billion.

This final case study is a story of the transformation of Ireland's 'miraculous' export-led growth of the 1990s into unsustainable debt-led growth in the 2000s. I explore this shift, as I did in the previous case studies, by situating the Irish banking crisis within the country's experience of divergence via Europeanisation. I begin by briefly framing the argument in relation to two important explanations of Ireland's Celtic Tiger and financial crisis. The first and arguably most dominant perspective argues that we should make an analytical distinction between the Celtic Tiger of the 1990s and the property bubble of the 2000s. The former was hijacked, squandered, and supplanted by immature political and economic governance from the late 1990s onwards. The second perspective emerges as a critique of this analysis, as well as in an earlier iteration, a critique of the self-congratulatory readings of Ireland's growth during the 1990s (O'Hearn 1998). It claims that the lightly regulated, low tax regime that was so successful at attracting FDI, during the 1990s, contained the seeds of the property boom and banking crisis during the 2000s. The property boom, in other words, is the other side of the Celtic Tiger coin. Challenging each of these perspectives, I show that an analytical split should indeed be made between Ireland's export boom and debt-led boom, but I also suggest that more attention needs to be paid to the European, and pre-2000 origins of the Irish property boom.

In the second and third sections I develop the argument that the Irish property boom emerged in a context of Ireland's deepening European integration. The second section discusses the rise and fall of Ireland's export-led model of growth. In the 1990s Ireland's Celtic Tiger economy was growing at a rate that was three times higher than that of any other EU state, yet from 2000 onwards this growth became undermined by the dot-com crash, registering a significant decline in growth and falling investment between 2001 and 2003. Although it recovered after this period, new forms of economic growth sidelined export-led growth for most of the 2000s. This downturn reveals the limitations of Ireland's export-led growth, in that it was always highly vulnerable to international shocks and, in particular, the performance of the US economy. In very different ways, Ireland shares limits to its export-led growth with Greece and Portugal. I argue, however, that it is misleading to locate the origins of the property boom, specifically, in the institutions and polices that made the export boom possible.

The third section discusses the parallel emergence of the conditions for the property and banking crisis during the 1980s and 1990s. Ireland's banking and financial sectors transformed from the late 1980s as a result of preparing for the Single Market and EMU. This boom could not have occurred without the changes to the Irish banking and financial sector following the liberalisation and deregulation associated with the re-launched European project in the late 1980s. The experience of Ireland presents an intriguing conclusion. 'Following the rules' of European integration, as Ireland was widely considered to have done, does not necessarily lead to sustainable economic growth. In fact, doing so actually threatened sustainable economic growth in Ireland. As Paul Krugman notes, Ireland got into its current bind "[b]y being just like us, only more so" (Krugman 2009).

The Irish boom and bust: contesting the link between export-led and debt-led growth

Was the Irish banking crisis a departure from the export-led growth of the 1990s, or an unintended outcome of it? Scholarly opinion is divided. Most narratives of the Irish property boom and bust begin with the election of the 1997 Fianna Fáil–Progressive Democrat (PD) coalition government.[1] This is typically cited as the moment where the export-led growth of the 1990s began to be undermined by a decade of expansionary, short-sighted misgovernment during the 2000s.[2] As the argument goes, Irish politicians helped generate the bubble through changes in national and investment politics. The 1997 coalition government combined the populist 'growth machine' approach of the centre–right Fianna Fáil party with the liberalising economic policies of the conservative-liberal PD party. As early as 1998 this government had slashed capital gains tax in half, with the explicit intention of injecting untapped capital into the economy. They more than succeeded in this goal and capital flowed into property and construction; signalling a newly emerging dynamic in Irish investment politics (Ó Riain 2012, 506).

Irish governments are often accused of actively encouraging, rather than restraining credit-fuelled property development during this period (Kirby 2010, 9; Oireachtas 2016). Dellepiane and Hardiman (2012) note that Irish politics has consistently tended to use taxation to garner political support. This continued into the 2000s when the former Irish Minister for Finance Charlie McCreevy, now infamous for his 'when I have it I spend it, when I don't I don't' aphorism on fiscal policy, pursued politically-driven reductions in income tax, damaging the profile of exchequer returns and contributing to inflationary spending (Dellepiane and Hardiman 2012). The theoretical explanation that is implied within this narrative (the Irish version of the immaturity thesis) is that the property boom of the 2000s represents a discontinuity with the export boom of the 1990s; and, moreover, it represents the overwhelming of the productive, sustainable growth Ireland had worked hard to achieve in the 1990s (Ó Riain 2012). In a manner of speaking, there is no contradiction between Ireland's status as the poster child for European integration in the 1990s, and its membership of the so-called PIIGS in 2010. Immature patterns of governance hijacked and reversed the mature growth of the 1990s. Ireland's Celtic Tiger was squandered, it was sunk by "stupidity and corruption" (O'Toole 2010).

Like the clearly evident 'dysfunctions' of the Greek crisis, this narrative is accurate but not the whole story. It is an explanation that is grounded in an earlier and still influential literature on the origins of the Celtic Tiger export boom. Honohan and Walsh (2002) and others (see Lane 2011; Ahearne, Schmitz, and von Hagen 2008; for overviews, see Ó Riain 2014, 36–8; Kinsella 2012) understand the unprecedented growth of the Celtic Tiger era as a case of 'delayed convergence'. Since the late 1950s, the institutions and polices set up as part of the 'great switch' (as I discuss in the second section) should have led to convergence with Western Europe. However, in the 1960s and 1970s, successive Irish government's 'got the policies wrong' – they followed fiscal expansion as a response to the oil crisis, which caused inflation, raised wages, and thereby damaged competitiveness and discouraged productive growth (see Ó Riain 2014, 36).

In 1987, when the newly elected Fianna Fáil government finally 'got the policies right', expansionary fiscal contraction took place (Kinsella 2012; Barry 2003), and convergence flowed rapidly, as if it had been water building up behind a dam that had just been demolished. As Ó Riain (2014) notes, this is in many respects the standard account of Ireland's Celtic Tiger, and remains a key reference point for accounts of the crisis, when after the 2000s, policymakers 'got the policies wrong' once again. (36).

The 'delayed convergence' reading explains economic transformation as having been achieved through market liberalisation. This has been strongly and frequently contested by a literature that focuses instead on the crucial role played by the state in generating Ireland's convergence. Scholars have correctly pointed out that Ireland's success cannot be reduced simply to the liberalisation of markets (Murphy and Kirby 2007). Critical political economists such as O'Hearn (1998, 2001) and others (Wickham 1980; Crotty 1987; Mac Laughlin 1994) stress the central role played by the state in reshaping the Irish economy. They often argue that Ireland has gone through a pattern of dependent export-oriented development (Kirby 2010, 95) where indigenous industry is neglected by the state in favour of attracting FDI through opening up and free trade. Irish governments have attempted to attract multinational corporations (MNCs) to invest in Ireland by offering low taxes and a 'hands off' government attitude towards business (O'Hearn 1998). O'Hearn notes that Irish governments have fostered a liberal environment for US MNCs to accumulate substantial wealth, but despite its high profile, these sectors have never created substantial numbers of jobs (O'Hearn 1998, 165; Central Bank of Ireland 1991, 1992, 1993, 1994). Moreover, in reshaping the Irish state to be as attractive as possible to US MNCs, successive Irish governments have pitted economic growth against social prosperity (O'Hearn 1998, 165).

These approaches also typically shed light on the inequality that has accompanied the Celtic Tiger boom, and point out the various ways in which GDP growth (as opposed to GNP growth, which is not so distorted by the MNC sector) has been illusory, oftentimes an artefact of corporate accounting and a conflation of 'growth' with 'development' (Kirby 2010, 92). One author within this literature recalls how such analysis was received as 'begrudgery' during the boom years (O'Hearn 1998), and notes that refrains about how such arguments were akin to 'talking down the economy' became a common accusation during the 2000s. Former Taoiseach of Ireland, Bertie Ahern, who was very much at the helm during the property boom, infamously remarked when addressing an Irish Congress of Trade Unions (ICTU) conference in Belfast that:

> sitting on the sidelines, cribbing and moaning is a lost opportunity. I don't know how people who engage in that don't commit suicide because frankly the only thing that motivates me is being able to actively change something.
> (RTÉ News 2007)

In the wake of the crisis, this critique of the Celtic Tiger period has led authors such as Kirby (Kirby 2004, 2008, 2010; Murphy and Kirby 2007; Kirby and Murphy 2011a, 2011b) to emphasise the continuity between the Celtic Tiger export model and the speculative property bubble. As this argument goes, the property bubble should not be understood as a departure from the patterns of the 1990s. Free market principles, deliberately weak regulation and low levels of taxation and expenditure may have underpinned the export-led growth of the 1990s, but these policies and institutions also left Ireland particularly vulnerable to financial crisis in 2008 (Ó Riain 2014, 37; Kirby and Murphy 2011a; Kitchin et al. 2012). Kirby sums up this argument:

> The reliance on stimulating an unsustainable construction boom to replace the growth model based on FDI and the role of the very lightly regulated banks in facilitating this, was the proximate cause, but the vulnerabilities this has exposed in the capacity and resilience of the Irish state derive from the low-tax regime that was seen as the central policy mechanism for attracting foreign investment. Behind these lie the role of the state and the ways in which it understood the opportunities of globalisation. *What has collapsed therefore is Ireland's dependent low tax model of state led development.*
>
> (Kirby 2010, 9 [italics added])

Kirby's work on the Celtic Tiger highlights the limitations and contradictions in a model of growth that was overly reliant on FDI; less a Celtic Tiger and more a "U.S Tiger caged in a Celtic Zoo" (Kirby 2010, 149); as well as illuminating social and welfare failures that accompanied the Irish 'competition state' (Kirby 2010; Kirby and Murphy 2011a).

Yet, Ó Riain (2004, 2014) criticises Kirby for having no positive account of the causes of change in the Celtic Tiger. Although he welcomes Kirby's critique of the cheerleading for the Celtic Tiger, he criticises the overall thrust of the argument for failing to take seriously the extensive change that has occurred in Ireland, whether or not the character of it should be taken to task (Ó Riain 2004, 9). This critical approach is successful in highlighting some of the reasons why export-led growth did not continue during the 2000s. Yet, it is less convincing in explaining the origins of the debt-led boom that replaced it. It tends to assume that the demand-led growth and low tax regime that accompanied the Celtic Tiger would inevitably lead to a housing bubble. As we have seen, this was not straightforwardly the case in either Greece or Portugal following similar demand-led growth in the 1990s.

As Kirby himself recognises, criticising the dependency theory approach of O'Hearn (1998), the notion that multinationals are simply 'draining capital' from the Irish national economy is difficult to support. In fact, far from a relationship of dependence, Ireland has received substantial net economic and financial gains to its economy (Kirby 2010, 95). It is clear that dismissing the Celtic Tiger boom as simply illusory, or as preamble before the speculative boom, is limiting. As I show in the second section, brand new patterns of economic activity emerged across Ireland during this period, and as the empirical thrust of Kirby's (2010) analysis concedes, we still require some sort of proximate explanation for the dramatic shift that this model went through circa 2000.

These competing perspectives leave us with a puzzle for explaining the link between the Celtic Tiger and the Irish banking crisis.[3] The existing debate has left us with a choice between problematically conflating these two very distinctive patterns of growth and falling back upon the narrow internalist assumptions of the immaturity thesis to account for an analytical distinction. As a way out of this puzzle, I show in the second section that during the 1990s the Irish economy did indeed undergo a significant transformation, which the challenges of Kirby (2002, 2010) and O'Hearn (1998, 2001) downplay by reinterpreting the decline of the Celtic Tiger as bound up in the 'logics' of its initial, illusory, success. I go on to show in the third section that the immaturity narrative has in turn downplayed the impact of European integration on this transformation. I first focus on how Ireland managed to succeed in achieving genuine, albeit vulnerable, export-led growth that should be understood as distinct from the property boom. This distinction is important to make because, as I later show, it clears the ground for an alternative explanation of the origins of Ireland's property boom. As was the case with Greece and Portugal, in doing so, I draw out the key role played by Ireland's divergence via Europeanisation.

The Celtic Tiger: vulnerable export-led growth at Europe's periphery

A 1980s advertisement by the Industrial Development Authority (IDA)[4] aimed to attract US businesses to invest in Ireland – "we're the young Europeans", it ventured (*New York Times* 1984). By 1994, the young Europeans were overtaking the old as their Celtic Tiger model of export-led growth gained Ireland international acclaim that it was quite unaccustomed to. As Kitchin et al. note:

> [p]oliticians, policy makers, economists, academics, practitioners, think-tank gurus, and journalists from around the world flocked to Ireland to be inducted in the art of best practice in fast-track growth, and former Irish leaders have gone on global lecture tours espousing the so-called benefits of the 'Irish model' of neoliberal economic reform for countries wishing to fast-track modernisation.
>
> (Kitchin et al. 2012, 1302–3)

In this section I trace the rise and decline of Ireland's export-led pattern of growth during the period 1987–2001. I briefly account for some 'pre-history' – tracing the institutional innovations of the great switch in 1959 that marked the beginning of Ireland's attempts to develop export-led strategies of modernisation. I then offer an account of the unprecedented growth of the Celtic Tiger era from 1987 to 2001, when Ireland began to experience growth rates and falling unemployment that set it very much apart from its Southern European, and at times its Western European, neighbours. I subsequently highlight some of the limitations of this pattern of growth, drawing particular attention to its vulnerability to changing international economic circumstances. Finally, I emphasise the distinction between the Celtic Tiger, and the banking crisis that was to follow.

The 'great switch': from economic nationalism to export-led growth

As late as 1990, Irish historian Joe Lee declared Ireland to be the 'economic laggard of Europe' (1990). Breznitz notes that, even as late as 1995, "observers considered Ireland's economic performance one of continuous failure" (Breznitz 2012, 87). The legacy of Ireland's colonial past had weighed heavily on its fledgling projects of economic modernisation. Agriculture accounted for almost half of the Irish economy, and the vast majority of exports went to Britain. Ireland had little control over its monetary policy as the new Irish currency, the punt, was tied to the sterling. Non-agricultural activity in the economy was characterised by little to no industry (O'Hearn 1998; Kirby 2010; Crotty 1987; Lynn 2010, 64–74).

By the mid-1950s various projects of economic nationalism aimed at modernising and industrialising Ireland had little success, creating political and economic crises for the new state. The first Fianna Fáil government of 1932, led by Éamon de Valera, instigated economic programmes that promised economic self-sufficiency (O'Hearn 1998, 36). Wide-ranging protectionist measures on Irish industry were pursued by de Valera, with the average tariff level rising from 9 percent in 1931, to 45 percent in 1945 (Kirby 2010, 17). Despite initial success, the developmental nationalism project was in chaos by the 1950s. As O'Hearn notes, by 1955 industrial production had fallen by 3 percent, agricultural production by 7 percent, and GNP by 1.3 percent. Employment fell by almost 10 percent between 1951 and 1956, and census results revealed that Ireland's population had declined by 2.11 percent over the same period (O'Hearn 1998, 38).[5] The Irish state was facing mounting pressure to address this economic situation. This led ultimately to the great switch of 1959 – the period when Ireland began to actively follow a project of export-led growth, facilitated through the successful attraction of FDI, coming primarily from the US. This was channelled into high-technology sectors that were new to Ireland, namely computing, pharmaceuticals, chemicals, metals, and engineering (Kirby 2010).

A young generation of Irish politicians pioneered a radical strategy of modernisation during the 1950s and 1960s that favoured export orientation and the promotion of free trade. Éamon de Valera retired as Taoiseach in 1959 and was replaced by Seán Lemass. This marked a new era for Ireland's political economy, which was signalled by the publication of the *First Programme for Economic Expansion*, covering the period 1959–63 (Kirby 2010, 19). Lemass and his secretary of the Department of Finance, T. K. Whitaker, are largely credited with setting in motion the three elements that characterise the liberal export-led model of Irish growth, which kicked off the Celtic Tiger decades later: the use of grants and tax concessions to encourage the development of an export-oriented sector, the attraction of FDI (especially in manufacturing), and the dismantling of protection in order to gain greater access to international markets (Kirby 2010, 20). Ireland unilaterally reduced tariffs by 10 percent on two occasions during the 1960s, and also negotiated the Anglo–Irish free trade agreement, which came into effect in 1966. EEC accession in 1973 provided a five-year window for Ireland to establish free trade with all EEC member states (Kirby 2010, 20). The Irish state also offered grants and, crucially, tax concessions to manufacturing and later financial services companies – in a number of predecessor arrangements to Ireland's well-known 12.5 percent corporation tax rate. The IDA[6] became a key (semi-state) agency, with similarities to the agencies of East Asian Tigers, and played a 'hunter–gatherer' role in attracting foreign firms (Kirby 2010, 20;

O Hearn 1998; Ó Riain 2004, 2014). Crucially, the IDA identified electronics as a key sector in 1974, and focused on attracting investment from the US in that sector, meaning that investment in post-1973 Ireland was decidedly 'modern' (O'Hearn 1998, 40).

Kirby (2010) notes that initially, this programme was expected to make indigenous industry more attractive, and few foresaw the pivotal role that FDI would ultimately play (20). In 1983 there were almost 1,000 foreign firms in Ireland and they had invested over I£4 billion in the economy (Kirby 2010, 20).[7] The shift to US investment came during a period of rapid worldwide investment in high-technology sectors such as electronics. Ireland's membership of the EEC proved to be a powerful attraction for American-based firms (O'Hearn 1998, 41). Yet, this export-oriented strategy, while somewhat successful, did not lead anywhere close to the kind of growth levels that would eventually characterise the Celtic Tiger. By the 1970s and 1980s "Ireland was in kind of a funk" (O'Hearn 1998, 55). Initial optimism over EC membership quickly subsided as industrial growth appeared to be short term. Also, while some (mostly larger) farmers experienced a rise in incomes, in the early decades Ireland's export-orientation strategy "turned into a nightmare of emigration and unemployment" (O Hearn 1998, 55).

The Celtic Tiger – 1987–2001

Few could have predicted the turnaround of the 1990s. The country found itself in a position to use the institutions and policies of the great switch to take advantage of a booming US economy, together with the new opportunities and increased attractiveness of Ireland as a destination for FDI due its membership of the recently 'completed' European Single Market (Cahill and O'Donnell 2010). Existing literature tends to split Ireland's export-led boom into three phases (Ó Riain 2014, 2008; Kirby 2010, 32). The first phase begins in 1987 when the newly elected Fianna Fáil government led by the charismatic and divisive Charles J. Haughey (Joyce and Murtagh 1983) introduced a number of significant new policies and institutions, including social partnership, "one of the longest historical unbroken series of corporatist national social pacts" (Ó Riain 2014, 177); as well as an ambitious project of fiscal consolidation, representing "the moment Ireland got its house in order" (Kinsella 2012, 233). Ireland succeeded in reducing its public debt levels from 112 percent of GDP in 1986 to 25 percent in 2007 (Kinsella 2012, 233). Yet, at first recovery was quite modest. From 1990 to 1993 Ireland was experiencing 'jobless growth', sluggish domestic demand, a legacy of public finance problems, and low levels of credit expansion. During this period, net exports were the primary source of growth, partly attributable to the MNC sector, which had a very limited impact on the Irish domestic economy (Central Bank of Ireland 1995, 7).

The second phase of the Celtic Tiger is best represented by the GNP[8] growth, and the dramatic decline in unemployment, of 1994–2000. There was a cumulative GNP increase from 1994 to 1996 of about 23 percent (Central Bank of Ireland 1997) and unemployment fell from 15 percent in 1994 to 4 percent in 2000. From

1980 to 2000 Ireland attracted 40 percent of US electronics FDI that went to Europe (Ó Riain 2014, 52). Firms were undoubtedly attracted by corporate tax rates of zero 0–12.5 percent at different time periods, pools of skilled labour, a highly supportive state, and increasingly improved technological and innovation capacities (Ó Riain 2014, 52; Lynn 2011 67). Remarkably, throughout all of this, wage pressure and inflation remained relatively modest, and government finances continued to be consolidated (Ó Riain 2014, 54). Ó Riain refers to this period as Ireland's 'developmentalist phase' (Ó Riain 2014, 184–6). Ireland became the second richest country in the EU (after Luxembourg), moving from a position of about 60 percent of EU per capita income (a place it had held since EEC accession in 1973) to 145.4 percent in 2006 (Kirby 2010, 32–3). Unlike Greece and Portugal during the 1990s, Irish growth was well balanced by domestic demand and exports, facilitated largely by US FDI in high-technology sectors (Ó Riain 2014, 55). Ireland was certainly in the right place at the right time, but the long-term institutional and policy legacy of the great switch made such growth possible during the 1990s. As such, its 1990s boom should be set apart from that of the other cases in this study. All three countries experienced unprecedented GDP growth during the 1990s, but Ireland was the only one that appeared to be doing so from a position of institutional advantage (Central Bank of Ireland, various years).[9]

The decline of Ireland's export-led growth

The massive influence and importance of US FDI for economic growth in Ireland is unquestionable. This meant that the profile of Irish growth during the 1990s was incredibly vulnerable to fluctuations in the US economy and to changing levels of FDI. Denis O'Hearn (1998) has noted that perhaps the most startling thing about Ireland's increased dependence on MNCs is not simply their share of GDP but their domination of economic growth. He notes that MNCs were responsible for 45 percent of GDP growth during the period 1990–5, and were indirectly responsible for an unknown additional amount of growth (O'Hearn 1998, 72, 73). Ireland's vulnerability was made apparent during the third period of the Celtic Tiger, 2001–3, when export growth began to decline. This was in large part due to Ireland's exposure to those sectors affected by the dot-com crash. After a decade of sustained growth, Ireland was losing the inflows that had characterised, and arguably defined the economic success of the Celtic Tiger era, as Figure 6.1 shows.

A 2002 IDA Annual Report reveals also that the year 2001 marked the first time since 1993 that employment dropped in IDA supported companies, never to come close to recovering the same percentage employment (IDA Ireland 2002) (see Figure 6.2). In the year 2000, employment in IDA supported companies increased from the previous year by 11.7 percent. In 2001 it fell by 3.2 percent, and again by 3.2 percent in 2002 and by 2.5 percent in 2003. Percentage change in full time employment averaged at 1 percent from 2001 until 2008. This is in contrast to the period from 1994 to 2000, where it averaged at 8.2 percent.

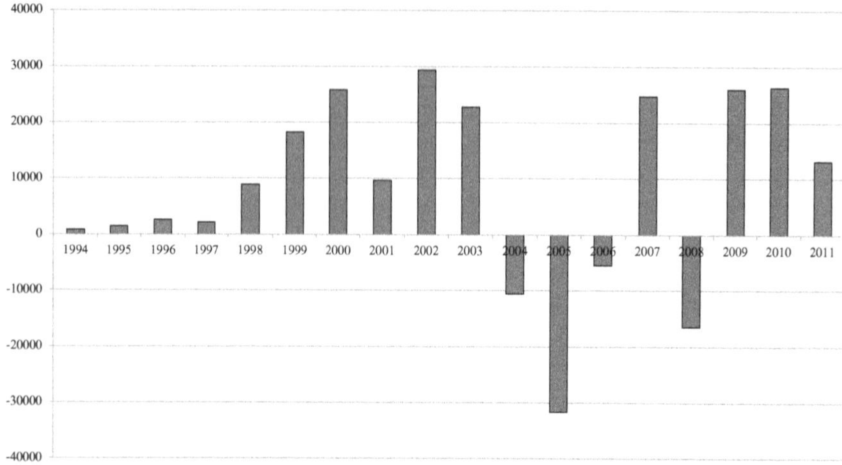

Figure 6.1 Amount of FDI inflows (in US$) from the US to Ireland
Source: UNCTAD

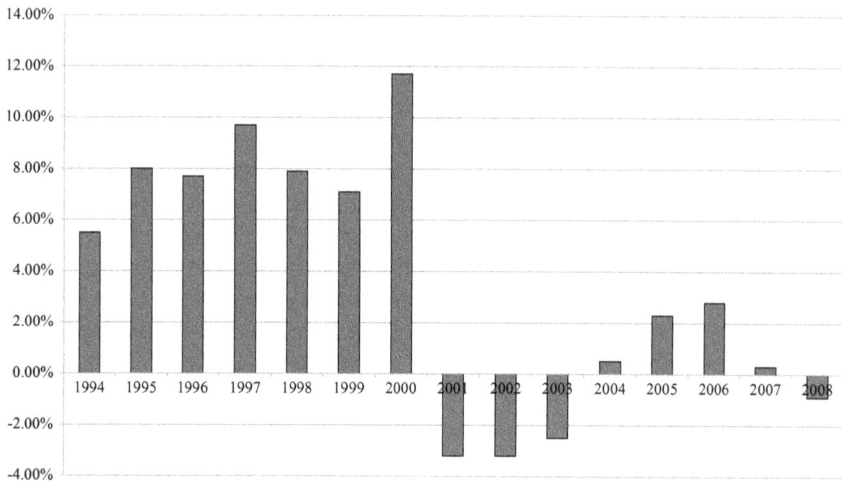

Figure 6.2 Percentage change in net employment in IDA supported companies
Source: IDA Annual Reports

In addition to falling investment and employment, the value of Ireland's merchandise exports in 2006 was less than it was in 2002 and crucially, for an 'export-led country', Ireland's balance of payments moved from a position of balance in 2003 to a deficit of 3.3 percent of GDP in 2006 (Kirby 2010, 35; see Figure 6.3).

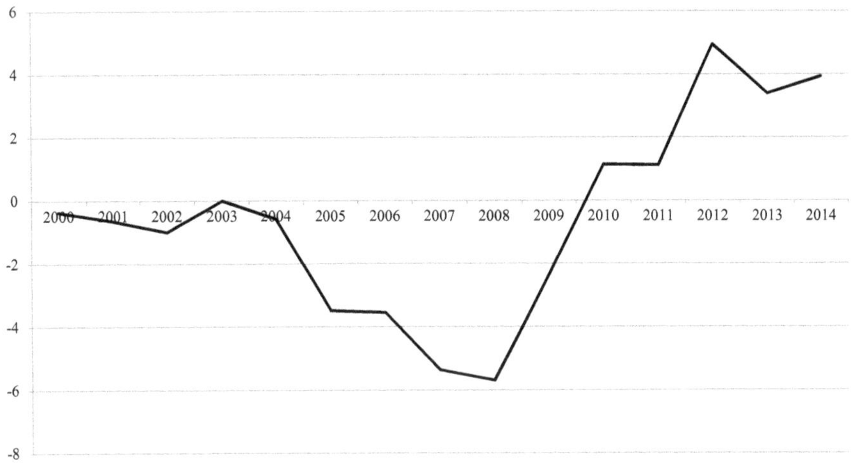

Figure 6.3 Ireland's current account balance (percentage of GDP)
Source: IMF Balance of Payments Statistics

As Tansey (2007) put it: "the Celtic Tiger economy met its end in 2001" (quoted in Kirby 2010, 35). Export-led growth was to pick up again, and arguably underpinned Ireland's recovery from the eurozone crisis from 2015 onwards (Brazys and Regan 2015). But at the time, vulnerability to falling FDI contributed to a massive shift away from Ireland's 'developmentalist phase', and the economy has seen nothing like the Celtic Tiger since 2001. Yet, as was the case for Greece and Portugal, the limitations of Ireland's export-led growth should not be understood as the same as the causes of its debt-led growth.

A boom without a bubble: towards a new account of Ireland's debt-led growth

It was during this period of uncertainty and downturn (2001–3) that the Irish property bubble began to kick off. As I argued in the first section, Kirby and others claim that the origins of the speculative property boom are to be found in the weaknesses of the Celtic Tiger export-led model of the 1990s. There are a number of problems with this argument. Firstly, it tends to under-specify the linkages between the Celtic Tiger's institutional set up and the origins of the property bubble. Secondly, in conflating the Celtic Tiger and the property boom into a singular, non-interrupted trajectory, the genuine promise of the Celtic Tiger that authors such as Ó Riain (2004, 2014) recognise is denied. This is a particular problem, because it misses out on a fundamental critique of Ireland's relationship with European integration. Certain aspects of Ireland's European integration contributed to the undermining and damaging of a peripheral economy that had effectively 'done everything right'.

The links between the various market and non-market state-led strategies of attracting inward investment and credit-fuelled property development are not usually clearly defined by critical analysis of Ireland's crisis (see Kirby 2010, 156–60 especially). Neoliberalism is often evoked as a 'black box' to account for the increasing prevalence of market logics across both the Celtic Tiger period and the 2000s (Kirby 2010, 164). Yet, authors such as Kirby fail to trace, historically, the concrete linkages between "a particular type of market economy . . . highly dependent on high levels of FDI and ever attentive to the needs of these foreign corporations" (Kirby 2010, 164) and the property boom; instead, the linkage is taken for granted. In fact, such analysis tends to need to rely on assumptions of the immaturity thesis to bridge their critique of the Celtic Tiger with their analysis of the origins of the property bubble. Kirby and others tend to over emphasise the significance of certain 'market forms' of FDI attraction when discussing the Celtic Tiger period. Light touch regulation is a clear linkage between both periods and was an important strategy for the attraction of the financial services sector, but less so for other sectors such as manufacturing and software. In fact, a strong and reliable regulatory infrastructure has been argued to be a central reason why Ireland managed to hang on to its pharmaceutical sector in the wake of the EU's enlargement to the CEE countries (Barry 2004, 844). Similarly, although low corporation tax is more clearly important across sectors, the link between Ireland as a 'low tax regime' in this respect, and the damaging of Ireland's fiscal profile in the 2000s does not stack up well with the reality that when the export boom was at its height, the tax base was not skewed towards unsustainable revenues, and fiscal consolidation was being strongly pursued.

Additionally, as Brazys and Regan (2015) argue, 'non-market' forms of FDI attraction were just as important as the well-known 'market forms'. Of key significance is the long-standing institutional commitment by public sector agencies to attract inward investment from global firms in high-technology sectors (Brazys and Regan 2015, 6). The authors emphasise the 'non-market forms' of coordination that have been instrumental in attracting large global firms to Ireland, including:

> informal networking, hard political bargaining and the active marketing of Ireland's low corporate tax regime, and their willingness to partner in a readymade business model.
>
> (Brazys and Regan 2015, 6)

Viewing the property boom as caused by the Celtic Tiger belies an important distinction that ought to be made between Ireland's export-led growth and its latter-day debt-led growth (see Kinsella 2012, 572). Certainly, Kirby and colleagues are correct to highlight some of the social and economic limitations of the Celtic Tiger model of growth. Yet, the elision of Ireland's debt-led and export-led growth does a disservice to some of the more positive aspects of the modernisation that was achieved during the 1990s. Neglecting this distinction is a problem, because it serves to downplay just how significant a discontinuity of the property bubble was in the context of Ireland's recent economic trajectory.

In this section I traced Ireland's transformation from a beleaguered peripheral European economy to an international success story (Lynn 2011). Despite the limitations of Irish export success, especially with respect to its vulnerability to the fortunes of the US economy, the Celtic Tiger was a symbol of Ireland's hard-won modernisation and its overcoming of postcolonial institutional path dependencies. The third and final section shows that Ireland's adaptation to European financial integration contributed greatly to the protracted derailment of this peripheral country's successful (at least temporarily) development of export-oriented growth.

Ireland adapts to Europe: debt-led growth via Europeanisation

While the second section discussed the evolution of Ireland's export-led model of growth and its place in the narrative of Ireland's crisis, this section traces the parallel emergence of Ireland's debt-fuelled property bubble. Fiscal mismanagement, weak regulation, and poor supervision by Irish authorities played an indisputable role in the shift from the Celtic Tiger to the housing bubble. But this is not the whole story. Such accounts have overlooked the important European dimensions of Ireland's banking crisis, many of which predate the expansionary fiscal policies of the late 1990s and 2000s. Some background to the property boom and banking crisis is first provided, before going on to trace the longer-term European origins of the Irish property boom. The narrative presented in this chapter provides an alternative reading of the Irish crisis as developing *alongside* the Celtic Tiger rather than because of it. The Celtic Tiger was not straightforwardly 'hijacked'. Ireland's commitment to participation in the euro and the European Single Market set the scene for the emergence of a radically transformed and highly competitive banking sector.

The Irish property boom: historical background

From about 2003 to 2008, domestic demand replaced export-led demand as the main driver of Ireland's economic growth.[10] Aggressive lending by the Irish banking system propelled a property boom during this period, which began to overwhelm all other sectors of the economy (Lane 2012, 2). Following the international recession of 2001 and because of Ireland's particular exposure to the dot-com sector, there were expectations that Ireland would return to a more 'normal' European growth path (Lane 2012, 6). Instead, a drastic transformation occurred. White (2010) notes that capital stock in Ireland soared by 157 percent in real terms between 2000 and 2008, and that housing accounted for almost two-thirds of this (1). House prices began to break the link with demand in ways they had not done during the 1990s. Ó Riain (2014) notes that 89 percent of all ghost estates in 2010 were granted planning permission in the period

2002–8 (87). A 2006 census, carried out at the height of the boom, found that there were 250,000 empty houses in Ireland, an astonishing figure for a country with a population of just over four million (Lynn 2011, 65).

The property bubble was the proximate cause of Ireland's banking and fiscal crisis (Hardiman 2012; Whelan 2013). Following the global credit crunch and falling house prices circa 2008, the banking system collapsed, leading the Dáil (Irish Parliament) to pass a blanket bank guarantee, effectively converting private bank debt into sovereign debt. In 2007 Ireland's gross debt to GDP ratio was 25 percent. By 2012 that had risen to 120 percent of GDP (Whelan 2013). The notorious bank guarantee has resonated through the popular Irish imagination as 'economic treason'[11] (O'Halloran 2011) and it played a key role in making Ireland's debt appear unsustainable to international markets (Whelan 2013, 1, 18); effectively ensuring the arrival of the troika to Dublin in November 2011.

The property bubble also contributed to a fiscal crisis (Dellepiane and Hardiman 2012, 91). Over the course of the late 1990s and 2000s, the Irish tax base became skewed towards construction related taxes, as governments from 1997 onwards reduced income taxes and promoted the inflation of the construction sector in various ways (Regling and Watson 2010, 5). Taxes on economic activities related to the construction boom – namely stamp duty, capital gains tax (although this was cut in half in 1997), and VAT – began to dominate the tax base, all of which fell dramatically after the property crash, no longer becoming effective sources of revenue (Dellepiane and Hardiman 2012, 95–6). This left the exchequer in serious trouble once the property bubble burst and those receipts stopped flowing. As Whelan argues (2013, 18) even though bank debts contributed hugely to this figure, Ireland's debt to GDP ratio was likely to be well over 80 percent of GDP by 2013. This was due to the gap between government receipts and expenditure, not to mention declining GDP. As such, Ireland's second great switch to debt-led growth in the 2000s damaged the competitiveness and sound public finances that had characterised the export-led growth of the Celtic Tiger era. In this section I locate the origins of this property bubble not just in the 'immaturity' of late 1990s Irish governance, but in the country's divergence via Europeanisation.

The origins of the Irish banking crisis: Ireland's adaptation to Europe

As I mentioned in the first section, scholarship on the Irish crisis (Whelan 2013; Lane 2011; Ahearne et al. 2008; Hardiman 2012; Hardiman and Dellepiane 2010; Hardiman 2010; see Ó Riain 2014, 36–8 and Kinsella 2012 for overviews), media coverage (for instance, *The Economist* 2011; English 2013; *The Belfast Telegraph* 2012; Sheahan 2010), and an Oireachtas (parliamentary) banking inquiry (Oireachtas 2016; Regling and Watson 2010; Nyberg 2011) tend to situate the origins of the banking crisis in the four- to five-year period from 2003 to 2008 (Ó Riain 2014, 61). As the story goes, increased, pro-cyclical government spending contributed to overheating, as did rising wages across the public and private sectors, and timid, ineffectual regulation failed to put the brakes on reckless bank lending. After 2000, euro membership resulted in an interest rate shock, adding fuel to an already blazing fire through unprecedented access to cheap capital.

This narrative establishes a clear analytical distinction between the Celtic Tiger and the property boom. While this distinction is important and correct, it nevertheless neglects the longer historical origins of the Irish banking crisis. In fact, we can trace the origins of the banking crisis back to the late 1980s, as Ireland began to make dramatic reforms to its banking and financial sector. This sub-section draws on Central Bank of Ireland annual reports (various years), quarterly bulletins (various years), and other publications (2013), as well as the work of Sinéad Kelly (2014), John Kelly, and Mary Everett (2004) to fill this gap.

The Irish banking system underwent a period of unprecedented transformation from the mid-1980s onwards and a key driver of this change was the preparations for the European Single Market (Kinsella and Bourke 2002). Although the Irish banking system was already relatively open and liberal since the 1960s, the Single Market programme accelerated this process (Kinsella and Bourke 2002). During the 1970s and 1980s, Irish governments issued credit controls and many other restrictions, which were reinforced to varying extents throughout the 1980s.[12] Following EEC accession in 1973, Irish banks were advised not to increase private-sector credit to non-productive sectors, including financial, property companies, and property sectors (Ferriter 2012, 465–73). This was in part a response to the debt and inflation crisis Ireland found itself in during the 1970s. Governments were concerned that increased levels of private spending and borrowing were damaging Ireland's competitiveness and widening its current account deficit. T. K. Whitaker was concerned that "for all the new opportunities, ill-judged and reckless policies could lead to a return to the dark days that had propelled his original foray into Irish economic policy formulation" (Ferriter 2012, 467). In 1974, credit restrictions on banks were reinforced by provisions for special deposits at non-commercial rates of interests, and banks were required to have a special 50 percent deposit requirement on capital outflows during these years (Central Bank of Ireland 2013). Stricter guidelines on loans to non-productive lending were enforced in October 1978 and, after briefly being discontinued, these guidelines were re-imposed in 1982.

In anticipation of Ireland's signing of the SEA these formal guidelines were ended in 1984. This began a process of dramatic financial liberalisation, driven by Ireland's adaptation to European integration. In 1988 there was a major relaxation of credit controls, and Ireland began to liberalise and deregulate the entire financial sector in accordance with preparation for the completion of the Single Market in 1993 (Kelly and Everett 2004, 95–8; see also Central Bank of Ireland 2013). Just like Greece and Portugal, Ireland's participation in the 're-launch' of Europe from the 1980s onwards signalled considerable changes for the terms and conditions for capital movements, domestic banking, and stock-market trading. Restrictions on credit-growth and interest rate rules were progressively dismantled by 1992, capital controls were removed, and banks' reserve requirements were reduced from 10 percent to 6 percent in 1992, falling further to 2 percent in 1999 (Kelly 2014, 42). Additionally, as was happening across the EU as a result of Single Market reforms, Irish banks expanded their operations overseas and widened their deposit bases (Kelly 2014, 43). Irish banks such as Anglo Irish Bank, Allied Irish Bank, and Bank of Ireland opened branches in the UK and elsewhere, contributing to massive flows of lending from the UK into Ireland (Kelly 2014, 43; Dooley 2014, 945). In other words, the seeds of Ireland's notorious 'light touch regulation' and highly liberalised banking sector were sown from as early as this period; and crucially, this transformation was driven by changes at the EU level.

In addition to the dismantling of controls, adaptation to European integration during this period drove the development of a more competitive banking environment in Ireland, which increased the availability of credit and reduced its cost (Central Bank of Ireland, various years). During the 1980s, the Irish banking sector was characterised by high levels of market concentration, an institutional segregation, and a limited set of capital market services (Kinsella and Bourke 2002, 166). The Single Market led to major changes to the competitive environment of Irish banking. Deregulation and EU policies including, but not limited to, the Single Passport for banking enabled new entrants to the Irish market. In fact, just months after the Second Banking Directive came into effect (early 1993) numerous UK credit institutions signalled their intention to provide banking services on a cross border basis in Ireland (Kinsella and Bourke 2002, 172). Halifax Bank of Scotland (HBOS), Rabobank, Northern rock, Royal Bank of Scotland (RBS) (trading as Ulster Bank), and Danske Bank (trading as National Irish Bank), were all operating in Ireland by 2003. This transformed the landscape of Irish retail banking, creating imperatives for growing competition (Kelly 2014, 44). RBS, on entering the mortgage market in 1999, had an immediate effect on the margins of competitors, and according to Bourke and Kinsella, writing as early as 2002, this had transformative effect on bank management's strategic thinking (175). Irish banks faced imperatives to defend their market share against foreign entrants like RBS (ibid) (Central Bank of Ireland 2002a). This new competition drove a transformation of banking practice, leading to expanding balance sheets 'regardless of risk' (Kelly 2014, 44). For instance, the introduction by HBOS of a 3.99 percent mortgage rate in 2001 had dramatic knock-on effects (Kelly 2014; see also Ross 2010) as other banks reduced their own mortgage rates in line. Banks also began to compete with new innovations, offering longer-term loans and higher loan-to-value ratios (Kelly 2014, 45). All the major banks were offering 90 percent mortgages by 2005, and First Active, a building society acquired by RBS in 2004, pioneered the notorious 100 percent mortgage soon after (Kelly 2014, 45; Cooper 2012, 239). Equity release loans became more common, and vetting of customer's ability to repay became laxer (Kelly 2014, 45). Domestic and these new foreign banks operating in Ireland were now free to compete in terms of the interest rates they could charge. All of this had a considerable impact on Ireland's mortgage markets (Kelly and Everett 2004, 97). 'Shareholder value' became a "strategic imperative" for Irish banks, who were suddenly operating on a European, rather than domestic scale, with all of the attendant competitive pressures (Kinsella and Bourke 2002, 175; Central Bank of Ireland 2002a).

Of particular importance, as Kelly (2014) notes, was the entrance of RBS into the Irish residential mortgage market in August 1999, trading as Ulster Bank, which resulted in a significant reduction in mortgage interest rates (Kelly and Everett 2004, 97; Cooper 2012, 239–41; Central Bank of Ireland 2002a). With the increasing presence of foreign banks in Ireland, Irish financial institutions faced more pressure to be competitive and this promoted the practice of short-term lending, and a culture of bonus payments to financial managers who could successfully meet or exceed targets through short-term lending (Kelly 2014, 37). This promoted the kind of reckless lending practices that were to characterise the transformation of Ireland from an export-led model of growth to a debt-led model in the 2000s with the property boom.

Such reckless lending was further propelled by the increasing availability of cheap foreign capital following waves of capital market liberalisation in Europe, which subsequently exploded following the introduction of the euro. Irish banks found themselves having much greater freedom to set their own liquidity management and interest rate policies since the Single Market (Kelly 2014, 42). Borrowing decisions also began to become affected from 1998 onwards when it was announced that Ireland would join EMU. Against the background of capital liberalisation and structural change in the financial sector, Irish banks were able to respond quickly when demand for credit strengthened (Kelly and Everett 2004, 98). Even before EMU membership provided Irish banks with significant sources of cheap foreign capital, the provisions of the Single Market meant that Irish banks were becoming increasingly internationalised.

In addition to the domestic banking sector that was most clearly implicated in fuelling the property bubble (mainly through banks such as Anglo Irish Bank, Bank of Ireland, and Allied Irish Bank), a brand new transnational banking sector emerged in Ireland from the mid-1980s and 1990s onwards. Much as Irish state agencies had identified the high-technology sector as an emerging sector that could be attracted to Ireland, the financial services industry began to be courted to set up firms in Ireland (Hendrikse 2013; Ó Riain 2014; Kelly 2014, 42). This was most emblematic in the International Financial Services Centre (IFSC), which was established in Dublin's docklands area in the late-1980s. Financial companies such as Citibank, Mellon Investment, Merrill Lynch, Chase Manhattan, and Deutsche Bank set up in the IFSC, bringing with them knowledge of new technologies of financial innovation as well as new and lucrative channels of access to international financial markets (Kelly, 2014, 42). Hendrikse (2013) writes about how the attraction of financial services enterprises was an explicit developmental strategy for Ireland, as Ó Riain (2014, 2012, 508) has also noted. The presence of these enterprises and the Irish government's desire to continue to develop the financial services sector created incentives for light touch regulation, as well as favourable tax incentives to the banking and financial sector – a regime that extended much beyond the 'City of London' style offshore IFSC (Hendrikse 2013). Hendrikse argues that the Irish property bubble grew in the shadows of the IFSC:

> as much as the Irish regulator did not police transnational finance in Dublin, it equally failed to detect the huge risks built up in its domestic banks. In other words, national and transnational financial institutions made use of the same institutional setting.
>
> (Hendrikse 2013, 191)

Accordingly, public bodies that were responsible for the regulation of the banking sector became heavily committed to the promotion of increased competition and liberalisation (Kelly 2014, 42). This dual role resulted in the timidity and complacence that Irish regulatory bodies have been accused of by the former governor of the Irish Central Bank in the course of an ongoing Irish banking inquiry into the causes of the crisis (Honohan 2010; Nyberg 2011). The Irish Financial Services Regulatory Authority (IFSRA), established in 2003, had an explicit goal to "foster an internationally competitive and successful financial services industry" within the context of its regulatory practice (Kelly 2014, 43). There has, unsurprisingly, been clear evidence of regulatory capture (McGrath 2010).

Ireland's debt-led growth as an outcome of European integration

The narrative in this chapter suggests that we cannot fully understand the property bubble of the 1990s without accounting for the EC/EU encouraged deregulation and liberalisation of the banking sector in Ireland from the late 1980s onwards. As was the case for Greece and Portugal, Ireland's participation in the EU's 'one market, one money' project since 1986 has had a dramatic transformative effect on its economy. While the role of credit in Ireland's export-led boom is disputed (Kelly and Everett 2004; Honohan 2006) – the EU reforms discussed here were setting the scene for a parallel pattern of growth that was to become fully activated following the EMU interest rate shock of the 2000s and the separate decline of the export-led growth following the dot-com crash of 2001–3. We cannot understand the unprecedented property bubble during this period without accounting for the EU reforms of the 1980s and 1990s. This suggests that existing explanations that focus only on pro-cyclical government policy during the 2000s are incomplete. While this undoubtedly contributed to the boom, former Central Bank governor John Hurley is correct when he claimed in the Oireachtas banking inquiry (2016) on 21st May 2015 that he didn't believe that "regulation could have prevented the crash and said international factors played a crucial role" (*The Irish Times* 2015). Irish governments in the early 2000s certainly encouraged the bubble when they could have reigned it in (Regling and Watson 2010). Yet, it is crucial to recognise that, in the decade before, European integration had already helped create an aggressive banking sector capable of driving debt-led growth. Irish governments may have failed to halt the bubble, but European financial integration helped it to emerge in the first place (Dooley 2015c).

Thus, just like Greece and Portugal, Ireland's crisis is intimately bound up in its adaptation to the project of European integration. This conclusion makes it possible to recognise that European integration can have a distinctly paradoxical impact on a small peripheral economy such as Ireland. As I suggested in the second section the Single Market and EMU are widely considered to have, at the very least, facilitated Ireland's export-led boom during the 1990s, and were certainly a significant factor in increasing overall US FDI to Europe from the late 1980s onwards (Cahill and O'Donnell 2010). It is reasonable to assume that Ireland would not have emerged as the prominent destination for US FDI into Europe without this deepening of European integration. Yet, as I have argued in this section; pursuing export-led growth via the specific blueprint of the Single Market and EMU also led to unintended transformations in the Irish economy. The specific reforms, policies, and institutions that were involved in Ireland's adaptation to Europe from the late 1980s onwards did far more than simply complement its export-led development strategy. They also set the scene for a banking crisis so severe that Ireland found itself returning to the periphery of Europe. Ireland thus owes a great deal of its success, but also its crisis, to its Europeanisation.

Conclusion

In this final case study, I traced Ireland's remarkable economic trajectory from the 'sick man of Europe' in its first 50–60 years of independence, to its status as the 'poster child' of European integration in the 1990s, to an apparent full circle return as one of the worst-hit economies of the European PIIGS in the 2000s. I make two important claims to account for this trajectory. First of all, Ireland's Celtic Tiger boom should be analytically separated from the property bubble of the 2000s. Since the 1950s, the Irish state, through a variety of institutional and policy innovations, consolidated a model of export-led development that allowed Ireland to take advantage of the 1990s US boom and the completion of the Single Market between 1994 and 2001. If 'institutional stickiness' has been a key characteristic of Greece and Portugal's inability to generate successful export-led growth in the 1990s and 2000s, Ireland is a contrasting story of a long, relatively successful period of institutional transformation.

This narrative represents a challenge to the beggar-thy-neighbour thesis. Since the late 1950s Ireland managed to negotiate its European integration to generate a high-technology, export-oriented model of modernisation. Ireland's relationship with Europe has thus never been straightforwardly negative. Nevertheless, as a small, open liberalised economy, Ireland was clearly exposed to any potential downturn in the US economy, and the Celtic Tiger model suffered a major crisis in the early years of the 2000s. It is showing clear signs of recovery since 2015, but vulnerabilities relating to the impact of Brexit and EU competition policy loom on the Irish horizon.

The second important claim that I make is that the parallel pattern of debt-fuelled property speculation has its origins in the capital market liberalisation, deregulation, and financial integration associated with Ireland's adaptation to the re-launched European project since the 1980s. Ireland's participation in the 'one market, one money' project was taken for granted, as it was viewed as a vital aspect of the Celtic Tiger export-led growth. Yet, somewhat ironically, the specific reforms that were introduced as part of this project set the scene for Ireland's banking crisis. Existing accounts that limit their analysis to domestic policy errors in the 2000s have tended to overlook this longer history, and in doing so, fail to recognise how new and more aggressive lending strategies by banks emerged quite directly as a result of these transformations in the late 1980s and 1990s.

This suggests an intriguing conclusion. Despite Ireland's mature, 'core European' style export-led growth in the 1990s, it was not invulnerable to the deleterious effects of 'following the rules' of European financial integration during this period. Ireland certainly benefitted in the earlier decades from European integration, and the success of its export-led model was almost certainly unthinkable outside of the EC/EU and indeed outside of the euro and the Single Market. Yet, financial integration in Europe led to unintended consequences in Ireland, catalysing parallel patterns of growth from the late 1980s onwards. Just like Greece and Portugal, adhering to a one-size-fits-all model of integration contributed to unexpected, and detrimental patterns of divergence in Ireland. Contrary to the claims of the immaturity thesis, Ireland's difficulties do not stem entirely from its 'getting the policies wrong' in the 2000s. They also stem from its following of those EU driven policies deemed to be 'right' since the late 1980s.

Notes

1 For overviews, see the following accounts: Honohan and Walsh 2002; Whelan 2013; Lane 2011; Ahearne, Schmitz, and von Hagen 2008; Hardiman 2010; Honohan and Leddin 2005; Ó Riain 2014, 36–38; Kinsella 2012.
2 This is a widely influential assessment. See Honohan 2010; O'Toole 2010; Ross 2010; Byrne 2012; Carswell 2012; Cooper 2012; Hardiman 2012; Ó Riain 2012, 2014.
3 See Kirby (2010, 71–217) for a close to exhaustive account of the different perspectives.
4 Renamed the Industrial Development Agency (Ireland), or IDA Ireland, in 1994.
5 Fears about the 'vanishing Irish' were common, see O'Brien (1953).
6 Later renamed the Industrial Development Agency Ireland.
7 £ refers to the Irish punt.
8 GNP is a better measure than GDP due to the key role of FDI in Ireland's economy.
9 But naturally, as I show in the third section, Ireland's export-led growth is not the only story to be told about this period.
10 For overviews, see Ó Riain 2014, 61; Kirby 2010; Lane 2011; Regling and Watson 2010; Cooper 2012; Drudy and Collins 2011; European Commission 2012b; Whelan 2013; Rae and van den Noord 2006.
11 A charge first levelled by Eamon Gilmore, former leader of the Irish Labour Party and Tánaiste (deputy Prime Minister) from 2011 to 2014, at the Fianna Fáil–Green Party coalition government responsible for the bill; although the guarantee is not without its defenders, see Donovan and Murphy (2013).
12 See O'Sullivan and Kennedy 2009; Kelly 2014; and also see Kelly and Everett 2004, 91 for how little attention has been paid to this.

7 Conclusion

Divergence via Europeanisation

In the foregoing chapters, I have shown how EU reforms and 'following the rules' of European financial integration have, counter-intuitively, helped propel the European periphery down divergent paths; paths that ultimately led them to their respective crises. The origins of the eurozone crisis were investigated across three of the worst-hit countries; Greece, Portugal, and Ireland. By bringing literature on Europeanisation studies into dialogue with the insights of CPE, this book has examined the ways in which 'divergence via Europeanisation' has resulted in the generation of fragile economic trajectories in each country.

In this concluding chapter, I bring together the three case studies to draw out the concept of 'divergence via Europeanisation', which was first introduced in Chapter 3. In doing so, I set out the central contribution of this book. I show that the eurozone crisis cannot be fully explained by narratives that stress the 'immaturity' of the countries of the European periphery. Neither can it be explained by more critical narratives that understand the periphery as a victim of German or core 'economic domination'. Instead, the European periphery got into trouble just as much by 'following the rules' of European integration as it did by failing or being unable to.

I conclude this argument over three sections. First, I recap the central research question that has animated this study: what explains the asymmetry of the eurozone crisis? In other words, why were the countries of the European periphery affected more severely than the core, and what explains the multiple paths to crisis experienced by Greece, Portugal, and Ireland? Second, I bring together the findings of the three case studies to outline the concept of 'divergence of Europeanisation'. I show how a CPE approach reveals the role of institutional stickiness in placing limits on the ability of the European periphery to converge with the core in terms of developing patterns of export-led growth. However, at the same time, I show how the Europeanisation of banking and finance led to different, yet equally damaging processes of institutional transformation in each case. Finally, I bring the book to a close by drawing out the broader significance of my argument for important debates on the origins – and future development – of the eurozone crisis.

Explaining the asymmetry of the eurozone crisis

I began this book by recognising that existing literature on the eurozone crisis has been unable to account for its asymmetric impact. The eurozone crisis has had a detrimental impact across Europe, but the countries of the European periphery have been affected more severely than others (Hardiman and Dellepiane 2010, 473). Moreover, the individual countries of the European periphery have followed considerably different paths to crisis, making it more difficult than might be expected to speak of the eurozone crisis as a single phenomenon. If there have been multiple paths to the eurozone crisis, it follows that any policy response will need to take this asymmetry into account. Yet, existing debates have tended to downplay, or explain away, this asymmetry.

Chapter 2 explored a tendency, common to both mainstream and more critical accounts of the eurozone crisis, to fall back upon and reproduce one of two problematic narratives on the asymmetry of the eurozone crisis. These were labelled the 'immaturity' and the 'beggar-thy-neighbour' theses. The immaturity thesis accounts for the relative severity of the crisis in the PIIGS by stressing the central roles of fiscal profligacy, corruption, and pathological patterns of national and political culture. Had the periphery introduced 'painful but necessary' structural reforms in the decades before the crisis, the sovereign debt crisis could perhaps have been avoided. Such assumptions continue to generate reams of commentary on Greece, and more recently Italy (Fleischhauer 2018), but the following analysis of Portugal exemplifies this argument as well as anything else:

> [t]here is a social psychological explanation for . . . [the low productivity of the Portuguese economy] . . . related to the lack of transformation of the values of Portuguese society, which tend to go counter with a competitive ethos and emphasize a lack of ambition in pushing through major objectives.
>
> (Magone 2004, 223)

The second perspective challenges the immaturity thesis by reinterpreting the eurozone as a region characterised by a beggar-thy-neighbour hierarchy between the economic growth of the core, which leads to precarious, 'financialised' growth in the periphery. Germany's economic strategy is centred on low domestic demand, export-led growth, and a firm commitment to ordoliberal values. Germany has reputedly used the euro to advance this strategy at the direct expense of the European periphery. Proponents of this approach have seemingly been vindicated, time and again, by Germany's intransigent response to the crisis. It makes perfect sense that Germany should be so inflexible in its negotiations with Greece; it has directly profited from the very unfairness that Syriza and others want so desperately to change (Dooley 2015b).

I have shown that each of these underlying assumptions have acted as obstacles to our understandings of the asymmetry of the eurozone crisis, primarily due to their deductive approach to identifying 'obstacles to convergence' in Greece, Portugal, and Ireland. Perspectives underpinned by assumptions of peripheral 'immaturity' share meta-theoretical assumptions with modernisation theory, they have propagated analysis that is insensitive to the ways in which development is pursued and achieved differently across societies (Lyberaki and Tsakalotos 2002, 93, 95; Eisenstadt 2000; Rosenberg 2006) – thereby merely offering explanations as to why the periphery failed to generate export-oriented patterns of growth, rather than accounting for the three dramatically different forms of divergence that emerged. On the other hand, core–periphery analysis was found to have overstated the 'structural role' of the periphery for Germany and the core in their generation of trade surpluses and as a destination for capital outflows. The empirical case for a beggar-thy-neighbour relationship between Germany and the periphery was exposed as seriously limited. Moreover, while the immaturity thesis conflates a 'failure to converge' with an explanation of divergence (Hancké 2009) narratives of German/core domination account for all divergence as a passive function of external economic domination. To adequately understand the asymmetry of the eurozone crisis, I claimed that we need to move beyond limiting narratives of blame.

To this end, in Chapter 3 I proposed an analytical framework, which combined Europeanisation studies focus on the 'domestic adaptation to European regional integration' (Vink and Graziano 2007) with CPE focus on capitalist diversity and institutional path dependence. While Europeanisation and CPE have both long been sensitive to the differential impact of Europeanisation, each literature has tended to account for this difference with reference to the 'persistence' of national diversity. In other words, asymmetry is explained as continuity with the past, and, in a theoretically meaningful sense, a lack of transformation in the face of the pressures of European integration. In Chapter 3 I developed an analytical framework that would investigate how Europeanisation has in fact been generative of institutional transformation in the European periphery, while at the same time recognising the role of institutional 'stickiness' highlighted by CPE. Combining these two literatures proved very productive, as it made it possible to study the ways in which domestic adaptation to European integration (Europeanisation) lead to institutional transformation – the fundamental transformation of existing domestic structures – and to the emergence of radically new hybrid domestic structures and patterns of growth. The periphery diverged from the core in terms of patterns of economic growth, due to its Europeanisation. At the same time, institutional stickiness placed obstacles in the path of Greece, Portugal, and Ireland's attempts to converge with the core in terms of export-led growth.

Divergence via Europeanisation

The central argument of this book is that the Europeanisation of banking sectors in Greece, Portugal, and Ireland has acted as a catalyst for the emergence of multiple patterns of precarious, non-competitive debt-led growth. The three case studies can thus be drawn together to develop the concept of 'divergence via Europeanisation'. Drawing on CPE, this book recognises that institutional stickiness played a role in limiting the convergence of the periphery with the core in terms of generating export-led growth. However, path dependence of national VoC is not the entire story. Each case study revealed the crucial role of institutional transformation in the origins of the eurozone crisis. The European periphery's attempt to adapt to Europe in terms of reforming its banking and financial sector was generative of non-uniform, but decidedly fragile, crisis-prone patterns of debt-led growth.

Beginning with the supposed epicentre of the eurozone crisis, Chapter 4 investigated the case of Greece. Much existing literature tends to emphasise the 'exceptional' character of the Greek crisis, setting it apart from not just Western Europe, but also, at times, from its fellow peripheral states. Jason Manolopoulos has perhaps been less equivocal than many when outlining a nevertheless familiar sentiment – 'Greece is not a Western country' (Manolopoulos 2011, 61). In contrast, this book has emphasised how the crisis in Greece is better understood as having both 'exceptional' and 'non-exceptional' roots. While it would be misguided to downplay Greece's poor record in reforming, *inter alia*, its public sector, welfare system, tax collection, and pension provision, it was shown that these putatively 'immature' processes only tell part of the story. First, ambitious attempts by successive Greek governments in the 1980s to reverse processes of deindustrialisation contributed to a legacy of chronic public finances, and did little to realise aspirations of high-technology, export-led growth in the decades to follow. Second, recognising that Greece's current difficulties have a fiscal and a competitiveness component, I have shown that we can best trace the origins of the latter by studying the impact of Europeanisation during the 1990s and 2000s.

In the early years of the Third Hellenic Republic, the Greek banking sector was highly regulated, controlled, and subject to state intervention. Preparations for the European Single Market and the euro led to its wholesale transformation. Liberalisation and deregulation made it possible for the Greek banking sector to drive a decade of above average GDP growth (Pagoulatos 2014). Between 2004 and 2008, private consumption was responsible for about 72 percent of Greece's GDP growth, and much of this was made possible through access to easy credit provided by a competitive banking sector (Bank of Greece 2010, 21). By the time the global financial crisis hit, Greece's economy was therefore highly vulnerable to a sudden stop of capital and a subsequent recession. Debt-led domestic demand also widened Greece's current account deficit in the years before the eurozone crisis, further signalling vulnerability to international speculators. Greece's trade deficit certainly reflected a lack of impressive export performance, but it was import penetration driven by buoyant domestic demand that was pivotal. Thus, the Europeanisation of Greece's banking sector contributed to its recession, current account deficit, and even to the country's fiscal problems as, from 2007 onwards, tax receipts related to private consumption dried up.

Nevertheless, Chapter 4 also showed how the impact of European integration on Greece has not been entirely consistent. Greece's poor reform capacity certainly contributed to its fiscal and sovereign debt crisis in 2009. Furthermore, although economic growth in Greece became driven by credit-fuelled domestic demand, as was the case in Ireland and Portugal, Greece ended up with one of the lowest levels of private and household debt in the eurozone and, unlike Ireland, Greece was quite clearly not a banking crisis (Pagoulatos and Triantopoulos 2009; Pasiouras 2012). Indeed, Greece's poor reform capacity worked in its favour, as Pagoulatos and Triantopoulos (2009) note. The performance of the Greek banking sector was relatively lacking when compared with other EU member states. "This relative 'underdevelopment', including the lack of exposure of Greek banks to 'toxic' products, proved beneficial during the current financial crisis" (37). As such, Greece's problems – somewhat incongruously – were caused just as much by the EU-driven reforms it succeeded in introducing, as by those it failed to. This suggests that, although the fiscal and debt crisis may have been greatly mitigated, there is little guarantee that the introduction of 'painful but necessary reforms' from the 1980s onwards would have ensured the good economic health of Greece today. Greece's crisis can be understood as stemming from a combination of adopting certain EU driven changes, while resisting others.

Chapter five turned to the 'difficult story' of Portugal (Krugman 2011). Much like Greece, Portugal lacked the various institutional advantages of core European economies such as Germany, which could have aided the development of export-led growth. Characterised by a predominance of SMEs, an uneven system of skill formation, non-coordinated wage bargaining systems, and a historical specialism in low- to medium-technology manufacturing exports, Portugal was always highly vulnerable to negative developments in its external environment. During the 2000s Portugal faced fierce competition from low-cost manufacturers in East Asia, North Africa, Eastern Europe, and other areas (Corkill 1999, 158; Lains 2007), which contributed to a decade of stagnant growth, trade deficits, and ultimately helped signal the weakness of Portugal to international speculators following the Greek and Irish bailouts. However, the institutional limits to Portuguese export success were not exhaustive of its path to crisis. The Europeanisation of Portugal's banking sector contributed to the generation of a damaging period of debt-led growth.

Following the Carnation Revolution, Portugal's banking sector was virtually completely nationalised. There were strict controls on new entrants, interest rates were fixed, and consumer lending was practically non-existent (Pinho 2002). The Single Market project led to the dramatic transformation of Portuguese banking. Liberalisation, privatisation, and deregulation were swift and profound, and by the mid-1990s a newly invigorated banking sector intensified competition for mortgage, consumer, and private lending. The Portuguese economy grew by an average of close to 4 percent between 1997 and 2000, and approximately 70 percent of this growth was attributable to private consumption, which in turn was driven to an important extent by bank lending (Royo 2012a, 206); Banco de Portugal 2009, 2010). This new pattern of debt-led growth contributed to the widening of Portugal's current account deficit from the 1990s, over-indebtedness dampened consumer demand and acted as an obstacle to investment from the 2000s, and credit tended to be allocated to the less productive, non-tradable sector throughout. The Europeanisation of Portuguese banking set a number of 'structural weaknesses' in motion, which helped make Portugal appear as the next domino to fall at the height of the eurozone crisis. This experience sets Portugal apart from Greece and Ireland. As the 'good pupil' of Europe (Delors 2013), Portugal's rapid adoption of EU reforms relating to banking and finance led to a relatively early pattern of private indebtedness during the 1990s. This suggests that, unlike the other cases, Portugal did not experience the interest rate shock of EMU with an increase in domestic demand or an acceleration of GDP (Deutsche Bank 2010). Portugal exhausted its domestic demand-led growth at a much earlier stage that Ireland and Greece (Lagoa et al. 2014, 66). In other words, like Greece, the Europeanisation of Portugal's economic trajectory during the 1990s catalysed a divergent and fragile trajectory of growth. Implementing the reforms necessary to take part in the Single Market and EMU helped transform Portugal's economy into one that was increasingly inward looking and debt driven; and fated to burn out rapidly.

The final case study departed Southern Europe for the North Atlantic. Chapter six traced the decline of Ireland's export-led 'Celtic Tiger' boom of the 1990s, and the emergence of a credit-fuelled property boom in the 2000s. For Ireland, participating in the Single Market and EMU emerged as 'a new zone of consensus' (Antoniades 2010, 146) that had much to do with Ireland's export-oriented strategy of modernisation – which would have been unthinkable outside of the Single Market and EMU (Ahern 2004). Ireland's experience of the 'one market, one money' project was initially highly positive, and especially so during the 1990s. It was during this period that Greece and Portugal were beginning to find their economies dominated by domestic demand; while in contrast, Ireland was experiencing more balanced economic growth underpinned by an unprecedented export boom. Ireland's Celtic Tiger was made possible by long-standing state-led institutional innovations in FDI attraction, but only fully activated once Ireland joined the Single Market, thus becoming a uniquely attractive location for inward investment from the USA. Path dependency characterised the fortunes of export-led growth in Greece and Portugal, whereas the role of long-term institutional transformations proved crucial in the case of Ireland.

Nevertheless, as a small open peripheral economy, Ireland's export sector is always vulnerable to shifts in its external environment. Ireland's recovery since its economic crisis has largely been driven by the relative buoyancy of its export sector, which is lacking in Portugal and Greece. In the early 2000s the dot.com crash resulted in declining FDI in Ireland, and two major threats loom on Ireland's contemporary horizon. First, Ireland is exposed to Brexit in a way that no other EU member state is. Bilateral trade between the Republic of Ireland and the UK amounts to approximately €1 billion per week (McGrane 2016), and Ireland's goods and services exports to Britain amount to about 17 percent of its total exports (RTÉ News 2017). The risk of a 'hard Brexit', if Britain leaves both the Single Market and the Customs Union, is profound for Ireland's economic recovery. Second, Ireland is vulnerable to developments coming from the European Commission relating to how Ireland taxes MNCs. The decision that Ireland had breached EU competition rules by providing Apple with an effective corporation tax rate of close to 0 percent exposes potential conflict between Ireland's 'industrialisation by invitation' growth model, and the European Commission's agenda (Nienaber 2018). Ireland's export success sets it apart from Greece and Portugal, but its vulnerabilities are nonetheless apparent.

European integration was seen (not without warrant) as a necessary and indispensable part of Ireland's modern and vibrant export-led growth, and yet, at the same time, Ireland's eagerness to adapt to the European model created the conditions for a severe banking crisis a decade later. 'Light touch' regulation and a pro-cyclical fiscal policy undoubtedly played a major role in spurring on the property bubble when it could have been reigned in (Regling and Watson 2010), just as 'debt-fuelled clientelism' played an important role in Greece. Yet Ireland's adaptation to the Single Market and EMU also facilitated the emergence of a highly liberalised and increasingly aggressive banking sector, a process beginning as early as the late 1980s. In anticipation of joining the European Single Market and preparing for EMU, Ireland began to dismantle its relatively regulated and controlled banking sector, which was nevertheless fairly liberal when compared with Greece and Portugal. With the increasing presence of foreign banks in Ireland, partially as a result of the EU's 'Single Passport' directive, Irish financial institutions faced more pressure to be competitive and this promoted the practice of lending funds and "a culture of bonus payments to financial manages on the basis of short-term success in meeting or exceeding lending targets" (Kelly 2014, 37). Ireland also set itself apart from Greece and Portugal by explicitly attracting a transnational financial sector to set up in Dublin's docklands from the 1980s onwards, as part of a broader developmental strategy of FDI attraction (Ó Riain 2012, 508). Each of these factors promoted the kind of reckless lending practices that were to characterise the transformation of Ireland from an export-led model of growth to a debt-led model in the 2000s with the property boom. The scene was set for the Irish property boom in the fifteen years before it began. Ireland may have eagerly participated in the Single Market and EMU to promote its export-oriented modernisation strategy, but in doing so it unintentionally created the conditions for a property boom and a banking crisis. While the Celtic Tiger boom may almost certainly have been unthinkable (Ahern 2004) without a strong commitment to European integration, the very same commitment also contributed to Ireland's banking crisis a decade later. The Irish case suggests that the consolidation of sustainable, putatively mature trajectories of export-led growth were little defence against the emergence of EU-facilitated, precarious patterns of debt-led growth.

The preceding case studies reflect the different ways in which the 'one size fits all' model of European integration was adapted domestically in Greece, Portugal, and Ireland. Paying attention to the differential impact of Europeanisation in this way is important because it makes it possible to explain sources of economic divergence, in a way that approaches emphasising passive external restructuring are ill-equipped to recognise. The periphery certainly experienced disastrous consequences from its attempt to adapt to the 'one market, one money' project. But these consequences played out in very different ways and took on very distinct, not at all consistent, forms. Each country can be said to have encountered crisis through a combination of following some of the rules of European integration and not following others. Chronic public finances and grossly inadequate financial regulation played a pivotal role in Greece and Ireland respectively. But those stories are incomplete without recognising the processes set in motion by the Europeanisation of banking across the European periphery.

Rethinking the eurozone crisis

The argument of this book has clear significance for scholars working on the origins of the eurozone crisis. Above all it has stressed the need for existing literature to take the asymmetry of the eurozone crisis more seriously, and to move beyond the problematic and limiting paradigm of 'immaturity' versus German/core 'economic domination'. Neither approach was capable of adequately accounting for the many different paths to crisis taken by the countries of the European periphery. The significance of 'divergence via Europeanisation' for narratives of immaturity and victimisation can be interpreted as follows. First, while overcoming the important limitations of each narrative, I do not suggest that Greece, Portugal, and Ireland are fully absolved from responsibility for their own crises. Second, neither do I propose that the absence of beggar-thy-neighbour dynamics between core and periphery should shut down important debates about inequality and hierarchy within the EU and the eurozone, or regarding Germany's possibly (re-)emergent role as a hegemon, reluctant or otherwise (Bulmer and Paterson 2013).

Rather, in overcoming some of their limitations, my argument aims to contribute to these existing debates in two main ways. First, although I have stressed the hitherto overlooked 'non-exceptional' catalysts of divergence in Greece, Portugal, and Ireland, to ignore parallel 'exceptional' catalysts of divergence would be to simply invert the problem. For instance, it would be misleading to ignore the role of 'poor reform capacity' in driving Greece's fiscal crisis, just as it would be equally limiting to downplay the role of Europeanisation in driving its competitiveness crisis. The argument presented can potentially act as a complement to domestic-level approaches by inviting them to broaden their analytical scope to consider more than simply the readily apparent 'exceptional' causes of peripheral crises. Such an approach can offer a deeper understanding of the crises in Greece, Portugal, and Ireland that a straightforward rejection of the 'official narrative' would miss out on. As it turns out, 'exceptional' factors are more useful at explaining asymmetry between the periphery themselves (poor reform capacity in Greece versus procyclical fiscal policy in Ireland) than they are at explaining divergence between the core and periphery.

Second, although I have challenged narratives of German/core economic domination, the concept of divergence via Europeanisation speaks to important debates surrounding the role of Germany, the design flaws of the EU, and the production of hierarchies within Europe. Beggar-thy-neighbour dynamics between core and periphery have been theoretically and empirically challenged, but this does not mean that Germany has not still, perhaps uniquely, benefitted from the institutional character of the euro. As I made clear in Chapter 2, the European project has certainly been tailored to a specific, one size fits all model of development in mind. We do not need beggar-thy-neighbour assumptions to recognise that this model may reflect the interests and work to the benefit of certain member states while disadvantaging others. Indeed, my argument has the potential to deepen these existing debates and hierarchy in Europe by inviting critical scholars to jettison empirically limited assumptions of 'dependency'. Europeanisation shows the variety of ways in which the periphery managed to follow, or not to follow, the rules of European integration, which explains their multiple forms of crisis. The consequence of this is that the periphery was not passively reshaped by European integration. Yet, it is nevertheless vital to remember that the countries of Western Europe have long been synonymous with being both 'modern' and 'European'. The countries of the European periphery were thus situated at the bottom of a foundational inequality, because they were seeking to confirm their 'Europeanness' and modernity by reforming and converging with or towards a model of development that has been defined by 'core' Europe (Giurlando 2012). The burden of adjustment and convergence was thus on these peripheral states and not the core (an inequality well-articulated in this way by Triandafyllidou, Gropas, and Kouki 2013). As such, the concept of 'divergence via Europeanisation' has the potential to enhance existing debates on hierarchy, the role of Germany, and the unequal position of the periphery in a more dynamic way. It is better able to recognise capitalist diversity between the core and periphery, and among the countries of the periphery themselves. Above all, it is capable of showing the unintended consequences of 'following the rules'.

The approach I have developed accepts the invitation extended by Bache, Bulmer, and Gunay (2011) for Europeanisation studies and CPE to engage more closely with one another (Dooley 2017b, 16). The authors note that Europeanisation literature has portrayed itself as an analytical framework or a valuable 'attention-directing device' rather than a theory in its own right. This framing has led to the neglect of meta-theoretical reflection (although see recent important exceptions from Exadaktylos and Radaelli 2012; Graziano and Vink 2007). This insight echoes the points made in this book – in that it has tended to smuggle in unilinear conceptions of development into its debates regarding divergence and convergence. CPE approaches such as VoC are highly productive at identifying the perfect storm of sticky national institutions and a flawed in design EMU. However, an excessive focus on path dependence can be rectified by bringing it into dialogue with Europeanisation's focus on institutional transformation. Bache, Bulmer, and Gunay note that Europeanisation literature has "not yet caught up with the Eurozone crisis"; however, to place it within the limitations of a conventional understanding "would be a very incomplete account" (2011, 18). This book suggests that it may be just as important for IPE and CPE literature on the eurozone crisis to catch up with the study of Europeanisation. The concept of 'divergence via Europeanisation' clearly shows the potential of a dialogue between these two literatures to do just that.

Similarly, this book speaks to ongoing debates within IPE and CPE regarding capitalist diversity. Scholars working within critical political economy (Ebenau, Bruff, and May 2015), VoC (Johnston 2016; Hall 2018; Johnston and Regan 2016), and Uneven and Combined Development (Sandbeck and Schneider 2013) have all attempted to understand the eurozone crisis by bringing their respective sensitivity to the diversity of economic development to existing debates. Similarly, Bruff (2010) notes the need for IPE to reconcile the role of the 'international' in accounting for distinctive national trajectories of development. Yet, the persistence of narratives of immaturity and core economic domination in existing accounts suggests that the modernisation versus dependency theory debate hasn't fully gone away, at least for analysis of the eurozone crisis. While discussions on capitalist diversity suggest intriguing alternatives to this debate, Bruff and Ebenau (2014, 4) recognise that there has only recently been a reflection within discourse on capitalist diversity on the implications of the eurozone crisis for their respective frameworks (see Hall 2018; Ebenau, Bruff, and May 2015; Clift 2014). Although it remains for future research to investigate more fully, the concept of divergence via Europeanisation, together with the case studies of Greece, Portugal, and Ireland, provide a useful reference point for deeper reflection on issues of diversity and the role of the institutional transformation in contemporary CPE. There is potential for the empirical contributions offered here to complement these kinds of debates on the eurozone crisis, but to also contribute to theoretical debates on capitalist diversity within CPE more generally.

If the eurozone crisis is neither solely a crisis of Greece nor Germany, the argument presented here could be brought fruitfully in relation to literature on the 'design flaws' of the eurozone. In various ways, these approaches emphasise that the eurozone crisis was an institutional one, stressing that we need to understand the crisis in the periphery in that context. The argument presented here invites 'design flaw' perspectives to interrogate the notions of asymmetry that underpin their own arguments. While these approaches focus on how EMU lacked the requisite discipline or how it did not promote a 'genuine' union involving banking, fiscal, and perhaps federal union, I have argued that the real institutional flaw in the European project was not that it lacked *enough* convergence. It is that the very promotion of convergence has generated multiple and unexpected patterns of divergence. Hence the distinction made in the introduction between convergence as a *process* and convergence as a *project*. National and supranational projects of convergence were prophesised to create pressures towards a process of convergence of the periphery with the core (Hall 2014). I argue instead that these very projects of convergence set in motion real processes of *divergence*.

This book also speaks to contemporary debates on the policy response to the eurozone crisis. The ongoing official reaction to the crisis in the periphery has centred on the correction of peripheral immaturity. The PIIGS got into difficulty because of their failure to reform in the decades before the crisis, risking their own stability and the very survival of the eurozone. If this diagnosis is accepted, it is easy to sympathise with claims that without economic and social reforms such as those prescribed by the troika, Greece will remain a relatively poor country: so, if the Greeks chose poverty, "let them have their way" (Giavazzi 2015). By illuminating the central and adverse role of Europeanisation in catalysing non-productive, debt-led patterns of growth across three peripheral countries, this book adds to the already long list of reasons why such a response is gravely misguided. Addressing only the 'exceptional' origins of the crisis fails to tackle the 'non-exceptional' causes. And if Greece, Portugal, and Ireland's crises were, to an important extent, an outcome of a flawed project of convergence, obliviously attempting to impose that same project is unlikely to ensure that all will be well for the eurozone.

Bibliography

Abdelal, Rawi. 2007. "Writing the Rules of Global Finance: France, Europe, and Capital Liberalization." SSRN Scholarly Paper ID 1007268. Rochester, NY: Social Science Research Network. http://papers.ssrn.com/abstract=1007268.

Abreu, Orlando. 2006. "Portugal's Boom and Bust: Lessons for Euro Newcomers." *ECFIN Country Focus* 3 (16): 1–6.

Adler-Nissen, Rebecca. 2017. "Are We 'Lazy Greeks' or 'Nazi Germans'?" In *Hierarchies in World Politics*, 198–218. Cambridge Studies in International Relations. Cambridge: Cambridge University Press. doi:10.1017/9781108241588.011.

Ahearne, Alan, Birgit Schmitz, and Jürgen von Hagen. 2008. "Current Account Imbalances in the Euro Area." In *Challenges of Globalization: Imbalances and Growth*, edited by Anders Åslund, and Marek Dabrowski. Washington DC: Peterson Institute for International Economics Centre for Social and Economic Research..

Ahern, Bertie. 2004. "Ireland and Europe: Embracing Change." In *Ireland and the European Union: The First Thirty Years*, edited by James Hourihane. Dublin: The Lilliput Press Ltd.

Alogoskoufis, George. 2000. "The Greek Economy and the Euro." In *Contemporary Greece and Europe*, edited by Achilleas Mitsos and Elias Mossialos. Aldershot; Burlington: Ashgate Publishing Limited.

———. 2012. "Greece's Sovereign Debt Crisis: Retrospect and Prospect." Monograph. January 2012. Hellenic Observatory's GreeSE Discussion Paper Series. London: LSE. http://www2.lse.ac.uk/europeanInstitute/research/hellenicObservatory/pubs/GreeSE.aspx.

Andreou, Alex. 2012. "Some Racism, It seems, Is Acceptable." *The Huffington Post UK* (blog). 5th January, 2012. http://www.huffingtonpost.co.uk/alex-andreou/racism-angelos-epithemiou_b_1181694.html.

Antoniades, Andreas. 2010. *Producing Globalisation: Politics of Discourse and Institutions in Greece and Ireland*. Manchester: Manchester University Press.

———. 2013. "At the Eye of the Cyclone: The Greek Crisis in Global Media." In *Greece's Horizons*, edited by Pantelis Sklias and Nikolaos Tzifakis, 11–25. The Konstantinos Karamanlis Institute for Democracy Series on European and International Affairs. Berlin; Heidelberg: Springer Nature.

Apeldoorn, Bastiaan van. 2012. "The European Capitalist Class and the Crisis of Its Hegemonic Project." In *Socialist Register 2013: The Question of Strategy*, edited by Leo Panitch, Gregory Albo, and Vivek Chibber. New York: Monthly Review Press.

Apeldoorn, Bastiaan van, Jan Drahokoupil, and Laura Horn. 2009. *Contradictions and Limits of Neoliberal European Governance: From Lisbon to Lisbon*. Basingstoke, UK; New York: Palgrave Macmillan.

Arnold, Jens. 2015. "Boosting Export Performance in Portugal," *OECD Economics Department Working Papers* no. 1257. OECD. https://doi.org/10.1787/5jrw21nm480q-en.

Baccaro, Lucio, and Jonas Pontusson. 2016. "Rethinking Comparative Political Economy: The Growth Model Perspective." *Politics & Society* 44 (2): 175–207. https://doi.org/10.1177/0032329216638053.

Bache, Ian, Simon Bulmer, and Defne Gunay. 2011. "Metatheory and Europeanization Research: Let's Get Critical!" Conference Paper presented at the 6th European Consortium for Political Research General Conference. Reykjavík.

Bache, Ian, Stephen George, Simon Bulmer, and Owen Parker. 2015. *Politics in the European Union*. 4th edition. Oxford: Oxford University Press.

Baer, Werner, and Antonio Nogueira Leite. 2003. "The Economy of Portugal within the European Union: 1990–2002." *The Quarterly Review of Economics and Finance* 43 (5): 738–54. https://doi.org/10.1016/S1062-9769(03)00047-4.

Bakker, Age. 1996. *The Liberalization of Capital Movements in Europe: The Monetary Committee and Financial Integration, 1958–1994*. Dordrecht, the Netherlands: Kluwer Academic Publishers.

Banco de Portugal. 1998. "Annual Report 1997." Lisbon: Banco de Portugal.

———. 1999. "Annual Report 1998." Lisbon: Banco de Portugal.

———. 2000. "Annual Report 1999." Lisbon: Banco de Portugal.

———. 2001. "Annual Report 2000." Lisbon: Banco de Portugal.

———. 2002. "Annual Report 2001." Lisbon: Banco de Portugal.

———. 2003. "Annual Report 2002." Lisbon: Banco de Portugal.

———. 2004. "Annual Report 2003." Lisbon: Banco de Portugal.

———. 2005. "Annual Report 2004." Lisbon: Banco de Portugal.

———. 2006. "Annual Report 2005." Lisbon: Banco de Portugal.

———. 2007. "Annual Report 2006." Lisbon: Banco de Portugal.

———. 2008a. "Annual Report 2007." Lisbon: Banco de Portugal.

———. 2008b. "The Portuguese Economy in the Context of Economic, Financial and Monetary Integration." https://www.bportugal.pt/en-US/BdP%20Publications%20Research/AllItems.aspx. Banco de Portugal.

———. 2009. "Annual Report 2008." Lisbon: Banco de Portugal.

———. 2010. "Annual Report 2009." Lisbon: Banco de Portugal.

———. 2011. "Annual Report 2010." Lisbon: Banco de Portugal.

———. 2012. "Annual Report 2011." Lisbon: Banco de Portugal.

———. 2013. "Annual Report 2012." Lisbon: Banco de Portugal.

———. 2014. "Annual Report 2013." Lisbon: Banco de Portugal.

Bank of Greece. 1999. "Report of the Governor for the Year 1998." Athens: Bank of Greece.

———. 2000. "Report of the Governor for the Year 1999." Athens: Bank of Greece.

———. 2001. "Report of the Governor for the Year 2000." Athens: Bank of Greece.

———. 2002. "Report of the Governor for the Year 2001." Athens: Bank of Greece.

———. 2003. "Report of the Governor for the Year 2002." Athens: Bank of Greece.

———. 2004. "Report of the Governor for the Year 2003." Athens: Bank of Greece.

———. 2005. "Report of the Governor for the Year 2004." Athens: Bank of Greece.

———. 2006. "Report of the Governor for the Year 2005." Athens: Bank of Greece.

———. 2007. "Report of the Governor for the Year 2006." Athens: Bank of Greece.

———. 2008. "Report of the Governor for the Year 2007." Athens: Bank of Greece.

———. 2009. "Report of the Governor for the Year 2008." Athens: Bank of Greece.

———. 2010. "Report of the Governor for the Year 2009." Athens: Bank of Greece.

———. 2011. "Report of the Governor for the Year 2010." Athens: Bank of Greece.

———. 2012. "Report of the Governor for the Year 2011." Athens: Bank of Greece.

———. 2013. "Report of the Governor for the Year 2012." Athens: Bank of Greece.

———. 2014. "Report of the Governor for the Year 2013." Athens: Bank of Greece.

Barry, Frank. 2003. "Economic Integration and Convergence Processes in the EU Cohesion Countries." *Journal of Common Market Studies* 41 (5): 897–921.

———. 2004. "Prospects for Ireland in an Enlarged EU." *World Economy* 27 (6): 829–52. https://doi.org/10.1111/j.1467-9701.2004.00631.x.

Bastasin, Carlo. 2012. *Saving Europe: How National Politics Nearly Destroyed the Euro*. 1st edition. Washington, DC: Brookings Institution Press.

BBC News. 2015. "Did Greeks Fail to Pay 89.5% of Taxes?" BBC News. 11th July 2015. http://www.bbc.co.uk/news/magazine-33479946.

Beck, Ulrich. 2013. *German Europe*. Translated by Rodney Livingstone. 1st edition. Cambridge, UK; Malden, MA: Polity Press.

Becker, Joachim, and Johannes Jäger. 2012. "Integration in Crisis: A Regulationist Perspective on the Interaction of European Varieties of Capitalism." *Competition & Change* 16 (3): 169–87. https://doi.org/10.1179/1024529412Z.00000000012.

Belke, Ansgar Hubertus, and Christian Dreger. 2011. "Current Account Imbalances in the Euro Area: Catching Up or Competitiveness?" SSRN Scholarly Paper ID 1769550. Rochester, NY: Social Science Research Network. http://papers.ssrn.com/abstract=1769550.

Bellofiore, Riccardo. 2013. "'Two or Three Things I Know about Her': Europe in the Global Crisis and Heterodox Economics." *Cambridge Journal of Economics* 37 (3): 497–512. https://doi.org/10.1093/cje/bet002.

Bellofiore, Riccardo, Francesco Garibaldo, and Joseph Halevi. 2010. "The Great Recession and the Contradictions of European Neomercantilism." Bergamo: University of Bergamo.

Bibow, Jörg. 2012. "The Euro Debt Crisis and Germany's Euro Trilemma." SSRN Scholarly Paper ID 2060325. Rochester, NY: Social Science Research Network. http://papers.ssrn.com/abstract=2060325.

Bieling, Hans-Jürgen. 2003. "Social Forces in the Making of the New European Economy: The Case of Financial Market Integration." *New Political Economy* 8 (2): 203–24.

Blanchard, Olivier. 2007. "Adjustment within the Euro. The Difficult Case of Portugal." *Portuguese Economic Journal* 6 (1): 1–21. https://doi.org/10.1007/s10258-006-0015-4.

Bois, Nick de. 2014. "The EU Had 30 Years to Create a Single Market, and Failed – We Need Change." *Spectator Blogs* (blog). 14th January 2014. http://specc.ie/JY77oR.

Börzel, Tanja, and Thomas Risse. 2003. "Conceptualizing the Domestic Impact of Europe." In *The Politics of Europeanization*, edited by Kevin Featherstone and Claudio M. Radaelli. Oxford; New York: Oxford University Press.

Botsiou, Konstantina E. 2009. "New Policies, Old Politics: American Concepts of Reform in Marshall Plan Greece." *Journal of Modern Greek Studies* 27 (2): 209–40. https://doi.org/10.1353/mgs.0.0063.

Bovens, Mark, and Paul 't Hart. 1998. *Understanding Policy Fiascoes*. New Jersey: Transaction Publishers.

Brazys, Samuel, and Niamh Hardiman. 2013. "From Tiger to PIIGS: Ireland and the Use of Heuristics in Comparative Political Economy." Working Paper. University College Dublin. Geary Institute. http://researchrepository.ucd.ie/handle/10197/4928.

Brazys, Samuel, and Aidan Regan. 2015. "These Little PIIGS Went to Market: Enterprise Policy and Divergent Recovery in European Periphery." Working Paper 201517. Geary Institute, University College Dublin. https://ideas.repec.org/p/ucd/wpaper/201517.html.

Breznitz, Dan. 2012. "Ideas, Structure, State Action and Economic Growth: Rethinking the Irish Miracle." *Review of International Political Economy* 19 (1): 87–113. https://doi.org/10.1080/09692290.2010.514260.

Bruff, Ian. 2010. "European Varieties of Capitalism and the International." *European Journal of International Relations* 16 (4): 615–38. https://doi.org/10.1177/1354066109344379.

Bruff, Ian, and Matthias Ebenau. 2014. "Critical Political Economy and the Critique of Comparative Capitalisms Scholarship on Capitalist Diversity." *Capital & Class* 38 (1): 3–15. https://doi.org/10.1177/0309816813510371.

Buch-Hansen, Hubert, and Angela Wigger. 2011. *The Politics of European Competition Regulation: A Critical Political Economy Perspective*. London: Routledge.

Bulmer, Simon. 2007. "Theorizing Europeanization." In *Europeanization: New Research Agendas*, edited by Paolo Graziano and Maarten P. Vink. Basingstoke, UK; New York: Palgrave Macmillan.

———. 2014. "Germany and the Eurozone Crisis: Between Hegemony and Domestic Politics." *West European Politics* 37 (6): 1244–63. https://doi.org/10.1080/01402382.2014.929333.

Bulmer, Simon, and William E. Paterson. 2013. "Germany as the EU's Reluctant Hegemon? Of Economic Strength and Political Constraints." *Journal of European Public Policy* 20 (10): 1387–405. https://doi.org/10.1080/13501763.2013.822824.

Byrne, Elaine. 2012. *Political Corruption in Ireland 1922–2010: A Crooked Harp?* Manchester, UK: Manchester University Press.

Cahill, Noel, and Rory O'Donnell. 2010. "The Role of the Internal Market in Ireland' Economic Growth." Background Paper no. 75. NESC.

Cardoso, Pedro L. 2005. "Household Behaviour in a Monetary Union: What Can We Learn from the Case of Portugal?" 20. Country Focus. *Brussels:* European Commission Directorate General for Economic and Financial Affairs. http://ec.europa.eu/economy_finance/publications/publication_summary1353_en.htm.

Carswell, Simon. 2012. *Anglo Republic*. Dublin: Penguin Ireland.

Central Bank of Ireland. 1991. "Annual Report: Report of the Central Bank of Ireland for the Year Ended 31 December 1990." Annual Report. Dublin: Central Bank of Ireland.

———. 1992. "Annual Report: Report of the Central Bank of Ireland for the Year Ended 31 December 1991." Annual Report. Dublin: Central Bank of Ireland.

———. 1993. "Annual Report: Report of the Central Bank of Ireland for the Year Ended 31 December 1992." Annual Report. Dublin: Central Bank of Ireland.

———. 1994. "Annual Report: Report of the Central Bank of Ireland for the Year Ended 31 December 1993." Annual Report. Dublin: Central Bank of Ireland.

———. 1995. "Annual Report: Report of the Central Bank of Ireland for the Year Ended 31 December 1994." Annual Report. Dublin: Central Bank of Ireland.

———. 1996. "Annual Report: Report of the Central Bank of Ireland for the Year Ended 31 December 1995." Annual Report. Dublin: Central Bank of Ireland.

———. 1997. "Annual Report: Report of the Central Bank of Ireland for the Year Ended 31 December 1996." Annual Report. Dublin: Central Bank of Ireland.

———. 1998. "Annual Report: Report of the Central Bank of Ireland for the Year Ended 31 December 1997." Annual Report. Dublin: Central Bank of Ireland.

———. 1999a. "Annual Report: Report of the Central Bank of Ireland for the Year Ended 31 December 1998." Annual Report. Dublin: Central Bank of Ireland.

———. 1999b. "Bulletin Winter 1999." Quarterly Bulletin Article. Dublin: Central Bank of Ireland.

———. 2000a. "Annual Report: Report of the Central Bank of Ireland for the Year Ended 31 December 1999." Annual Report. Dublin: Central Bank of Ireland.

———. 2000b. "Bulletin Winter 2000." Quarterly Bulletin Article. Dublin: Central Bank of Ireland.

———. 2001a. "Annual Report: Report of the Central Bank of Ireland for the Year Ended 31 December 2000." Annual Report. Dublin: Central Bank of Ireland.

———. 2001b. "Bulletin Winter 2001." Quarterly Bulletin Article. Dublin: Central Bank of Ireland.

———. 2002a. "Annual Report: Report of the Central Bank of Ireland for the Year Ended 31 December 2001." Annual Report. Dublin: Central Bank of Ireland.

———. 2002b. "Bulletin Winter 2002." Quarterly Bulletin Article. Dublin: Central Bank of Ireland.

———. 2003. "Annual Report: Report of the Central Bank of Ireland for the Year Ended 31 December 2002." Annual Report. Dublin: Central Bank of Ireland.

———. 2004a. "Annual Report: Report of the Central Bank of Ireland for the Year Ended 31 December 2003." Annual Report. Dublin: Central Bank of Ireland.

———. 2004b. "Bulletin Winter 2004." Quarterly Bulletin Article. Dublin: Central Bank of Ireland.

———. 2005a. "Annual Report: Report of the Central Bank of Ireland for the Year Ended 31 December 2004." Annual Report. Dublin: Central Bank of Ireland.

———. 2005b. "Bulletin Winter 2005." Quarterly Bulletin Article. Dublin: Central Bank of Ireland.

———. 2006a. "Annual Report: Report of the Central Bank of Ireland for the Year Ended 31 December 2005." Annual Report. Dublin: Central Bank of Ireland.

———. 2006b. "Bulletin Winter 2006." Quarterly Bulletin Article. Dublin: Central Bank of Ireland.

———. 2007a. "Annual Report: Report of the Central Bank of Ireland for the Year Ended 31 December 2006." Annual Report. Dublin: Central Bank of Ireland.

———. 2007b. "Bulletin Winter 2007." Quarterly Bulletin Article. Dublin: Central Bank of Ireland.

———. 2008. "Annual Report: Report of the Central Bank of Ireland for the Year Ended 31 December 2007." Annual Report. Dublin: Central Bank of Ireland.

———.2013. "History of the Central Bank". Dublin. Central Bank of Ireland.

Cesaratto, Sergio. 2013. "Controversial and Novel Features of the Eurozone Crisis as a Balance of Payment Crisis." In *Post-Keynesian Views of the Crisis and Its Remedies*, edited by Óscar Dejuán, Eladio Febrero Paños, and Jorge Uxo Gonzalez. Hoboken, NJ: Taylor & Francis.

Cesaratto, Sergio, and Antonella Stirati. 2011. "Germany and the European and Global Crises." Department of Economics University of Siena 607. Department of Economics, University of Siena. https://ideas.repec.org/p/usi/wpaper/607.html.

Christodoulais, Nikos. 2013. "Market Reforms in Greece, 1990–2008: External Constraints and Domestic Limitations." In *From Stagnation to Forced Adjustment: Reforms in Greece, 1974–2010*, edited by Stathis Kalyvas, George Pagoulatos, and Haridimos Tsoukas. New York: Oxford University Press.

Clerc, Jean-Pierre. 1985. "Entretien Avec Mário Soare." *Le Monde*, 06 1985, no. 12 554 edition.

Clift, Ben. 2014. *Comparative Political Economy: States, Markets and Global Capitalism*. Basingstoke, UK: Palgrave Macmillan.

Clogg, Richard. 1993. *Greece, 1981–89: The Populist Decade*. New York: Palgrave Macmillan.

———. 2002. *A Concise History of Greece*. 2nd edition. Cambridge, UK; New York: Cambridge University Press.

Clogg, Richard, and Nikos Diamandouros. 1993. "Politics and Culture in Greece, 1974–1991: An Interpretation." In *Greece, 1981–89: The Populist Decade*. New York: Palgrave Macmillan.

Cockfield, Lord. 1994. *The European Union: Creating the Single Market*. London: John Wiley & Sons.

Cooper, Matt. 2012. *How Ireland Really Went Bust*. Dublin: Penguin Ireland.

Copeland, Paul, and Dimitris Papadimitriou. 2012. *The EU's Lisbon Strategy: Evaluating Success, Understanding Failure*. Basingstoke, UK: Palgrave Macmillan.

Corkill, David. 1999. *The Development of the Portuguese Economy a Case of Europeanization*. London; New York: Routledge.

Crotty, Raymond. 1987. *Ireland in Crisis: A Study in Capitalist Colonial Undevelopment*. Dingle, Co. Kerry, Ireland; Dover, NH: Brandon Books.

Decressin, J, and P Mauro. 1998. "The Portuguese Banking System: Feeling Its Pulse on the Eve of EMU Membership." 98/127. IMF Country Report.

Deeg, Richard. 2012. "Innovation Financing in Europe: What Has Financial Market Integration Brought?" In *Europe and National Economic Transformation: The EU After the Lisbon Decade*, edited by Mitchell P. Smith. New York: Palgrave Macmillan.

Dejuán, Óscar, Eladio Febrero Paños, and Jorge Uxo Gonzalez. 2013. *Post-Keynesian Views of the Crisis and Its Remedies*. Hoboken, NJ: Taylor & Francis.

Dellepiane, Sebastian, and Niamh Hardiman. 2012. "Governing the Irish Economy: A Triple Crisis." In *Irish Governance in Crisis*, edited by Niamh Hardiman. Manchester, UK; New York: Manchester University Press; distributed in the USA exclusively by Palgrave Macmillan.

Dellepiane, Sebastian, Niamh Hardiman, and Jon Las Heras. 2013. "Building on Easy Money: The Political Economy of Housing Bubbles in Ireland and Spain." Working Paper. University College Dublin. Geary Institute. http://researchrepository.ucd.ie/handle/10197/4929.

Delors, Jacques. 2013. "Rebuilding Greater EuropeNotre Europe: Jacques Delors Institute Tribune." http://www.institutdelors.eu/media/rebuildinggreatereurope-delors-ne-jdi-june13.pdf?pdf=ok.

Deutsche Bank. 2010. "Global Markets Research: Portugal's Difficulties Come from Afar."

Diamandouros, Nikos. 2011. "Politics, Culture, and the State: Background to the. Greek Crisis." Conference paper presented at *SEESOX International Conference*. May 27–8. St. Antony's College, Oxford.

Directorate-General for Economic and Financial Affairs. 2004. "The Portuguese Economy after the Boom – Directorate-General for Economic and Financial Affairs – European Commission." 8. Occasional Papers. Brussels: European Commission. http://ec.europa.eu/economy_finance/publications/publication_summary1004_en.htm.

Donovan, Donal, and Antoin E. Murphy. 2013. *The Fall of the Celtic Tiger: Ireland and the Euro Debt Crisis*. Oxford; New York: Oxford University Press.

Dooley, Neil. 2014. "Growing Pains? Rethinking the 'Immaturity' of the European Periphery." *Millennium – Journal of International Studies* 42 (3): 936–46. https://doi.org/10.1177/0305829814531059.

———. 2015a. "Bad Things Can Still Happen to 'Good Pupils' in the Eurozone." *SPERI* (blog). 2015. http://speri.dept.shef.ac.uk/2015/12/09/bad-things-can-still-happen-to-good-pupils-in-the-eurozone/.

———. 2015b. "Beyond the PIIGS and the Big Bad Wolf – Le Monde Diplomatique – English Edition." *Le Monde Diplomatique* (blog). 14th March 2015. http://mondediplo.com/blogs/beyond-the-piigs-and-the-big-bad-wolf.

———. 2015c. "The Real Political Economy of Ireland." *SPERI* (blog). 2nd September 2015. http://speri.dept.shef.ac.uk/2015/09/02/real-political-economy-ireland/.

———. 2017a. "Who's Afraid of the Big Bad Wolf? Rethinking the Core and Periphery in the Eurozone Crisis." *New Political Economy* 0 (0): 1–27. https://doi.org/10.1080/13563467.2017.1417363.

———. 2017b. "Divergence via Europeanisation: Rethinking the Origins of the Portuguese Debt Crisis." *Third World Thematics: A TWQ Journal* 0 (0): 1–22. https://doi.org/10.1080/23802014.2017.1381571.

———. 2018. "Portugal's Economic Crisis: Overheating Without Accelerating." In *Crisis in the Eurozone Periphery: The Political Economies of Greece, Spain, Ireland and Portugal*, edited by Owen Parker and Dimitris Tsarouhas. Basingstoke, UK: Palgrave Macmillan.

Draenos, Stan. 2009. "United States Foreign Policy and the Liberal Awakening in Greece, 1958–1967." *The Historical Review/La Revue Historique* 5 (0): 121–49.

Drudy, Patrick J., and Micheál L. Collins. 2011. "Ireland: From Boom to Austerity." *Cambridge Journal of Regions, Economy and Society* 4 (3): 339–54. https://doi.org/10.1093/cjres/rsr021.

Dullien, Sebastian, and Ulrike Guérot. 2012. "The Long Shadow of Ordoliberalism: Germany's Approach to the Euro Crisis." Policy Brief. European Council on Foreign Relations. http://www.ecfr.eu/publications/summary/the_long_shadow_of_ordoliberalism_germanys_approach_to_the_euro_crisis.

Ebenau, Matthias, Ian Bruff, and Christian May, eds. 2015. *New Directions in Comparative Capitalisms Research: Critical and Global Perspectives*. 2015 edition. Basingstoke, UK; New York: AIAA.

Egan, Michelle. 2012. "EUROPP – Twenty Years after the Completion of the EU's Single Market Programme, Member States Have Still Not Eliminated All Barriers to Trade." *LSE Europp Blog* (blog). http://blogs.lse.ac.uk/europpblog/2012/11/08/single-market-egan/.

Eichengreen, Barry, and Heather D. Gibson. 2001. "Greek Banking at the Dawn of the New Millennium." SSRN Scholarly Paper ID 269391. Rochester, NY: Social Science Research Network. https://papers.ssrn.com/abstract=269391.

Eisenstadt, S. N. 2000. "Multiple Modernities." *Daedalus* 129 (1): 1–29.

Elliott, Larry, Phillip Inman, and Helena Smith. 2013. "IMF Admits: We Failed to Realise the Damage Austerity Would Do to Greece." *The Guardian*, 5th June 2013, sec. Business. http://www.theguardian.com/business/2013/jun/05/imf-underestimated-damage-austerity-would-do-to-greece.

Emerson, Michael, Daniel Gros, and Alexander Italianer. 1992. *One Market, One Money: An Evaluation of the Potential Benefits and Costs of Forming an Economic and Monetary Union*. Oxford; New York: Oxford University Press.

English, Damien. 2013. "Column: Cowen Is Wrong – Ireland's Economy Was on Course for Collapse Even without the Global Crisis." *TheJournal.Ie* (blog). September 10,

2013. http://www.thejournal.ie/readme/brian-cowen-ireland-economy-property-crash-debt-crisis-1076197-Sep2013/.

European Commission. 2004. "The Portuguese Economy after the Boom." Occasional Papers, no. 8. *Brussels:* European Commission. http://ec.europa.eu/economy_finance/publications/pages/publication1000_en.pdf.

———. 2010. *The Economic Adjustment Programme for Greece: . . . Review*. European Economy. Occasional Papers, nos. 68, 72, 77, 82. Luxembourg: Publications Office of the European Union.

———. 2011. *The Economic Adjustment Programme for Portugal.* Luxembourg: Publications Office of the European Union.

———. 2012a. "20 Years of the European Single Market: Together for New Growth; Main Achievements." Luxembourg: Publications Office of the European Union.

———. 2012b. "Ireland's Economic Crisis: How Did It Happen and What Is Being Done about It?" *European Commission Representation in Ireland* (blog). http://ec.europa.eu/ireland/key-eu-policy-areas/economy/irelands-economic-crisis/index_en.htm.

European Council. 2000. "Lisbon European Council: Conclusions of the Presidency." http://www.europarl.europa.eu/summits/lis1_en.htm.

Exadaktylos, Theofanis, and Professor Claudio M. Radaelli, eds. 2012. *Research Design in European Studies: Establishing Causality in Europeanization.* Basingstoke, UK; New York: Palgrave Macmillan.

Featherstone, Kevin. 1998. "'Europeanization' and the Centre Periphery: The Case of Greece in the 1990s." *South European Society and Politics* 3 (1): 23–39. https://doi.org/10.1080/13608740308539524.

———. 2008. "'Varieties of Capitalism' and the Greek Case: Explaining the Constraints on Domestic Reform?" Working Paper, GreeSE: 11. Hellenic Observatory, London School of Economics and Political Science, London. http://www.lse.ac.uk/collections/hellenicObservatory/pubs/GreeSE.htm.

———. 2011. "The JCMS Annual Lecture: The Greek Sovereign Debt Crisis and EMU: A Failing State in a Skewed Regime*." *JCMS: Journal of Common Market Studies* 49 (2): 193–217. https://doi.org/10.1111/j.1468-5965.2010.02139.x.

Featherstone, Kevin, Georgios Kazamias, and Dimitris Papadimitriou. 2001. "The Limits of External Empowerment: EMU, Technocracy and Reform of the Greek Pension System." *Political Studies* 49 (3): 462–80. https://doi.org/10.1111/1467-9248.00321.

Featherstone, Kevin, and Dimitris Papadimitriou. 2008. *The Limits of Europeanization: Reform Capacity and Policy Conflict in Greece*. Basingstoke, UK; New York: Palgrave Macmillan.

Ferriter, Diarmaid. 2012. *Ambiguous Republic: Ireland in the 1970s*. London: Profile Books.

Flassbeck, Heiner, Costas Lapavitsas. 2015. *Against the Troika: Crisis and Austerity in the Eurozone*. London: Verso Books.

Flassbeck, Heiner, and Costas Lapavitsas. 2016. "Confusion is no Response to Economic Orthodoxy. The German Wage Moderation Discussion." *Flassbeck Economics International* (blog). 23rd February 2016. http://www.flassbeck-economics.com/confusion-is-no-response-to-economic-orthodoxy/.

Fleischhauer, Jan. 2018. "Italien: Die Schnorrer von Rom – Kolumne – SPIEGEL ONLINE." *Spiegel Online*, May 2018. http://www.spiegel.de/politik/ausland/italien-die-schnorrer-von-rom-kolumne-a-1209266.html.

Fligstein, Neil, and Iona Mara-Drita. 1996. "How to Make a Market: Reflections on the Attempt to Create a Single Market in the European Union." *American Journal of Sociology* 102 (1): 1–33.

Fourcade, Marion, Phillipe Steiner, Wolfgang Streeck, and Cornelia Woll. 2013. "The Economy as Morality Play and Implications for the Eurozone Crisis." *Socio-Economic Review* 11 (3): 601–27.

Fouskas, Vassilis K. 2012. "Insight Greece: The Origins of the Present Crisis." *Insight Turkey* 14 (2). http://www.insightturkey.com/insight-turkey-volume-14-no-2/issues/168#Greece.

Fouskas, Vassilis K., and Constantine Dimoulas. 2012. "The Greek Workshop of Debt and the Failure of the European Project." *Journal of Balkan and Near Eastern Studies* 14 (1): 1–31. https://doi.org/10.1080/19448953.2012.656929.

———. 2013. Greece, Financialization and the EU: The Political Economy of Debt and Destruction. Basingstoke, UK: Palgrave Macmillan.

Genito, Lorenzo. 2018. "The Ideological Shifts, Economics and Geopolitics of the Italian Elections | SPERI." *SPERI* (blog). 2018. http://speri.dept.shef.ac.uk/2018/06/12/the-ideological-shifts-economics-and-geopolitics-of-the-italian-elections/.

George, Alexander L., and Andrew Bennett. 2005. *Case Studies and Theory Development in the Social Sciences*. Cambridge, MA: MIT Press.

Gerakis, Andreas S., and Haskell P. Wald. 1964. "Economic Stabilization and Progress in Greece, 1953–61: Contribution of Foreign Exchange and Trade Reforms (Contribution Des Réformes de Change et de Commerce à La Stabilisation économique En Grèce, 1953–61) (El Aporte de Las Reformas Cambiarias y Comerciales a La Estabilización Económica de Grecia, 1953–61)." *IMF Staff Papers* 11 (1): 125–49.

Giavazzi, Francesco. 2015. "Greeks Chose Poverty, Let Them Have Their Way." *Financial Times*, 9th June 2015. http://www.ft.com/cms/s/0/2bc11fe8-0dd5-11e5-9a65-00144feabdc0.html?siteedition=uk#axzz3dJclYGNt.

Giavazzi, Francesco, and Luigi Spaventa. 2010. "Why the Current Account May Matter in a Monetary Union: Lessons from the Financial Crisis in the Euro Area." 8008. CEPR Discussion Papers. C.E.P.R. Discussion Papers. https://ideas.repec.org/p/cpr/ceprdp/8008.html.

Giordano, Francesco, and Sharda Persaud. 1998. *The Political Economy of Monetary Union: Towards the Euro*. 1st edition. London; New York: Routledge.

Giurlando, Philip. 2012. "Vicarious Evaluation: How European Integration Changes National Identities." SSRN Scholarly Paper ID 2155909. Rochester, NY: Social Science Research Network. http://papers.ssrn.com/abstract=2155909.

Goetz, Klaus, and Kenneth Dyson. 2003. *Germany, Europe, and the Politics of Constraint*. OUP/British Academy.

Goodin, Robert. 2003. "Choose Your Capitalism?" *Comparative European Politics* 1 (2): 203–14.

Gorstos, Christos. 2002. "Greece." In *Banking in the New Europe: The Impact of the Single European Market Programme and EMU on the European Banking Sector*, edited by Edward P. M. Gardener, Barry Moore, and Philip Molyneux. Basingstoke, UK: Palgrave Macmillan.

Gourgouris, Stathis. 2015. "The Syriza Problem: Radical Democracy and Left Governmentality in Greece." OpenDemocracy. 5th August 2015. https://www.opendemocracy.net/can-europe-make-it/stathis-gourgouris/syriza-problem-radical-democracy-and-left-governmentality-in-g.

Grauwe, Paul de. 2013. "Design Failures in the Eurozone: Can They Be Fixed?" LEQS Paper no. 57. Available at SSRN: https://ssrn.com/abstract=2215762.

Graziano, Paolo, and Maarten P. Vink, eds. 2007. *Europeanization: New Research Agendas*. Basingstoke, UK; New York: Palgrave Macmillan.

Hall, Peter A. 2012. "The Economics and Politics of the Euro Crisis." *German Politics* 21 (4): 355–71. https://doi.org/10.1080/09644008.2012.739614.

———. 2014. "Varieties of Capitalism and the Euro Crisis." *West European Politics* 37 (6): 1223–43. https://doi.org/10.1080/01402382.2014.929352.

———. 2018. "Varieties of Capitalism in Light of the Euro Crisis." *Journal of European Public Policy* 25 (1): 7–30. https://doi.org/10.1080/13501763.2017.1310278.

Hancké, Bob. 2009. *Debating "Varieties of Capitalism": A Reader*. Oxford: Oxford University Press.

———. 2013. Unions, Central Banks, and EMU: Labour Market Institutions and Monetary Integration in Europe. Oxford: Oxford University Press.

Hänska, Max. 2015. "The Politics of Blame." *Euro Crisis in the Press* (blog). http://blogs.lse.ac.uk/eurocrisispress/2013/03/22/the-politics-of-blame/.

Hardiman, Niamh. 2010. "Bringing Domestic Institutions Back into Understanding Ireland's Economic Crisis." Working Paper no. 201042. Geary Institute, University College Dublin. https://ideas.repec.org/p/ucd/wpaper/201042.html.

———. 2012. *Irish Governance in Crisis*. Manchester, UK; New York: Manchester University Press; distributed in the USA exclusively by Palgrave Macmillan.

———. Forthcoming. "Building on Easy Money: Housing Bubbles and the Financial Resource Curse in Spain and Ireland."

Hardiman, Niamh, Joaquim Araújo, Muiris MacCarthaigh, and Calliope Spanou. 2017. "The Troika's Variations on a Trio: Why the Loan Programmes Worked so Differently in Greece, Ireland, and Portugal." SSRN Scholarly Paper ID 3060346. Rochester, NY: Social Science Research Network. https://papers.ssrn.com/abstract=3060346.

Hardiman, Niamh, and Sebastian Dellepiane. 2010. "European Economic Crisis: Ireland in Comparative Perspective." SSRN Scholarly Paper ID 1642791. Rochester, NY: Social Science Research Network. http://papers.ssrn.com/abstract=1642791.

Hendrikse, Reijer P. 2013. "Entangled Geographies of 'Irish' Finance." *Eurasian Geography and Economics* 54 (2): 182–201. https://doi.org/10.1080/15387216.2013.809294.

Heritier, Adrienne, Dieter Kerwer, Christoph Knill, Dirk Lehmkuhl, Michael Teutsch, and Anne-Cecile Douillet. 2001. *Differential Europe: The European Union Impact on National Policymaking*. 1st edition. Lanham, MD: Rowman & Littlefield.

Hogan, John, Paul F. Donnelly, and Brendan O'Rourke, eds. 2010. *Irish Business and Society*. Dublin: Gill & Macmillan Ltd.

Hondroyiannis, George, Sarantis Lolos, and Evangelia Papapetrou. 1999. "Assessing Competitive Conditions in the Greek Banking System." *Journal of International Financial Markets, Institutions and Money* 9 (4): 377–91.

Honohan, Patrick. 1999. "Consequences for Greece and Portugal of the Opening-up of the European Banking Market." 29029. The World Bank. http://documents.worldbank.org/curated/en/1999/04/5146052/consequences-greece-portugal-opening-up-european-banking-market.

———. 2010. "The Irish Banking Crisis Regulatory and Financial Stability Policy 2003–2008." A Report to the Minister for Finance by the Governor of the Central Bank. Dublin: Central Bank of Ireland.

Honohan, Patrick, and Anthony J. Leddin. 2005. "Ireland in EMU: More Shocks, Less Insulation?" CEPR Discussion Paper 5349. C.E.P.R. Discussion Papers. http://ideas.repec.org/p/cpr/ceprdp/5349.html.

Honohan, Patrick, and Brendan Walsh. 2002. "Catching Up with the Leaders: The Irish Hare." *Brookings Papers on Economic Activity* 33 (1): 1–78.

Höpner, Martin, and Mark Lutter. 2014. "One Currency and Many Modes of Wage Formation: Why the Eurozone Is Too Heterogeneous for the Euro." *MPIfG Discussion Paper* 14 (14). https://www.researchgate.net/publication/264934518_Hopner_Martin_and_Mark_Lutter_2014_One_Currency_and_Many_Modes_of_Wage_Formation_Why_the_Eurozone_Is_Too_Heterogeneous_for_the_Euro_MPIfG_Discussion_Paper_1414_Cologne_Max_Planck_Institute_for_the_Stu.

IDA Ireland. 2002. "IDA Ireland Annual Report 2002." Annual Report. Dublin: IDA Ireland.

IMF. 2009. "Ireland: IMF Country Report." 09/195. Country Report. Washington, DC: IMF.

———. 2013. "Portugal: Selected Issues Paper." 13/19. Country Report. Washington, DC: IMF.

Inman, Phillip. 2018. "Eurozone Braces for Row with Greece over Bailout Exit Terms." *The Guardian*, 18th June 2018. https://www.theguardian.com/business/2018/jun/18/eu-eurozone-braces-for-row-with-greece-over-bailout-exit-terms.

Jacoby, Wade. 2015. "Europe's New German Problem: The Timing of Politics and the Politics of Timing." In *The Future of the Euro*, edited by Matthias Matthijs and Mark Blyth. New York: Oxford University Press.

Jäger, Johannes, and Elisabeth Springler. 2015. *Asymmetric Crisis in Europe and Possible Futures: Critical Political Economy and Post-Keynesian Perspectives*. London: Routledge.

Jessop, Bob. 2006. "State- and Regulation-Theoretical Perspectives on the European Union and the Failure of the Lisbon Agenda." *Competition & Change* 10 (2): 141–61. https://doi.org/10.1179/102452906X104213.

Johnston, Alison. 2016. *From Convergence to Crisis: Labor Markets and the Instability of the Euro*. Cornell Studies in Money. Ithaca, NY: Cornell University Press.

Johnston, Alison, Bob Hancké, and Suman Pant. 2014. "Comparative Institutional Advantage in the European Sovereign Debt Crisis." *Comparative Political Studies* 47 (13): 1771–1800. https://doi.org/10.1177/0010414013516917.

Johnston, Alison, and Aidan Regan. 2016. "European Monetary Integration and the Incompatibility of National Varieties of Capitalism." *JCMS: Journal of Common Market Studies* 54 (2): 318–36. https://doi.org/10.1111/jcms.12289.

Jones, E. 2015. "Getting the Story Right: How You Should Choose between Different Interpretations of the European Crisis (and Why You Should Care)." *Journal of European Integration*, 37 (7): 817–32. https://doi.org/10.1080/07036337.2015.1079376.

Jones, Erik. 2016. "Competitiveness and the European Financial Crisis." In *The Political and Economic Dynamics of the Eurozone Crisis*, edited by James Caporaso and Martin Rhodes, 79–99. Oxford: Oxford University Press.

Joyce, Joe, and Peter Murtagh. 1983. *The Boss: Charles J. Haughey in Government*. 1st edition. Dublin: Poolbeg Press Ltd.

Kalyvas, Stathis, George Pagoulatos, and Haridimos Tsoukas. 2013. *From Stagnation to Forced Adjustment: Reforms in Greece, 1974–2010*. New York: Oxford University Press.

Katsimi, Margarita, and Thomas Moutos. 2010. "EMU and the Greek Crisis: The Political-Economy Perspective." *European Journal of Political Economy* 26 (4): 568–76. https://doi.org/10.1016/j.ejpoleco.2010.08.002.

Kelly, John, and Mary Everett. 2004. "Financial Liberalisation and Economic Growth in Ireland." Quarterly Bulletin Article. Dublin: Central Bank of Ireland.

Kelly, Sinéad. 2014. "Light-Touch Regulation: The Rise and Fall of the Irish Banking Sector." In *Neoliberal Urban Policy and the Transformation of the City*, edited by Andrew MacLaran and Sinéad Kelly. Basingstoke, UK: Palgrave Macmillan. http://www.palgrave.com%2Fpage%2Fdetail%2FNeoliberal-Urban-Policy-and-the-Transformation-of-the-City%2F%3FK%3D9781137377043.

Khan, Mehreen, and Paul McClean. 2017. "Dijsselbloem under Fire after Saying Eurozone Countries Wasted Money on 'Alcohol and Women.'" *Financial Times*, March 21, 2017. https://www.ft.com/content/2498740e-b911-3dbf-942d-ecce511a351e.

Kinsella, Ray, and Phillip Bourke. 2002. "Ireland." In *Banking in the New Europe: The Impact of the Single European Market Programme and EMU on the European Banking Sector*, edited by Edward P. M. Gardener, Barry Moore, and Philip Molyneux. Basingstoke, UK: Palgrave Macmillan.

Kinsella, Stephen. 2012. "Is Ireland Really the Role Model for Austerity?" *Cambridge Journal of Economics* 36 (1): 223–35. https://doi.org/10.1093/cje/ber032.

Kirby, Peadar. 2002. *The Celtic Tiger in Distress: Growth with Inequality in Ireland*. International Political Economy Series. Basingstoke, UK; New York: Palgrave Macmillan.

———. 2004. "Development Theory and the Celtic Tiger." *The European Journal of Development Research* 16 (2): 301–28. https://doi.org/10.1080/0957881042000220831.

———. 2008. "Explaining Ireland's Development: Economic Growth with Weakening Welfare | Publications | UNRISD." Poverty Reduction and Policy Regimes 37. Geneva: United Nations Research Institute for Social Development. http://www.unrisd.org/80256B3C005BCCF9/search/D35985C0845ED8F3C12575120031778C?OpenDocument.

———. 2010. *Celtic Tiger in Collapse: Explaining the Weaknesses of the Irish Model*. 2nd edition. Basingstoke, UK; New York: Palgrave Macmillan.

Kirby, Peadar, and Mary Murphy. 2011a. "Globalisation and Models of State: Debates and Evidence from Ireland." *New Political Economy* 16 (1): 19–39. https://doi.org/10.1080/13563461003789795.

Kirby, Peadar, and Mary P. Murphy. 2011b. *Towards a Second Republic: Irish Politics after the Celtic Tiger*. 1st edition. London: Pluto Press.

Kitchin, Rob, Cian O'Callaghan, Justin Gleeson, Karen Keaveney, and Mark Boyle. 2012. "Placing Neoliberalism: The Rise and Fall of Ireland's Celtic Tiger." *Environment and Planning A* 44 (6): 1302–26. https://doi.org/10.1068/a44349.

Knill, Christoph, Jale Tosun, and Michael W. Bauer. 2009. "Neglected Faces of Europeanization: The Differential Impact of the Eu on the Dismantling and Expansion of Domestic Policies." *Public Administration* 87 (3): 519–37. https://doi.org/10.1111/j.1467-9299.2009.01768.x.

Koo, Richard. 2011. "Learning the Wrong Lessons from the Crisis in Greece." *Unpublished*, May. http://s3.amazonaws.com/zanran_storage/ineteconomics.org/ContentPages/2512617019.pdf.

Kornetis, Kostis. 2010. "No More Heroes? Rejection and Reverberation of the Past in the 2008 Events in Greece." *Journal of Modern Greek Studies* 28 (2): 173–97. https://doi.org/10.1353/mgs.2010.0420.

Kouretas, Georgios, and Prodromos Vlamis. 2010. "The Greek Crisis: Causes and Implications." *Panoeconomicus* 57 (4): 391–404.

Kouvélakis, Stathis. 2012. "Introduction: The End of Europeanism." In *Crisis in the Eurozone*, by Costas Lapavitsas. London; New York: Verso.

Krugman, Paul. 2009. "PAUL KRUGMAN: Erin Go Broke." *The New York Times*, 19th April 2009. http://www.nytimes.com/2009/04/20/opinion/20krugman.html.

———. 2011. "Portugal? O Nao!" *The Conscience of a Liberal, The New York Times* (blog). 10th January 2011. http://krugman.blogs.nytimes.com/2011/01/10/portugal-o-nao/.

———. 2013a. "The Harm Germany Does." *The Conscience of a Liberal*, *The New York Times (blog)*. 1st November 2013. http://krugman.blogs.nytimes.com/2013/11/01/the-harm-germany-does/.

———. 2013b. "German Surpluses: This Time Is Different." *The Conscience of a Liberal, The New York Times* (blog). 3rd November 2013. http://krugman.blogs.nytimes.com/2013/11/03/german-surpluses-this-time-is-different/.

Kyriaki Kosmidou. 2008. "The Determinants of Banks' Profits in Greece during the Period of EU Financial Integration." *Managerial Finance* 34 (3): 146–59. https://doi.org/10.1108/03074350810848036.

Laffan, Brigid. 1998. "The European Union: A Distinctive Model of Internationalization." *Journal of European Public Policy* 5 (2): 235–53. https://doi.org/10.1080/135017698343965.

———. 2007. "Core Executives." In *Europeanization: New Research Agendas*, edited by Paolo Graziano and Maarten P. Vink. Basingstoke, UK; New York: Palgrave Macmilan.

Lagoa, Sergio, Emanuel Leao, Ricardo Mamede, and Ricardo Barradas. 2014. "Financialisation and the Financial and Economic Crises: The Case of Portugal." Working Paper 24. Studies in Financial Systems. Financialisation, Economy, Society and Sustainable Development (FESSUD). http://www.fessud.eu.

Lains, Pedro. 2007. "The Portuguese Economy in the Irish Mirror, 1960–2004." *Open Economies Review* 19 (5): 667–83. https://doi.org/10.1007/s11079-007-9070-4.

Lane, Philip R. 2011. "The Irish Crisis." SSRN Scholarly Paper ID 1794877. *Rochester, NY: Social Science Research Network*. http://papers.ssrn.com/abstract=1794877.

———. 2012. "The European Sovereign Debt Crisis." *The Journal of Economic Perspectives* 26 (3): 49–67. https://doi.org/10.1257/jep.26.3.49.

Lapavitsas, Costas. 2010. "The Greek Crisis – Politics, Economics, Ethics: A Debate Held at the Birkbeck Institute for the Humanities, Birkbeck College, University of London, 5 May 2010." *Journal of Modern Greek Studies* 28 (2): 293–310. https://doi.org/10.1353/mgs.2010.0422.

———. 2018. *The Left Case Against the EU*. Oxford: Polity Press.

Lapavitsas, Costas, and Jeff Powell. 2013. "Financialisation Varied: A Comparative Analysis of Advanced Economies." *Cambridge Journal of Regions, Economy and Society* 6 (3): 359–79.

Lapavitsas, C., A. Kaltenbrunner, G. Labrinidis, D. Lindo, J. Meadway, J. Michell, J. P. Painceira, E. Pires, J. Powell, N. Teles, and L. Vatikiotis. 2012. *Crisis in the Eurozone*. London: Verso.

Lavdas, Kostas A. 1997. *The Europeanization of Greece: Interest Politics and the Crises of Integration*. Basingstoke, UK: Palgrave Macmillan.

Lavdas, Kostas A., Spyridon N. Litsas, and Dimitrios V. Skiadas. 2013. *Stateness and Sovereign Debt: Greece in the European Conundrum*. 1st edition. Lanham, MD: Lexington Books.

Leão, Emanuel, Ricardo Barradas, Ricardo Mamede, and Sergio Lagoa. 2013. "Financialisation in the European Periphery and the Sovereign Debt Crisis: The Portuguese Case." In *FESSUD*. Oporto, Portugal. http://fessud.eu/?p=2297.

Lee, Joseph J. 1990. *Ireland, 1912–1985: Politics and Society*. Cambridge; New York: Cambridge University Press.

Louri, Helen, and Ioanna Pepelasis Minoglou. 2002. "A Hesitant Evolution: Industrialisation and de-Industrialisation in Greece over the Long Run." MPRA Paper. http://mpra.ub.uni-muenchen.de/29275/.

Lourtie, Pedro. 2011. "Understanding Portugal in the Context of the Euro Crisis." Paper prepared for "Resolving the European Debt Crisis", a conference hosted by Peterson Institute for International Economics and Bruegel, 13th–14th September. Chantilly, France: Peterson Institute for International Economics. http://www.iie.com/publications/papers/lourtie20110913.pdf.

Lyberaki, Antigone, and Euclid Tsakalotos. 2002. "Reforming the Economy without Society: Social and Institutional Constraints to Economic Reform in Post-1974 Greece." *New Political Economy* 7 (1): 93–114. https://doi.org/10.1080/13563460120115534.

Lynn, Matthew. 2010. *Bust: Greece, the Euro and the Sovereign Debt Crisis*. Hoboken, NJ: John Wiley & Sons.

Mac Laughlin, Jim. 1994. *Ireland: The Emigrant Nursery and the World Economy*. Cork: Cork University Press.

Macedo, Jorge Braga De. 1990. "External Liberalization with Ambiguous Public Response: The Experience of Portugal." In *Unity with Diversity in the European Economy: The Community's Southern Frontier*, edited by Jorge Braga De Macedo and C. J. Bliss. Cambridge: Cambridge University Press.

Magone, José M., Brigid Laffan, and Christian Schweiger. 2016. *Core-Periphery Relations in the European Union: Power and Conflict in a Dualist Political Economy*. London: Routledge.

Magone, José María. 2004. *The Developing Place of Portugal in the European Union*. London: Transaction Publishers.

Manolopoulos, Jason. 2011. *Greece's "odious" Debt: The Looting of the Hellenic Republic by the Euro, the Political Elite and the Investment Community*. London: Anthem Press.

Markantonatou, Maria. 2012. "The State and Modes of Regulation in Greece from the Post-War Period to the 2009 Financial Crisis." *Journal of Balkan and Near Eastern Studies* 14 (4): 416–32. https://doi.org/10.1080/19448953.2012.736225.

Matthijs, Matthias. 2016a. "Powerful Rules Governing the Euro: The Perverse Logic of German Ideas." *Journal of European Public Policy* 23 (3): 375–91. https://doi.org/10.1080/13501763.2015.1115535.

———. 2016b. "The Euro's 'Winner-Take-All' Political Economy: Institutional Choices, Policy Drift and Diverging Patterns of Inequality." *Politics & Society* 44 (3): 393–422.

Matthijs, Matthias, and Mark Blyth. 2011. "Why Only Germany Can Fix the Euro." *Foreign Affairs* (blog). 17th November 2011. https://www.foreignaffairs.com/articles/germany/2011-11-17/why-only-germany-can-fix-euro.

———, eds. 2015. *The Future of the Euro*. New York: Oxford University Press.

Matthijs, Matthias, and Kathleen McNamara. 2015. "The Euro Crisis' Theory Effect: Northern Saints, Southern Sinners, and the Demise of the Eurobond." *Journal of European Integration* 37 (2): 229–45. https://doi.org/10.1080/07036337.2014.990137.

Mavroudeas, Stavros. 2010. "Greece and the EU: Capitalist Crisis and Imperialist Rivalries." MPRA Paper. 10th September 2010. http://mpra.ub.uni-muenchen.de/25080/.

Maxwell, Kenneth. 1995. *The Making of Portuguese Democracy*. Cambridge; New York: Cambridge University Press.

McGrane, John. 2016. "Why Brexit Would Be Bad for Trade between Britain and Ireland." *The Irish Times*, 2016. https://www.irishtimes.com/opinion/why-brexit-would-be-bad-for-trade-between-britain-and-ireland-1.2693469.

McGrath, Conor. 2010. "Lobbying Regulation: An Irish Solution to a Universal Problem?" In *Irish Business and Society*, edited by John Hogan, Paul F. Donnelly, and Brendan O'Rourke. Dublin: Gill & Macmillan Ltd.

McMenamin, Iain. 2013. *If Money Talks, What Does It Say?: Corruption and Business Financing of Political Parties*. Oxford: Oxford University Press.

Mētsopoulos, Michalēs, and Theodōros K Pelagidēs. 2012. *Understanding the Crisis in Greece: From Boom to Bust*. Basingstoke, UK; New York: Palgrave Macmillan.

Michaelides, Panayotis G., Theofanis Papageorgiou, and Angelos T. Vouldis. 2013. "Business Cycles and Economic Crisis in Greece (1960–2011): A Long Run Equilibrium Analysis in the Eurozone." *Economic Modelling* 31 (C): 804–16.

Michael-Matsas, Savas. 2010. "Greece and the World Capitalist Crisis." *Critique* 38 (3): 489–502. https://doi.org/10.1080/03017605.2010.492691.

Michael Nienaber, and John Walsh. 2018. "Ireland May Have Helped Apple Cut Its EU Tax Rate to 0.7%." *The Times*, 21st June 2018, sec. Ireland. https://www.thetimes.co.uk/article/ireland-may-have-helped-apple-cut-its-eu-tax-rate-to-0-7-n3cvhfvmt.

Milios, John, and Dimitris P. Sotiropoulos. 2010. "Crisis of Greece or Crisis of the Euro? A View from the European 'Periphery.'" *Journal of Balkan and Near Eastern Studies* 12 (3): 223–40. https://doi.org/10.1080/19448953.2010.506806.

Mitsos, Achilleas, and Elias Mossialos. 2000. *Contemporary Greece and Europe*. Aldershot, UK; Burlington, VT: Ashgate Publishing Limited.

Monastiriotis, Vassilis, and Andreas Antoniades. 2009. "Reform That! Greece's Failing Reform Technology: Beyond 'vested Interests' and 'Political Exchange.'" GreeSE papers, no. 28. London School of Economics and Political Science, Hellenic Observatory, London. October. http://www2.lse.ac.uk/europeanInstitute/research/hellenicObservatory/pdf/GreeSE/GreeSE28.pdf.

Moravcsik, Andrew. 2012. "Europe after the Crisis: How to Sustain a Common Currency." *Foreign Affairs* 91: 54.

Morrison, Rodney J. 1981. *Portugal, Revolutionary Change in an Open Economy*. Boston, MA: Auburn House Pub. Co.

Münchau, Wolfgang. 2018. "Political Tale-Telling Is Splitting the Eurozone Apart." *Financial Times*, 10th June 2018. https://www.ft.com/content/087e3a12-6b1e-11e8-8cf3-0c230fa67aec.

Murphy, Mary, and Peadar Kirby. 2007. "Ireland as a 'Competition State.'" *IPEG Papers in Global Political Economy* 28. http://www.bisa-ipeg.org/.

Murphy, Neil B. 2000. "European Union Financial Developments: The Single Market, the Single Currency, and Banking." *FDIC Banking Review* 13.2000 (1).

New York Times. 1984. "In Ireland, a Host of Problems," 4th June 1984. http://www.nytimes.com/1984/06/04/business/in-irelanda-host-of-problems.html.

Newman, Abraham. 2015. "Germany's Euro Experience and the Long Shadow of Reunification." In *The Future of the Euro*, edited by Matthias Matthijs and Mark Blyth. New York: Oxford University Press.

Noeth, Bryan J., and Rajdeep Sengupta. 2012. "Global European Banks and the Financial Crisis." *Federal Reserve Bank of St. Louis Review* 94 (6) (November/December). http://research.stlouisfed.org/publications/review/article/9527.

Nölke, Andreas. 2016. "Economic Causes of the Eurozone Crisis: The Analytical Contribution of Comparative Capitalism." *Socio-Economic Review* 14 (1): 141–61. https://doi.org/10.1093/ser/mwv031.

Ntampoudi, Ioanna. 2014. "The Eurozone Crisis and the Politics of Blaming: The Cases of Germany and Greece." *Political Perspectives* 8 (2): 1–20.

Nyberg, Peter. 2011. "Misjudging Risk: Causes of the Systemic Banking Crisis in Ireland." Report of the commission of investigation into the banking sector in Ireland. Oireachtas Banking Inquiry Reports. Dublin: Oireachtas Banking Inquiry. http://www.bankinginquiry.gov.ie/Preliminary%20Report%20into%20Ireland's%20Banking%20Crisis%2031%20May%202010.pdf.

Ó Riain, Seán. 2004. *The Politics of High Tech Growth: Developmental Network States in the Global Economy*. 1st edition. Cambridge: Cambridge University Press.

———. 2012. "The Crisis of Financialisation in Ireland." *The Economic and Social Review* 43 (4, Winter): 497–533.

———. 2014. *The Rise and Fall of Ireland's Celtic Tiger: Liberalism, Boom and Bust*. Cambridge: Cambridge University Press.

O'Brien, John A. 1953. *The Vanishing Irish*. 1st edition. New York: McGraw-Hill.

OECD. 1994. "Greece." OECD Reviews of Foreign Direct Investment. Paris: OECD Publishing. http://www.oecd.org/greece/34383957.pdf.

———. 2013. *Portugal: Reforming the State to Promote Growth*. Paris: OECD. http://www.oecd-ilibrary.org/content/book/9789264207981-en.

O'Halloran, Marie. 2011. "Gilmore Repeats Economic Treason Charge." *The Irish Times*, 13th January 2011. http://www.irishtimes.com/news/politics/oireachtas/gilmore-repeats-economic-treason-charge-1.1277407.

O'Hearn, Denis. 1998. *Inside the Celtic Tiger: The Irish Economy and the Asian Model*. 1st edition. London; Sterling, VA: Pluto Press.

———. 2001. *The Atlantic Economy: Britain, the US and Ireland*. Manchester, UK; New York: Manchester University Press.

Oireachtas. 2016. "Volume 1: Report | Report of the Joint Committee of Inquiry into the Banking Crisis." Dublin: Oireachtas Banking Inquiry. https://inquiries.oireachtas.ie/banking/volume-1-report/contents/.

Oltheten, Elisabeth, Theodore Sougiannis, Nickolaos Travlos, and Stefanos Zarkos. 2013. "Greece in the Eurozone: Lessons from a Decade of Experience." *The Quarterly Review of Economics and Finance* 53 (4): 317–35. https://doi.org/10.1016/j.qref.2013.05.006.

Orsi, Roberto. 2015. "Weaponisation of War Memories and Anti-German Sentiment | Euro Crisis in the Press." *LSE: Euro Crisis in the Press* (blog). 14th August 2015. http://blogs.lse.ac.uk/eurocrisispress/2015/08/14/weaponisation-of-war-memories-and-anti-german-sentiment/.

O'Sullivan, K. P. V., and Tom Kennedy. 2009. "What Caused the Irish Banking Crisis?" *Journal of Financial Regulation and Compliance*, September. http://papers.ssrn.com/abstract=1888342.

O'Toole, Fintan. 2010. *Ship of Fools: How Stupidity and Corruption Sank the Celtic Tiger*. London: Faber & Faber.

Pagoulatos, George. 2003. *Greece's New Political Economy: State, Finance and Growth from Postwar to EMU*. New York: Palgrave Macmillan.

———. 2005. "The Politics of Privatisation: Redrawing the Public–Private Boundary." *West European Politics* 28 (2): 358–80. https://doi.org/10.1080/01402380500060031.

———. 2014. "State-Driven in Boom and in Bust: Structural Limitations of Financial Power in Greece." *Government and Opposition* 49 (3): 452–82. https://doi.org/10.1017/gov.2014.6.

Pagoulatos, George, and Lucia Quaglia. 2013. "Turning the Crisis on Its Head: Sovereign Debt Crisis as Banking Crisis in Italy and Greece." In *Market-Based Banking and the International Financial Crisis*, edited by Iain Hardie and David Howarth. 1st edition. Oxford: Oxford University Press.

Pagoulatos, George, and Christos Triantopoulos. 2009. "The Return of the Greek Patient: Greece and the 2008 Global Financial Crisis." *South European Society and Politics* 14 (1): 35–54. https://doi.org/10.1080/13608740902995844.

Panageotou, Steven. 2011. "A Critical Literature Review of the Greek Financial Crisis." In *Academia.Edu* (Unpublished Draft).

Papadimitriou, Dimitri B., and L. Randall Wray. 2012. "Euroland's Original Sin." Economics Policy Note Archive 12–08. Levy Economics Institute. http://ideas.repec.org/p/lev/levypn/12-08.html.

Papadimitriou, Dimitris, and Sotirios Zartaloudis. 2014. "European Discourses on Managing the Greek Crisis: Denial, Distancing and Blaming." *LSE: Euro Crisis in the Press* (blog). 2014. http://blogs.lse.ac.uk/eurocrisispress/2014/05/01/european-discourses-on-managing-the-greek-crisis-denial-distance-and-blame/.

Pappas, Takis S. 2013. "Why Greece Failed." *Journal of Democracy* 24 (2). https://doi.org/10.1353/jod.2013.0035.

Pasiouras, Fotios. 2012. *Greek Banking: From the Pre-Euro Reforms to the Financial Crisis and Beyond.* Basingstoke, UK: Palgrave Macmillan.

Paterson, William E. 2011. "The Reluctant Hegemon? Germany Moves Centre Stage in the European Union*." *JCMS: Journal of Common Market Studies* 49 (September): 57–75. https://doi.org/10.1111/j.1468-5965.2011.02184.x.

Patomäki, Heikki. 2013. *The Great Eurozone Disaster: From Crisis to Global New Deal.* London: Zed Books.

Pedroso, Paulo. 2014. "Pedroso, P. (2014) – Portugal and the Global Crisis – The Impact of Austerity on the Economy, the Social Model and the Performance of the State." Study published by the Friedrich Ebert Stiftung, Berlin. http://library.fes.de/pdf-files/id/10722.pdf.

Pellegrin, Julie. 2001. *The Political Economy of Competitiveness in an Enlarged Europe*. Basingstoke, UK: Palgrave Macmillan. http://www.loc.gov/catdir/bios/hol058/2001021883.html.

Pereira and Wemans. 2012. "Portugal and the Global Financial Crisis – Short-Sighted Politics, Deteriorating Public Finances and the Bailout Imperative." Working Papers Department of Economics 2012/26. ISEG – School of Economics and Management, Department of Economics, University of Lisbon. http://econpapers.repec.org/paper/iseisegwp/wp262012.htm.

Pérez-Caldentey, Esteban, and Matías Vernengo. 2012. "The Euro Imbalances and Financial Deregulation: A Post-Keynesian Interpretation of the European Debt Crisis." *702*. Working Paper, Levy Economics Institute. http://www.econstor.eu/handle/10419/57064.

Pinho, Paulo Soares de. 2002. "Portugal." In *Banking in the New Europe: The Impact of the Single European Market Programme and EMU on the European Banking Sector*, edited by Edward P. M. Gardener, Barry Moore, and Philip Molyneux. Basingstoke, UK: Palgrave Macmillan.

Pisani-Ferry, Jean, and André Sapir. 2006. "Last Exit to Lisbon." March 2006. Bruegel Policy Contribution. http://www.econstor.eu/handle/10419/72133.

Pisani-Ferry, Jean, Andre Sapir, and Benedicta Marzinotto. 2010. "Two Crises, Two Responses. Bruegel Policy Brief 2010/01, March 2010." Policy Paper. March 2010. http://aei.pitt.edu/13469/.

Radaelli, Claudio M. 2000. "Whither Europeanization? Concept Stretching and Substantive Change." SSRN Scholarly Paper ID 302761. Rochester, NY: Social Science Research Network. http://papers.ssrn.com/abstract=302761.

———. 2004. "Europeanisation: Solution or Problem?" SSRN Scholarly Paper ID 601163. Rochester, NY: Social Science Research Network. http://papers.ssrn.com/abstract=601163.

Radaelli, Claudio M., and Romain Pasquier. 2007. "Theorizing Europeanization." In *Europeanization: New Research Agendas*, edited by Paolo Graziano and Maarten P. Vink. Basingstoke, UK; New York: Palgrave Macmillan.

Rae, David, and Paul van den Noord. 2006. "Ireland's Housing Boom: What Has Driven It and Have Prices Overshot?" OECD Economics Department Working Paper no. 492. OECD Publishing. https://ideas.repec.org/p/oec/ecoaaa/492-en.html.

Regling, Klaus, and Max Watson. 2010. "A Preliminary Report on The Sources of Ireland's Banking Crisis." Oireachtas Banking Inquiry Reports. Dublin: Oireachtas Banking Inquiry. http://www.bankinginquiry.gov.ie/Preliminary%20Report%20into%20Ireland's%20Banking%20Crisis%2031%20May%202010.pdf.

Reis, Ricardo. 2013. "The Portuguese Slump and Crash and the Euro Crisis | Brookings Institution." *Brookings* (blog). 21st March 2013. https://www.brookings.edu/bpea-articles/the-portuguese-slump-and-crash-and-the-euro-crisis/.

Reisenbichler, Alexander, and Kimberley J. Morgan. 2013. "How Germany Won the Euro Crisis and Why Its Gains Could Be Fleeting." *Foreign Affairs*, 20th June 2013. http://www.foreignaffairs.com/articles/139520/alexander-reisenbichler-and-kimberly-j-morgan/how-germany-won-the-euro-crisis.

Rodrigues, João, and José Reis. 2012. "The Asymmetries of European Integration and the Crisis of Capitalism in Portugal." *Competition & Change* 16 (3): 188–205. https://doi.org/10.1179/1024529412Z.00000000013.

Rodrigues, João, Ana C. Santos, and Nuno Teles. 2016. "Semi-Peripheral Financialisation: The Case of Portugal." *Review of International Political Economy* 23 (3): 480–510. https://doi.org/10.1080/09692290.2016.1143381.

Rodrik, Dani. 2013. "Europe's Way Out." Project Syndicate. 12th June 2013. http://www.project-syndicate.org/commentary/saving-the-long-run-in-the-eurozone-by-dani-rodrik.

Rosenberg, Justin. 2006. "Why Is There No International Historical Sociology?" *European Journal of International Relations* 12 (3): 307–40. https://doi.org/10.1177/1354066106067345.

Ross, Shane. 2010. *The Bankers: How The Banks Brought Ireland to Its Knees*. London: Penguin Ireland.

Royo, Sebastian. 2012a. "Portugal and Spain in the EU: The Paradox of Economic Divergence." In *Portugal in the Twenty-First Century: Politics, Society, and Economics*, edited by Sebastián Royo. Lanham, MD: Lexington Books.

———. 2012b. "The Europeanization of Portuguese Interest Groups? Trade Unions and Employers' Associations." In *The Europeanization of Portuguese Democracy*, edited by Antonio Costa Pinto and Nuno Severiano Teixeira. 1st edition, 139–82. Boulder, CO; New York: Columbia University Press.

RTÉ News. 2007. "Ahern Apologises for Suicide Remark." Articles. *RTE.Ie*, 4th July 2007. http://www.rte.ie/news/2007/0704/90808-economy/.

———. 2017. "Majority of EU Goods Most Exposed to UK Are Irish." *RTE.Ie*, September. https://www.rte.ie/news/business/2017/0913/904427-irish-exports-to-uk/.

RTÉ Prime Time. 2010. Brian Lenihan "We All Partied" on *Prime Time*, 24th November 2010. https://www.youtube.com/watch?v=YK7w6fXoYxo&feature=youtube_gdata_player.

Sandbeck, Sune, and Etienne Schneider. 2013. "From the Sovereign Debt Crisis to Authoritarian Statism: Contradictions of the European State Project." *New Political Economy* 0 (0): 1–25. https://doi.org/10.1080/13563467.2013.861411.

Sapelli, Giulio. 1995. *Southern Europe since 1945: Tradition and Modernity in Portugal, Spain, Italy, Greece and Turkey*. London: Longman.

Selassie, Abebe Aemro. 2012. "Portugal's Economic Crisis: Diagnostics and Remedies." presented at the Ordem dos Economistas – presentation for the IMF, Lisbon, 12th December. https://www.imf.org/external/country/PRT/rr/2012/121212.pdf.

Sepos, A..2016. "The Centre-Periphery Divide in the Eurocrisis: A Theoretical Approach" in *Core-Periphery Relations in the European Union: Power and Conflict in a Dualist Political Economy*, edited by Magone et. al. London: Routledge, 35–55.

Sheahan, Fionnan. 2010. "Lenihan Says 'Sorry' for Role of Fianna Fail in Crisis." *Independent.Ie*, 16th April 2010. http://www.independent.ie/irish-news/lenihan-says-sorry-for-role-of-fianna-fail-in-crisis-26650169.html.

Sinn, Hans-Werner. 2014. *The Euro Trap: On Bursting Bubbles, Budgets, and Beliefs*. Oxford: Oxford University Press.

Skidelsky, Robert. 2014. "Germany's Current-Account Surplus Is Partly to Blame for Eurozone Stagnation | Business | The Guardian." *The Guardian* (blog). 24th July 2014. https://www.theguardian.com/business/2014/jul/24/germany-surplus-part-blame-eurozone-stagnation.

Smith, Mitchell P., ed. 2012a. *Europe and National Economic Transformation: The EU After the Lisbon Decade*. New York: Palgrave Macmillan.

———. 2012b. "Introduction: Evaluating the Lisbon Process: A Soft Approach to Hard Objectives." In *Europe and National Economic Transformation: The EU After the Lisbon Decade*, edited by Mitchell P. Smith. New York: Palgrave Macmillan.

Snaith, H. and Nedergaard, P. 2015. "From Washington Consensus to 'Berlin Consensus'?: The Political Role of Austerity in Global Context". Paper prepared for BISA 40th Annual Conference, 18 June 2015, London. Soares, António Goucha. 2012. "Portugal: An Incomplete Europeanization." In *Portugal in the Twenty-First Century: Politics, Society, and Economics*, edited by Sebastián Royo. Lanham, MD: Lexington Books.

Stiglitz, Joseph. 2016. *The Euro: And Its Threat to the Future of Europe*. London: Allen Lane.

Stockhammer, Engelbert. 2011. "Peripheral Europe's Debt and German Wages: The Role of Wage Policy in the Euro Area." *International Journal of Public Policy* 7 (1): 83–96. https://doi.org/10.1504/IJPP.2011.039577.

———. 2012. "Rising Inequality as a Root Cause of the Present Crisis." Working paper. https://www.peri.umass.edu/publication/item/464-rising-inequality-as-a-root-cause-of-the-present-crisis

Storm, Servaas. 2016. "German Wage Moderation and the Eurozone Crisis: A Critical Analysis." *Institute for New Economic Thinking* (blog). 8th January 2016. www.ineteconomics.org/ideas-papers/blog/german-wage-moderation-and-the-eurozone-crisis-a-critical-analysis.

Storm, Servaas, and C. W. M. Naastepad. 2015. "Crisis and Recovery in the German Economy: The Real Lessons." *Structural Change and Economic Dynamics* 32 (C): 11–24.

Streeck, Wolfgang. 2008. *Re-Forming Capitalism: Institutional Change in the German Political Economy*. Oxford; New York: Oxford University Press.

Streeck, Wolfgang, and Kathleen Thelen, eds. 2005. *Beyond Continuity: Institutional Change in Advanced Political Economies*. Oxford; New York: Oxford University Press.

Tansey, Paul. 2007. "Roaring Trade Required." *The Irish Times*, 2007. http://www.irishtimes.com/business/roaring-trade-required-1.1200589.

Távora, Isabel, and Pilar González. 2014. "The Reform of Joint Regulation and Labour Market Policy during the Current Crisis: National Report on Portugal." *Joint Regulation and Labour Market Policy in Europe during the Crisis*, 321.

Teixeira, Nuno Severiano. 2012. "Introduction: Portugal and European Integration, 1974–2010." In *The Europeanization of Portuguese Democracy*, edited by Antonio Costa Pinto and Nuno Severiano Teixeira, 1st edition. Boulder, CO; New York: Columbia University Press.

The Belfast Telegraph. 2012. "Fianna Fail 'Created Ireland's Worst Crisis since Famine.'" *BelfastTelegraph.Co.Uk*, 26th April 2012. http://www.belfasttelegraph.co.uk/news/republic-of-ireland/fianna-fail-created-irelands-worst-crisis-since-famine-28742303.html.

The Economist. 2011. "After the Race." *The Economist*, 17th February 2011. http://www.economist.com/node/18176072.

The Irish Times. 2015. "ECB 'Told Ireland' to Stand with Failing Banks." *The Irish Times*, 2015. http://www.irishtimes.com/business/financial-services/ecb-told-ireland-to-stand-with-failing-banks-1.2220886.

Thelen, Kathleen. 2009. "Institutional Change in Advanced Political Economies." *British Journal of Industrial Relations* 47 (3): 471–98. https://doi.org/10.1111/j.1467-8543.2009.00746.x.

Thompson, Helen. 2013. "The Crisis of the Euro: The Problem of German Power Revisited." *SPERI*, SPERI Papers, no. 8. http://speri.dept.shef.ac.uk/2013/12/10/speri-paper-no-8-published-crisis-euro-problem-german-power-revisited/.

———. 2015. "Germany and the Euro-Zone Crisis: The European Reformation of the German Banking Crisis and the Future of the Euro." *New Political Economy* 20 (6): 851–70. https://doi.org/10.1080/13563467.2015.1041476.

Triandafyllidou, Anna, Ruby Gropas, and Hara Kouki. 2013. "Introduction: Is Greece a Modern European Country?" In *The Greek Crisis and European Modernity*, edited by Anna Triandafyllidou, Ruby Gropas, and Hara Kouki. London: Palgrave Macmillan.

Tsakalotos, Euclid. 1991. *Alternative Economic Strategies: The Case of Greece*. Aldershot, UK; Brookfield, VT: Avebury.

———. 2014. "Contesting Greek Exceptionalism within the European Crisis." In *Europe in Modern Greek History*, edited by Kevin Featherstone. London: C. Hurst & Co Publishers Ltd.

Tsoukalas, C. 1995. "Free Riders in Wonderland; or of Greeks, in Greece." In *Greece Prepares for the Twenty-First Century*, by Dimitri Constas and Theofanis Stavrou. Washington, DC; Baltimore, MD: Woodrow Wilson Center Press.

Tziovas, Dēmētrēs. 2001. "Beyond the Acropolis: Rethinking Neohellenism." *Journal of Modern Greek Studies* 19 (2): 189–220. https://doi.org/10.1353/mgs.2001.0025.

Tziovas, Dimitris. 2014. *Re-Imagining the Past: Antiquity and Modern Greek Culture*. 1st edition. Oxford: Oxford University Press.

Umbach, Gaby, and Wolfgang Wessels. 2008. "The Changing Context of Economic and Monetary Union: 'Deepening', 'Widening', and Stability." In *The Euro at 10: Europeanization, Power, and Convergence*, edited by Kenneth H. F. Dyson. Oxford; New York: Oxford University Press.

Varoufakis, Yanis. 2017. *Adults in the Room: My Battle with Europe's Deep Establishment*. London: Bodley Head.

Vermeiren, M., 2017. "One-Size-Fits-Some! Capitalist Diversity, Sectoral Interests and Monetary Policy in the Euro Area." *Review of International Political Economy*, 24 (6): 929–57.

Vink, Maarten P., and Paolo Graziano. 2007. "Challenges of a New Research Agenda." In *Europeanization: New Research Agendas*. Basingstoke, UK; New York: Palgrave Macmillan.

Vossole, Jonas Van. 2016. "Framing PIGS: Patterns of Racism and Neocolonialism in the Euro Crisis." *Patterns of Prejudice* 50 (1): 1–20. https://doi.org/10.1080/0031322X.2015.1128056.

Wessels, Wolfgang. 2003. *Fifteen into One?: The European Union and Its Member States*. Manchester, UK; New York: Manchester University Press.

Whelan, Karl. 2013. "Ireland's Economic Crisis – The Good, the Bad and the Ugly." Working Paper 201306. Dublin: School of Economics, University College Dublin. https://ideas.repec.org/p/ucn/wpaper/201306.html.

White, Rossa. 2010. "Irish Macro Comment: Years of High Income Largely Wasted." Research Report: Irish Economy. Dublin: Davy Research.

Wickham, James. 1980. "The Politics of Dependent Capitalism: International Capital and the Nation State." In *Ireland, Divided Nation, Divided Class*, edited by Austen Morgan and Bob Purdie. London: Ink Links.

Wigger, Angela. 2015. "Enhancing 'competitiveness' in Response to the European Crisis: A Wrong and Dangerous Obsession." In *Asymmetric Crisis in Europe and Possible Futures: Critical Political Economy and Post-Keynesian Perspectives*, edited by Johannes Jäger and Elisabeth Springler. London: Routledge.

Wihlborg, Clas, Thomas D. Willett, and Nan Zhang. 2010. "The Euro Crisis: It Isn't Just Fiscal and It Doesn't Just Involve Greece." SSRN Scholarly Paper ID 1776133. Rochester, NY: Social Science Research Network. http://papers.ssrn.com/abstract=1776133.

Wolf, Martin. 2010. "Eurozone Plays 'Beggar My Neighbour.'" *Financial Times*, 18th May 2010. http://www.ft.com/cms/s/0/58ebec36-62aa-11df-b1d1-00144feab49a.html#axzz30w1P52Nd.

———. 2014. *The Shifts and the Shocks: What We've Learned –And Have Still to Learn– From the Financial Crisis*. London: Penguin Publishing Group.

Wren-Lewis, Simon. 2015. "Who Is Responsible for the Eurozone Crisis? The Simple Answer: Germany." *Independent.Co.Uk* (blog). 13th December 2015. http://www.independent.co.uk/voices/who-is-responsible-for-the-eurozone-crisis-the-simple-answer-germany-a6771536.html.

Xenakis, Sappho. 2013. "Normative Hybridity in Contemporary Greece: Beyond 'Modernizers' and 'Underdogs' in Socio-Political Discourse and Practice." *Journal of Modern Greek Studies* 31 (2): 171–92. https://doi.org/10.1353/mgs.2013.0017.

Young, Brigitte, and Willi Semmler. 2011. "The European Sovereign Debt Crisis: Is Germany to Blame?" *German Politics & Society* 29 (1): 1–24. https://doi.org/10.3167/gps.2011.290101.

Young, Tom. 1999. "The State and Politics in Africa." *Journal of Southern African Studies* 25 (1): 149–54.

Index

Page numbers in *italics* refer to figures. Page numbers in **bold** refer to tables.

For Product Safety Concerns and Information please contact our EU representative GPSR@taylorandfrancis.com
Taylor & Francis Verlag GmbH, Kaufingerstraße 24, 80331 München, Germany

www.ingramcontent.com/pod-product-compliance
Ingram Content Group UK Ltd.
Pitfield, Milton Keynes, MK11 3LW, UK
UKHW011017180926
475701UK00004B/797
9780367583552